Praise for *Becoming Cliterate*

"An excellent, thorough, inspiring, and much-needed guide to the source of our deepest energy, pleasure, and power—the clitoris. Everyone needs to read this book and become cliterate."

—Eve Ensler, author of *The Vagina Monologues* and
In the Body of the World

"This read doesn't just zero in on the politics of pleasure inequality, it also offers up solutions that help the reader become more hands on (literally) with their own sexuality."

—*Bust*

"Down with ill-cliteracy! The tongue is mightier than the sword! Brothers and sisters-in-arms (and legs and butts and hearts and souls), bring your huddled masses to this book and embrace orgasm equality! Think outside HER box! Viva la Vulva!"

—Ian Kerner, Ph.D., LMFT, *New York Times* bestselling
author of *She Comes First*

"Brilliant."

—*goop*

"*Becoming Cliterate* will change how we think and talk about female sexual pleasure. The orgasm gap isn't a consequence of women not knowing how—it's a cultural problem that we should be reading about to discover what went wrong in the first place."

—Betty Dodson, sex educator and author of *Sex for One*

"What a fascinating and deeply empowering book. I wish every woman could read what Dr. Laurie Mintz has to teach us about our bodies. It's strange that sometimes that which is a mystery to us is also that which is most intimate in our lives. Dr. Mintz demystifies a lot of things about women's sexuality. Education is the best way to dispel shame and fear, and [this] book really does a beautiful job."

—Sara Benincasa, comedian and auth~~~~~~~~~
*Have Day Jobs (And Other Aweso~~~~
Teach You in School)*

"Women experience sexual pleasure—and, often orgasm—from diverse ways of physical and mental stimulation. This book provides a wealth of information on the clitoris and ways of imagining and creating a more fulfilling sexual life."

—Debby Herbenick, Ph.D., associate professor at Indiana University and author of *Because It Feels Good*

"For too long, men and women have assumed that getting a penis inside a vagina is the holy grail of sex. For men, maybe, but women's sexual satisfaction depends on way more than this. Fortunately, Laurie Mintz provides dozens of helpful suggestions to increase women's sexual pleasure. I encourage both men and women to read this valuable and insightful book."

—Paul Joannides, Psy.D., author of *Guide to Getting it On*

"If you sometimes feel lost on the way to your orgasm, *Becoming Cliterate* is the map (and the cheering section) you need to find your way. Grounded in research and packed with real-world tips, readers will thank Mintz for her truth-telling."

—Dorian Solot, coauthor of *I Love Female Orgasm*

"This book is set up like a college textbook for female orgasm, with some philosophy and pep talks, and then some hands-on experimenting. And a chapter at the end for male partners to read. What more could you need?"

—*Book Riot*

"A fun and empowering reminder that sexual dissatisfaction is not inevitable. . . . *Becoming Cliterate* does a good job questioning these basic assumptions, reorienting us to another vision of what sex can be, and giving practical advice on how to be a boss bitch during sex."

—*Feministing*

"Laurie Mintz, a professor of psychology at the University of Florida, wins this year's award for best book title."

—*New York Times*

"You'll be reading for pleasure in more ways than one."

—*Bustle*

"A manifesto for today's orgasmic insurrection. . . . Mintz is unpretentious and intuitive. . . . *Becoming Cliterate* will help many women reach their orgasm objectives."

—*Los Angeles Review of Books*

"Fun, funny, and empowering. A must-read for people with clits, especially those who are having sex with people with penises."

—*BuzzFeed*

"Personable, witty, and easy to read. . . . *Becoming Cliterate* could be considered a book for anyone with a vulva, as well as anyone who is interested in having sex with someone with a vulva."

—*Journal of Sex & Marital Therapy*

"Dr. Laurie Mintz draws up biology, sociology, and sex therapy to provide a comprehensive manual for both achieving orgasm and raising awareness about female orgasm. Readers will walk away with suggestions for changing our culture of sexuality and, more specifically, female orgasm."

—*PsycCRITIQUES*

BECOMING
CLITERATE

Why Orgasm Equality Matters—
And How to Get It

LAURIE MINTZ

HarperOne
An Imprint of HarperCollinsPublishers

This book is dedicated to all the women and men who
embrace the idea that there is no quality without
equality in *all* realms—including the sexual—and who
are willing to take the revolutionary steps necessary
to make equal opportunity orgasms a reality.

HarperOne

HarperCollins books may be purchased for educational, business, or sales
promotional use. For information, please email the Special Markets Department at
SPsales@harpercollins.com.

FIRST HARPERCOLLINS PAPERBACK EDITION PUBLISHED IN 2018

Designed by SBI Books Arts, LLC
All illustrations by Kelsi E. Quicksall

Library of Congress Cataloging-in-Publication Data is available upon request.

ISBN 978-0-06-266455-6

23 24 25 26 27 LBC 14 13 12 11 10

CONTENTS

SEXTION FOUR

WAIT, THERE'S MORE (CUM AGAIN)

SEXTION FIVE

YOU DON'T HAVE TO HAVE A CLITORIS TO BE CLITERATE

HELLO AND I WANT YOU TO ORGASM

Mind-blowing, body-rippling, can't-help-screaming-out-loud orgasms— maybe your friends say they've had them or maybe you've seen them in movies and porn. But, you've rarely, if ever, experienced this seemingly common feeling, and you're starting to feel cheated and worried. Or maybe you're *pretty* sure you've had orgasms but wonder if they could be better, if there are pieces of the puzzle you're missing.

Congratulations! You've picked up the right book. By the time you finish reading, you'll have discovered the missing pieces of the orgasm puzzle. You'll be *sure* you're having orgasms and you won't be wondering if they could be better. They'll be awesome!

Perhaps you're wondering how I can say this with such certainty. Let me answer by telling you a bit about myself. I'm a middle-aged psychologist who has worked with hundreds of clients, and I teach human sexuality to about 150 students a year at the University of Florida. My students tell me that I remind them of the mother and sex therapist in the movie *Meet the Fockers*—likely because I have a large nose and curly hair, and tell lots of stories about both my personal life and my therapy practice. My students also describe me as quirky because I say things like "I've been having orgasms longer than you've been alive!" And—key to my statement that this book will lead you to orgasm—countless female students tell me that the information in my class has done so for them. A representative quote from my end-of-the-semester teaching evaluations is "Thanks to what I learned in this class, I am now orgasmic!"

My students' experiences, both their frustrations and successes, are the reason I wrote this book. Through teaching human sexuality to college students, I've become aware that a whopping 50 percent of eighteen- to thirty-five-year-old women say they have trouble reaching orgasm with a partner. While women struggling with this problem feel like something is wrong with them, these large numbers tell me that something is wrong with our culture. Based on my conversations with students and clients, I'm convinced I know what's wrong (it's not you) and, thankfully, how to fix it.

What's needed is a combination of cultural analysis (to understand why so many women are struggling) and key practical skills (to help individual women—*like you*—orgasm). That's what this book provides. In the first "sextion"—"Your Orgasm Problem Is a Cultural Problem"—you'll explore the bigger societal picture of why so many young women don't orgasm with partners. The next sextion—"Increase Your Cliteracy"—provides key information on your most important sexual organ. In the third sextion—"The Time Has Come for You to Cum"—you'll learn the attitudes and hands-on (pun intended!) ways *you* can reach orgasm. Then in the fourth sextion of the book—"Wait, There's More (Cum Again)"—you'll gain a few additional pieces of information about women's sexuality and will be encouraged to spread the word to empower other women to orgasm. The final sextion of the book—"You Don't Have to Have a Clitoris to Be Cliterate"—is about spreading the word to men, which includes a chapter you can give to male friends and sexual partners so they can have the same key knowledge of women's ways of orgasming. Cliteracy skills are truly the gift that keeps on giving!

As you read on, I hope you feel like a valued client in my private therapy practice or a treasured student in my classroom. While I already told you that my students say I'm quirky, I also feel really good about the fact that they describe me as both kind and passionate. They can tell I genuinely care about their well-being, and I'm excited to give them information that will make their sex lives better. Female students know that I want them to experience the unique and wonderful feeling of orgasm that has previously eluded so many of them. I want this for you too! I hope that as you read—and are led to those orgasms you've been wanting—you feel engaged, entertained, and cared about. Let's get started!

Caveat (One Book/One Problem)

This book is written to address the fact that when *cisgender women* have sexual encounters with *cisgender men*, they're having way fewer orgasms. By cisgender women, I mean people born with vaginas who identify as women, and by cisgender men, I mean people born with penises who identify as men. While we know for certain that there is an orgasm gap when cisgender folks get it on with each other, we don't yet have enough research to state with certainty if or how the orgasm gap affects people born with vaginas who identify as men (i.e., trans men), people born with penises who identify as women (i.e., trans women), or people born with penises and vaginas who don't identify on the male/female gender binary at all and identify instead, for example, as genderqueer. Similarly, we don't have any knowledge on if or how the orgasm gap affects people born with ambiguous genitalia (i.e., intersex individuals). In fact, we don't even have enough knowledge to say whether what is known about cisgender sexual pleasure can be applied to the sexual pleasure of gender-diverse individuals—although there are fantastic sex researchers, therapists, and educators working tirelessly to answer these questions and to develop sex-positive, pleasure-based resources for gender-diverse people. Gender-diverse communities are also educating themselves and sharing fantastic resources online (Tumblr blogs, YouTube videos, zines). In short, in writing this book to address a problem that occurs when cisgender men and cisgender women have sex with each other, I am not thoughtlessly ignoring the sexual relationships that gender-diverse individuals have with one another or with cisgender individuals—it's just that we don't have enough science or theory to know if the material in this book would be applicable or helpful for anyone but cisgender individuals having sex with other cisgender individuals.

Because the book is written to address a problem among cisgender women and men, when I use the words "women" and "men" or "female" and "male" in this book, I am referring to cisgender women and men, respectively. It's important to state this because when we use these words without explaining why we are using them, and instead assume they capture everyone, we are linguistically erasing gender-diverse individuals. Gender-diverse individuals face not only common cultural linguistic erasure (akin to the linguistic erasure of the clitoris you will read about in chapter 2), but enormous societal discrimination. This book is in no way intended to contribute to this discrimination and erasure; it is simply that its goal is to address one cultural problem (the orgasm gap), and what we know about this problem (including its existence, its causes, and its solutions) is known from research on cisgender individuals.

While I truly wish I could solve all our MANY cultural sexual problems in this book (actually, forget the book, I wish I had a magic wand), I can't. So, instead, I focus the more than 200 pages of this book on eradicating just one societal problem—the orgasm gap that occurs during sexual encounters between cisgender women and men.

YOUR ORGASM PROBLEM IS A CULTURAL PROBLEM

1.

THE PLEASURE GAP
Lies About Getting Laid

"Mm you feel so good. Does that feel good, baby?"

No, not really, you think. "Oh yeah!" you reply. You roll
your eyes because thankfully, in doggy style, he can't
see your face. You are so ready for it to be over.

He grunts enthusiastically, breathing hard. You sense he's
about to come so you start breathing hard and moaning too.

"Yes! Harder! Deeper!" you scream in
order to hurry him to climax.

He finally finishes and asks, "Did you come too?"

"Yes, it was amazing," you lie.

Can you relate? Sadly, most women can. Here's the deal: There's a huge
pleasure gap between women and men. Men are having way more orgasms than women are. And while this is true in all types of sex, it's especially true in casual or hookup sex.

What the F Is Going On?!?

- The F itself. There is **way too much emphasis on intercourse**—the
  way men reach orgasm.

- Movies and porn show women having fast and fabulous orgasms from male pounding. These images are lies!

- The idea that women should orgasm from intercourse is **the number one reason for the pleasure gap**.

- Other reasons, such as poor body image, slut shaming, the idea that women's role is to please men, and poor sexual communication, also contribute to the pleasure gap.

The Solutions!

- Truly understanding that for most women **penetration alone is not the route to ultimate pleasure!** Almost all women need clitoral stimulation to orgasm, which is not achieved during typical penetrative intercourse.

- Discovering an array of easily attainable, yet very powerful, skills and attitudes that will make your orgasm as much of a surefire thing as his.

THE PLEASURE GAP EXPOSED

You've likely already experienced the pleasure gap in your own life. Probably there's been a time or two (or more!) when your male partner—be it your friend, a guy you just met off Tinder, your boyfriend, your fiancé, or your husband—came for real, but your orgasm was either nonexistent or faked. What you may not know is just how many other women are experiencing the same problem, or just how wide this pleasure gap is:

> In one recent survey of thousands of women and men, 64 percent of women versus 91 percent of men said they'd had an orgasm during their most recent sexual encounter.

In another recent survey of over two thousand straight women:

> 57 percent said they orgasm most or every time they have sex with a partner, while 95 percent said their partner orgasms most or every time.

If this wasn't bad enough, things get much worse during hookup sex. As you likely know, "hooking up" is a vague term that can include anything from kissing to intercourse. But when I specifically asked my students (in anonymous polls) about first-time hookup sex involving intercourse or other activities (e.g., oral sex) that could lead to an orgasm:

> 55 percent of men versus 4 percent of women said they usually reach orgasm during first-time hookup sex!

These numbers make it clear that you're not alone. Your missing orgasm is a reflection of a broader cultural problem.

THE PLEASURE GAP EXPLAINED

So what's the problem here? We're doing too much of what we consider "fucking" (aka intercourse) and not enough of other sexual activities. The reason there's such a massive orgasm gap between the sexes is because we overvalue men's most common way of reaching an orgasm (intercourse) and undervalue women's most common way (clitoral stimulation). Our cultural over-focus on the importance of putting a penis into a vagina is screwing with women's orgasms.

You don't have to look far to see this focus—just watch almost any movie with a sex scene. To quote one of my male students, "In the porn I watch, it's male pounding that turns women on." To quote one of my

Relationship Issues and Orgasm Problems

Sometimes women have difficulty reaching an orgasm because of a relationship issue. Not wanting to be in a relationship with someone anymore, not trusting your partner, or not being attracted to a person can lead to orgasm problems.

While this book can give you tools to get to know your body and to get the stimulation you need, it can't solve relationship issues.

Counseling can help if you're feeling stuck or conflicted about your relationship. See appendix B, "Additional Resources," for tips on finding a counselor. The communication skills in chapter 8 could also be useful to help you talk to your partner.

female students, "In mainstream movies and in porn, all I see are women having orgasms during intercourse."

No wonder women tell me they want to orgasm this way! I've even had a good number tell me they think this is what's best for their relationships. No wonder the most common complaint women bring to sex therapists is the inability to orgasm during intercourse. It's also no surprise that the most frequent question asked by my human sexuality students and sent into *Cosmopolitan* magazine is "How do I have an orgasm during intercourse?"

Women's magazines often answer this question by recommending specific intercourse positions ("Try the woman-on-top position!"). This makes matters worse, because it implies that all women can orgasm during intercourse if only they do it right. But this isn't true. The vast majority of women cannot orgasm from the stimulation provided by intercourse alone. Unfortunately, very few women (and men) know this. So countless women end up thinking something is wrong with them, and like the woman portrayed in that all-too-familiar scene at the start of this chapter, they fake orgasms.

When researchers ask college women why they fake, one of the most common answers is to avoid appearing abnormal. Other common answers are to avoid hurting their partner's feelings and to build their partner's ego. Women are faking orgasms because they think a penis should get them off and they want the guy involved to think his penis has these powers. But it doesn't! No penis does.

THAT'S NOT ALL

The idea that women should orgasm from intercourse is the number one lie women are told about getting laid. It's the primary reason for the pleasure gap. Still, it's not the only reason. A lot of other cultural issues mess with women's ability to orgasm. Here are just a few:

- We have a double standard that judges women more harshly than men for having casual sex. This leaves many women feeling conflicted about the sex they're engaging in. It's hard to have an orgasm when you're guilt-ridden or ashamed.

- We're bombarded with media images of "sexy" women whose role is to attract and please men. These images are plentiful in porn, but they're not limited to porn—open any magazine and you'll find advertisements using gorgeous, provocatively posed, scantily clad women to sell everything from cars to clothes. Researchers have found that these images lead girls and women to constantly assess how they appear to others. This puts women's main focus on being sexually desirable *to others* rather than on their *own* sexual desires. It places women's emphasis on how they *look* rather than on how they *feel*. Even worse, some women (and men) come to believe—even subconsciously—that a woman's main role is to pleasure men, rather than believing sex entails equally giving and receiving pleasure. A logical consequence of this is that some women gauge how good a sexual encounter is by their partner's pleasure rather than their own (i.e., "If it was good for him, it was good for me").

- These same media images of sexy, beautiful—and thin—women are also the main culprit in the fact that many women dislike their own bodies. And a woman who dislikes her own naked body is not going to feel open and free during a sexual encounter. It's impossible to have an orgasm while trying to hold your stomach in (believe me, I spent my younger years trying).

- Sex education focuses almost exclusively on the dangers of sex, such as pregnancy and sexually transmitted infections (STIs). Stating the obvious, you're less likely to enjoy something that's been billed as perilous rather than pleasurable.

- Most women (and men) have zero training in sexual communication. Good communication is especially necessary when it comes to female orgasms. Most men pretty much reach orgasm the same way and it's not all that complex. It's a lot more complicated for women to orgasm, since there are vast differences between women in terms of what they need to orgasm. Also, what a woman needs can vary from one encounter to another. Men can't read minds—or vaginas. Sexual communication is needed for women's orgasms, yet it's a skill rarely taught in sex education.

Conflicted feelings about sex, a greater focus on attracting and pleasing a partner than on one's own needs, body self-consciousness, and poor communication all help explain why the orgasm gap is widest between the sexes during first-time hookup sex, but progressively narrows with subsequent hookup sex, friends-with-benefits sex, and relationship sex. It takes time to get to know an individual woman's body. Self-consciousness diminishes with familiarity; people are more apt to say what they need with familiarity and trust. Still, issues like body shame and people's difficulty in expressing what they want don't just disappear during relationship sex; they still take their toll on women's orgasms.

Can you relate to any of these problems? Have you ever felt self-conscious of your body during sex, maybe holding in your stomach or attempting to get into a position where a part you consider unattractive won't show? Have you ever wanted to tell your partner what you needed but just

Sexual Trauma and Orgasm Problems

Sometimes women have trouble reaching orgasm due to more personal reasons. Sadly, way too many women have been the victim of rape, sexual coercion, or childhood sexual abuse.

If you're one of these women, the information in this book might help you reach orgasm, but you're also likely to need information specific to reclaiming your sexuality after being sexually abused. A great book for this is *The Sexual Healing Journey* by Wendy Maltz. Counseling can also help. Appendix B, "Additional Resources," gives advice about locating a therapist.

didn't know what to say or do? I promise we'll conquer all these issues together! If you're already having orgasms, even good ones, the information in this book will help you take them up a notch, giving you information and skills to enhance your sexual expression and ecstasy. And if you've not yet had an orgasm or are having them only inconsistently, the information in this book will lead you to orgasm in any type of sexual encounter you choose to engage in, including hookup sex, friends-with-benefits sex, relationship sex, and everything in between. No matter where you're starting your orgasm journey, you'll find personalized solutions to make sure your orgasms are the best they can be—and you'll be part of the cultural revolution to eradicate that number one lie about getting laid!

THE PLEASURE GAP CLOSED

Since our cultural over-focus on intercourse is the main reason for your missing orgasm, the solution is to truly and deeply understand that the overwhelming majority of women don't reach orgasm through penetration alone. Most women need clitoral stimulation—either alone or coupled with penetration.

Perhaps you're wondering exactly what "the overwhelming majority" means. Most times when women's magazines talk about this they throw around the statistic that only 25 to 30 percent of women can reach orgasm during intercourse. But, as pointed out by a scholar who analyzed the studies that came up with this statistic, there's a big problem: most of these studies don't differentiate between women who can orgasm from *just* a thrusting penis and women who orgasm during intercourse by making sure their clitoris is also stimulated (e.g., by touching it with a hand or a vibrator). Interestingly, though, when this differentiation was made in two different recent surveys, both found that only about 15 percent of women have orgasms from thrusting alone. And the numbers decrease further when I ask my female students about their *most reliable* way to orgasm. Averaging across multiple years of anonymous polls, here's what the women in my classes say their most surefire route to orgasm is:

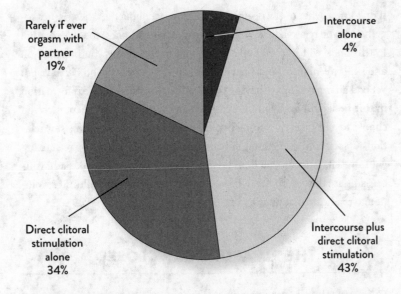

Even more striking, looking only at the women who can orgasm:

95 percent of women need clitoral
stimulation to reach orgasm!

The clitoris is *the key* to women's orgasms. We must raise awareness of the clitoris in our culture. Most important, I want to bring it front and center during *your* sexual encounters.

Allow me to put my long-standing love of the clitoris into further context. I already told you I'm middle-aged. This means I reached my sexual coming-of-age during an era (the '70s and early '80s) in which the clitoris was in the spotlight. One of my favorite moments during this clitoral-focused era was when three graduate school friends and I were out for dinner and four men kept approaching us. Although all heterosexual, we finally decided that to politely get rid of these men, we would tell them they were wasting their time, because we were two lesbian couples. They all looked a bit shocked and then one exclaimed (in quite a lovely accent, I might add), "But intercourse, it is the ultimate pleasure, no?" In complete unison, with no preplanning, we all loudly said, *"No!"* Thirty years later, we continue to laugh about this when we get together, saying to one another, "Intercourse, it is the ultimate pleasure, no?" *"No!"*

What troubles me is that much of this clitoral knowledge seems to have been lost to millennials. Most young women think they're abnormal if they don't reach orgasm during intercourse. Likewise, many of the men I teach say they feel pressured to make girlfriends and hookup partners reach orgasm with their penis. My clients and students are shocked to discover the truth: The vagina (by which I mean the *inside* canal of the female sexual organs, something we'll learn about in chapter 4) has very few touch-sensitive nerve endings. Instead, the overwhelming majority of the nerve endings that women need to reach orgasm are on the *outside*. I repeat: Penetration is not required. Clitoral stimulation is. This is why truly appreciating and attending to the clitoris is the simple secret to your orgasm!

The focus on clitoral stimulation is why women have more orgasms when they have sex with other women, as well as one of the reasons that women have more orgasms alone than with a partner. When two women get it on, they mostly focus on stimulating each other's clitorises; penetration (e.g., with a strap-on or dildo) is a *totally optional* activity, only incorporated if one of the women finds that it enhances her arousal and orgasm. Likewise, somewhere between 88 and 99 percent of women don't include *any* penetration in their masturbation—and those who do almost always pair it with clitoral stimulation. When pleasuring themselves, most women focus exclusively on their clitorises, using vibrators, fingers, pillows, and other external stimulation, resulting in over 94 percent reaching orgasm. Clearly, both solo and lesbian sex focus on the clitoris, but when penetration is involved, that becomes the main event and less attention is paid to the clitoris. In fact, regardless of whether the encounter takes place in the context of a hookup, a committed relationship, or anything else in between:

> During sexual encounters that include intercourse, 78 percent of women's orgasm problems are caused by not enough or not the right kind of clitoral stimulation.

The solution, then, seems pretty straightforward. Let's make both penetration and clitoral stimulation equally valued!

Let me be clear: I'm not trying to turn the tables and have us value clitoral stimulation *more* than intercourse. I'm just trying to level the playing field and have them be equally valued. *I'm not anti-intercourse; I'm just pro-clitoral-course!* And if you are one of those *rare* women (according to my class surveys, one of the approximately 5 percent) who most reliably reach orgasm from penetration alone, there's nothing wrong with this and I won't tell you to stop reaching orgasm that way. It's just that most women don't know how unusual this is—and (as you'll discover in a subsequent chapter) a biological impossibility for many women! Also, interestingly, I've had several women tell me that they thought they were having orgasms during intercourse—since intercourse does create really nice feelings—only to discover what an orgasm actually felt like when they took time to get to know their clitoris. The bottom line is that while many women love the emotional and physical feelings they get from intercourse, thrusting alone rarely results in orgasm. So to close the pleasure gap and have more women reach orgasm, we need to make internal

A Note to Women Who Have Sex with Women

As you can plainly see, a main focus of this book is to eradicate the myths about intercourse that are at the root of so many female orgasm concerns. Obviously, this concern is not as relevant to women who have sex only with other women. If this describes you, you can skip over the passages dedicated to squashing penetration-based myths. Or you might want to read them anyway, reveling in the fact that you're already a step ahead in the orgasm game! In this book you can still find useful information to enhance your orgasmic potential, such as the attitude and focusing skills taught in chapter 5 and the communication skills found in chapter 8. Additionally, you'll find advice for enhancing sex with a female partner in chapter 7. In short, I sincerely hope the focus on debunking myths about intercourse won't deter you, and instead you'll concentrate on the information that will benefit you the most!

stimulation (intercourse for him) and external stimulation (clitoral stimulation for you) equally important.

This is easier said than done. To make penetration and clitoral stimulation equal, you'll need more than just knowledge of the clitoris. I say this based on my experience as a therapist and on a fascinating study that found that women who knew about their clitorises had higher rates of orgasming during masturbation, but not during sex with a partner. To apply knowledge of the clitoris to sex with a partner, you'll need additional skills that go beyond anatomy. You'll need to feel positive, rather than guilty or ashamed, about the sex you have. You'll need to feel that your pleasure is as important as your partner's pleasure. You'll need to learn to relax and not feel self-conscious during sex. And you'll need good sexual communication skills. You'll find all of this in the pages that follow.

THE PLEASURE GAP:
REAL STORIES OF PERSONAL CLOSURE

Because I teach and counsel about sex, a lot of people tell me their sex problems, even outside my classroom and office walls. My twenty-seven-year-old hair stylist, Diane, confided in me that she really liked her new boyfriend, but she was worried because she never reached orgasm with him, as she had with her prior boyfriend, whom she didn't like as much. As we talked, I learned that her prior boyfriend had some difficulties with sustaining an erection, and so he "compensated" by giving her plenty of oral sex. Her new boyfriend had no such problems, and they thus focused on intercourse without much, or any, clitoral stimulation. I also learned that like most women, Diane touched her clitoris when she masturbated—and not surprisingly, she reached orgasm that way. Despite this, Diane and her new boyfriend focused on his penis, assuming it would bring both of them to orgasm. In other words, Diane knew about the importance of her clitoris during oral sex and masturbation, and she even knew how to make herself come, but she didn't make the connection that she also needed to focus on her clitoris during a sexual encounter that involved intercourse.

As soon as she made this connection in our conversations (and it was a serious *aha* moment!), things changed. Diane explained this to her boyfriend. They started having oral sex before they had intercourse, during which Diane started consistently having the Big O.

For Jasmine, it wasn't that easy. After learning about the clitoris in my class, Jasmine bought a clitoral vibrator and had an orgasm for the first time. But she was terrified to tell her boyfriend, Brandon, about this. "I don't want him to feel bad about himself," she said. Brandon was under the same false illusion that Jasmine had previously been—that his penis was central to her pleasure. And this was an illusion she had perpetuated during the several months of their relationship by faking the type of screaming, sheet-gripping orgasms she and Brandon had seen in porn. Eventually, Jasmine got up the courage to talk to

Brandon about her faked orgasms and what she needed for real ones. Things didn't go well. Brandon was mad that Jasmine had faked—and he said he didn't want a vibrator substituting for his penis. They broke up. But, happily, a few months later Jasmine met Kevin, and she was able to tell him from the start what she needed to orgasm. Thankfully, Kevin was completely on board and eager to give Jasmine lots of oral sex and to have her use her vibrator on herself during intercourse. He wanted to please her. At this point, her moans and orgasms were from real pleasure, not from attempting to mimic a porn star. (We'll talk all about vibrators in a later chapter.)

In my experience as an educator and a therapist, most men are more like Kevin than Brandon: they actually want to please women and are happy for information on how to do that. I've read articles claiming that men don't care about women's pleasure, especially during hookup sex. While this may be true of some men (run if you find one!), the men I talk to genuinely want to please women. They just don't know how—or, so many women have faked orgasms with them, they think they have the ticket to all women's orgasms.

Knowing how to bring all women to orgasm is impossible because, again, what each woman needs to orgasm is unique and also varies from one encounter to another—even with the same partner! Some women orgasm most reliably from oral sex. Some orgasm most reliably from manual stimulation without a penis in their vagina. Some orgasm most reliably from stimulation of their clitoris (by their own hand, their partner's hand, or a vibrator) while a penis (or dildo) is in their vagina. Oftentimes, a woman needs a variety of these activities. It also takes women a lot longer to reach orgasm with a partner than it does men (fifteen to forty-five minutes versus two to ten minutes). Fair or not, it simply takes more intricate knowledge for a woman to orgasm than it does for a man. And most of us are taught very little about how women actually orgasm; instead, we're fed lies about orgasms during intercourse. It's no wonder you and your friends have been searching for the secret to those mind-blowing, penis-induced orgasms. It's no wonder that almost *half* of eighteen- to thirty-year-old women are having trouble reaching orgasm!

I want this to change. I don't want any woman—*especially you*—to struggle to orgasm anymore. And I am 100 percent confident that every woman—*including you*—can orgasm if given the right information and skills.

By now you know that it's rare for women to orgasm from intercourse alone and, instead, **the clitoris is key**. Indeed, foreshadowing the focus on language in the next chapter, the word "clitoris" comes from a Greek word meaning "key." Yet despite its absolutely central role in the female orgasm, "clitoris" is a word many people feel uncomfortable saying. Read on to find out why.

2.

DIRTY TALK

Redefining the Language of Sex

"I hooked up with Jeremy last night,"
you confide to your best friend.

"Did you have sex?" she asks.

"No," you reply, since his penis didn't enter you.

Do you see anything wrong with these words? Most people don't. But by the time you finish reading this chapter, you'll understand how such language reflects our cultural disregard for women's orgasms. Yet, language can also shape culture. In other words, we are what we speak. So let's explore the language we use—and how a linguistic sexual revolution will help to bring about orgasm equality!

SCRUTINIZING "SEX"

Take a moment to think about how the word "sex" is used in our culture. Think of what the majority of people mean when they say "We had sex" or "I'd love to have sex with her!"

If you thought of the act of putting a penis into a vagina (i.e., intercourse), you nailed it (pun intended). You don't have to look very far to see that in modern Western culture the terms "sex" and "intercourse" are used as if they were one and the same. Popular magazines often feature stories on the "best sex" positions, and what these articles contain are positions for intercourse. Even the dictionary defines sex as intercourse.

Given all these examples, it isn't surprising that multiple studies reveal that most people in our culture define sex as intercourse as well. In these studies, researchers gave people a list of sex acts (e.g., penile-vaginal intercourse, oral sex given to a woman, oral sex given to a man) and then asked the participants to indicate if they consider each behavior to be sex. The results revealed the obvious: almost all people said intercourse is sex, while far fewer considered oral sex to be "official" sex. Also interesting is what the people in these studies said about having an orgasm during intercourse. Almost all said that even if the female doesn't have an orgasm during intercourse, it still counts as sex. The same isn't true if the male doesn't orgasm during intercourse—fewer people said this counts as sex. In short, in our culture, it's not "sex" unless intercourse happens and the male has an orgasm. Let that sink in for a moment.

As you likely know from experience (and psychological research confirms it), sex generally ends when the man ejaculates. Most heterosexual sexual encounters follow a familiar script: first there's "foreplay" and then there's "sex" (intercourse), during which the man has an orgasm, and then the action stops. Where in this familiar sequence of events is the female orgasm? It's often faked during intercourse alongside the male orgasm. If it occurs for real, it's generally either during intercourse because women are getting direct or indirect clitoral stimulation or it's during those activities (oral sex, manual stimulation) we call "foreplay."

FIGURING OUT "FOREPLAY"

Let's look at the term "foreplay." It goes hand in hand with the heterosexual penetrative way sex is defined in our culture. Merriam-Webster says that foreplay is the "erotic stimulation preceding sexual intercourse" or the "action or behavior that precedes an event." Foreplay is all that comes before the main event—again, the main event being heterosexual intercourse. A group of feminist women who briefly put the clitoris on the map (whom you'll learn about in the next chapter) said:

> The word foreplay implies that this sexual pleasure is not in itself important, but rather an exercise men need to go through to get us ready for intercourse.

Let's take a closer look at one sex act often used to get women ready: oral sex. Quoting Ian Kerner, author of the how-to oral sex manual for men *She Comes First,* "Most men consider cunnilingus an aspect of foreplay, an appetizer to be served before the main meal of genital intercourse." However, it's crucial to understand that this "appetizer" is actually *the main course* for many women—it's the way they orgasm! Despite this, oral sex isn't often considered to be sex. In one study in which people decided what counted as sex or not, among those in the eighteen-to twenty-nine-year-old age range:

> 68 percent of women said it counts as sex when a partner gives them oral sex, but only 33 percent of men said it counts when they give a partner oral sex.

Besides the chilling amount of potential for sexual miscommunication (two people get it on and one thinks they had sex and the other doesn't!), these results emphasize that the way a great number of women consistently reach orgasm isn't considered sex by about two-thirds of men and one-third of women. It's *just* foreplay.

REDEFINING THE LANGUAGE OF FOREPLAY AND SEX

What would the world be like if men's orgasms were "just foreplay" and women's orgasms were the main event? If this were the case, the clitoral caressing (with a finger, tongue, or vibrator) that often occurs in heterosexual encounters before intercourse would be called "sex" and intercourse would be called "post-play." Wouldn't that be revolutionary!

If we made this switch, however, we'd still have orgasm inequality because we'd be turning the tables and prioritizing female orgasms. So here's a more equitable solution:

> Let's define *both* clitoral stimulation *and* intercourse as sex!

If we as a society made this change, there'd be no need for the term "foreplay." There'd be no *one* main event. Men's and women's satisfaction and routes to orgasm would be equally valued.

Putting intercourse and clitoral stimulation on the same level would also solve another insidious word problem—the way magazines, and even some sex therapists, refer to women touching their own clitorises during intercourse. It's often called "extra clitoral stimulation." As you might recall from the prior chapter, in anonymous surveys in my class:

> Almost 45 percent of women said their most reliable route to orgasm was intercourse coupled with clitoral stimulation.

There's clearly nothing *additional* about this clitoral stimulation. It's not a superfluous add-on. It's a vital part of the main event!

Considering clitoral stimulation and intercourse as equally important has two obvious benefits. Central to what I've been saying up to this point, it would honor the way most women reach orgasm. But, just as important, what two women do together when they get it on would also count as sex. In a wonderfully provocative essay that the students in my class read—"Are We Having Sex Now or What?"—writer Greta Christina tells readers how easy it was for her to count sexual partners when she

Activities or Orientations?

While many women identify with a sexual orientation, others don't—and even if a woman identifies with an orientation (e.g., heterosexual), she still might engage in sexual activities outside this orientation (e.g., a hookup with another woman). Also, women's sexuality often encompasses interests and attractions that can change several times over a lifetime. There are a multitude of orientations people identify with. All of this is why, throughout this book, I will use words like "heterosexual" or "lesbian" as adjectives to describe *sexual activities*, rather than as nouns to describe *people*.

had sex only with men, and how confusion arose when she started having sex with women. Christina tells readers:

> I'd always made my list of sex partners by defining sex as penile-vaginal intercourse. . . . It's a pretty simple distinction, a straight-forward binary system. Did it go in or didn't it? Yes or no? . . . Granted, it's a pretty arbitrary definition; but it's the customary one, with an ancient and respected tradition behind it, and when I was just screwing men, there was no really compelling reason to question it. But with women . . . well, first of all there's no penis, so right from the start the tracking system is defective. . . . So when I started having sex with women, the binary system had to go, in favor of a more inclusive definition.

With the goal of a more inclusive definition—one that honors women's way of orgasming—I'd like to ask you to join me in ceasing to use the word "sex" for intercourse. But first I need to warn you: this is going to be hard (another pun intended). Honestly, even though I'm writing a book advocating a changed sexual language, I sometimes find myself automatically, reflexively using the word "sex" for intercourse. This is because it is so deeply ingrained in all of us to do so.

A good place to start in changing your language is by just noticing. As you read magazines and books and watch television and movies, pay attention to the word "sex." Notice how often it's used to mean intercourse. When you couple this with the knowledge that very few women orgasm from intercourse alone, the craziness will become clear to you. One example I spotted when I first started changing my language was an "orgasm quiz" in a reputable online magazine. This quiz asked, "How long does it take women to orgasm during sex?" While the quiz authors answered with a number, the actual answer is that it depends on how you're defining sex! For most women, the answer is about twenty minutes if they count clitoral stimulation as sex, but it's way less clear if they refer to sex only as a penis thrusting in a vagina, since few women reliably orgasm this way. Even crazier are the countless articles listing the "best sex" positions, which go over tons of intercourse positions that might indirectly stimulate the clitoris yet never mention direct clitoral stimulation (with fingers, a tongue, or a vibrator). As you begin to see this insidious language injustice more clearly, try to adjust your own language.

But what words should you use? Of course, you could keep using the word "sex" but mean it to signify the whole of a sexual encounter, not just intercourse. Another option is to use an entirely different term to convey a whole sexual encounter. One of my students tells me that she and her friends use the term "fucking around." However, because of the literal meaning of "fuck," this one doesn't quite sit well with me in terms of the language I'm trying to advocate. So here are a few words to get you started: "fooling around," "getting it on," or "hooking up" (a term you're probably using anyway). We could also go into a time capsule and start using the age-old "hanky-panky." Or if you're comfortable enough with your partner, try "making love." When you want to refer to just the act of intercourse, you could say the actual word or you could call it "P.V.I." (penile-vaginal intercourse). Less academic sounding, there is "screwing," "shagging," "banging," "boinking," "doing the horizontal bob," and "playing hide the salami." Or, despite its sometimes negative connotations, you could say you "fucked." Whatever words you choose, and as

How Does This Benefit Men?

In *She Comes First*, author Ian Kerner gives male readers a pep talk about how not equating sex and intercourse is to their benefit. He tells readers:

> *When we understand the role of the clitoris in stimulating that process, then sex becomes easier, simpler, and more rewarding, and we are compelled to create pleasure with our hands and mouths, bodies and minds. In letting go of intercourse, we open ourselves up to new creative ways of experiencing pleasure, ways that may not strike us as inherently masculine, but ultimately allow us to be more of a man. Sex is no longer penis-dependent, and we can let go of the usual anxieties about size, stamina, and performance. We are free to love with more of ourselves, with our entire self.*

> I'll be emphasizing this to the guys in your life in the "Cliteracy— For Him" chapter.

challenging as it may be, I hope you'll stop equating sex with intercourse exclusively. I promise that you, your partner, and society as a whole will reap the benefits.

IT'S ALL VAGINA "DOWN THERE"

Another related word problem we need to solve is what we call women's genitals. To understand this problem, a brief preview of what you'll learn in the next chapter is needed.

Both women and men have visible (outside) and invisible (inside) parts of their genitals. A man's visible parts include his penis and the sack that houses his testicles (his balls). Men's unseen parts include his actual testicles and a series of ducts that carry urine and semen. A woman's visible part is called the vulva, which includes her inner and outer lips, the tip of her clitoris, the opening to her urethra (where urine comes out), and the opening to her vagina (where the penis goes in and babies come out). A woman's inside parts include her inner clitoris and her vaginal canal (her vagina).

Despite all these distinct internal and external parts of women's genital anatomy, we call everything "down there" a vagina. I vividly recall being with a friend who had a four-year-old son and a six-year-old daughter. The daughter asked, "Why can't I pee standing up like Sammy?" Without hesitation, the mother said, "Because he has a penis and you have a vagina." This mother is a physician, one who did a rotation in ob-gyn in medical school. Yet even she could not find the words to tell her daughter that for boys, the pee comes out of the penis, which they can see, hold, and point at the toilet, whereas for girls, the pee comes out of a hole in their vulva and so there is no way to hold it or point it. Instead, she told her daughter that pee comes out of a place that it doesn't, the vagina! This is analogous to telling a child that the nose is for both eating and breathing—since, after all, the nose and the mouth are both on the face, so what's the difference?! This would be bizarre, but somehow we've taken to calling all women's genitals by one part and we don't even notice the absurdity of it.

This absurdity is especially notable when we consider Eve Ensler's feminist play *The Vagina Monologues*. As aptly written by Harriet Lerner in her *Psychology Today* blog, "Here was a play whose purpose was purportedly to restore pride in female genitals—including pride in naming—and it could not have been more confusing about genital reality. Shaving a vagina? *Really?* Much of the play didn't make sense unless you substituted the word vulva for vagina."

Lerner goes even further than pointing out the confusion created when we call the vulva by the wrong name; she also points out the harm of this misnaming. She tells us we're engaged in a linguistic genital mutilation. Using Lerner's words:

> We can be thankful for the fact that Americans don't excise the clitoris and ablate the labia, as is practiced in other cultures. Instead, we do the job linguistically—a psychological genital mutilation, if you will. Obviously the two are not equivalent, but language can be as powerful and swift as the surgeon's knife.

Lerner isn't the first to use the metaphor of linguistic genital mutilation. Feminist anthropologists have said that by calling all of women's genitals a vagina, we're relegating women's most important sexual organ—the clitoris—to nameless invisibility. These scholars say we're engaged in a cultural "symbolic clitoridectomy."

What's your reaction? Are you having an *aha* moment? Or perhaps you find phrases like "symbolic clitoridectomy" and "psychological genital mutilation" too strong. Let me rephrase this in a softer manner. As aptly pointed out by Rebecca Chalker, author of *The Clitoral Truth*, we shouldn't call all of women's genitals by the part (the vagina) that's sexually more useful to men than it is to women themselves. Plus, as was once stated on the online Tumblr site V Is for Vulva:

> What isn't named doesn't exist, and every time someone uses the word "vagina" when they really mean "vulva," they're erasing some of the parts of a woman's sexual organs that give them the most pleasure! It's time we stop making ourselves—and parts of our bodies—invisible, and that starts with using the right language.

WHAT *IS* THE RIGHT LANGUAGE?

What should we call the whole of women's anatomy? Maybe you're thinking, *I know, how about "vajayjay"?*

The history of this word is telling. The word was coined because in 2006 the network producers and executives of *Grey's Anatomy* decided that the word "vagina" was being said too often on the show, and they weren't sure it was appropriate. (Never mind that they didn't have this same concern with the word "penis.") So they created a new word and used it in a scene. The word "vajayjay" quickly made its way into mainstream culture. Oprah Winfrey told millions of viewers, "I think 'vajayjay' is a nice word, don't you?" "Vajayjay" appeared in online dictionaries, including Urban Dictionary and Merriam-Webster's Open Dictionary. In a *New York Times* article on the popularity of this word, one linguist said, "There was a need for a pet name, a name that women can use in a familiar way among themselves." In this same article, the famous feminist Gloria Steinem said, "I'm hoping that the use of this new word is part of the objection to only saying vagina since it doesn't include all of women's genitalia, for instance the clitoris, in the way that vulva does." Urban Dictionary doesn't support Ms. Steinem's hope. In this online source, "vajayjay" is defined as another word for vagina. So while you may like this word (it really does have a nice ring, I agree), it's actually another word for vagina, and this is what I'm hoping we can get away from—calling everything down there a vagina and, in so doing, ignoring the clitoris.

Here are a few words for women's genitals that don't originate or stand for just the vagina: "yoni," "coochie," "love taco," "cha-cha." "Yoni" is an ancient Hindu term that some writers use to signify the vulva (or even the whole of women's internal and external genitals), recommending it due to its respectful, even reverent, connotations. While I like the idea behind this word, it doesn't quite work for me. Truth be told, one of my best friends and I actually use the word "coochie," and I call my sex toys my "ac-coochie-ments" (pun for "accoutrements"). Still, one of my trusted students says the word "coochie" doesn't work for her due to its use in rap music. She also found the other words ("love taco," "cha-cha")

Get Off the Floor!

In June 2012, Michigan State Representative Lisa Brown used the word "vagina" when addressing a Democratic caucus. The next day, she was banned from speaking on the House floor. Protests grew. Those who banned her backtracked and gave other reasons for her being barred (e.g., she threw a temper tantrum, something that a videotape of the session doesn't support). Most news sources reported that it was clearly the word "vagina" that got Representative Brown banned.

ridiculous (as do I). So how about we keep it simple and just call it by its real name? Let's just start saying "vulva" until it becomes as commonplace as "penis"!

Betty Dodson, a famous feminist from the 1960s (an era when women learned about the power of the clitoris for reaching orgasm), has a DVD titled *Viva la Vulva*. *Viva* is a Spanish word often used to signify a celebration. So come on, ladies, let's follow Dodson's advice and name and celebrate the vulva!

Most imperative, let's start naming and talking about the clitoris. As stated by the writers of *I Love Female Orgasm*, "The word 'vagina' regularly steals some of the clit's limelight. Perhaps someday the lusty, trusty clitoris will get her own day to shine." Today is that day!

NICKNAMING THE CLITORIS

What should we call the clitoris to bring her into the spotlight? A few nicknames are out there and most refer to the external tip, or glans, of the clitoris. For example, there is "nub," "magic button," "love button," "bean," and "C-spot." There is also the "little man in the boat" and the "jelly bean." Betty Dodson uses the word "clitty." Still, the most commonly used term is "clit."

But even saying "clit" feels uncomfortable to many women. When talking to a trusted student about this, she told me, "We don't talk about it to guys. When we talk about it to our women friends, we call it 'the clit' and it feels weird and awkward." During this same conversation, my student and I tried to brainstorm words for the clitoris and none sounded right. In frustration she said, "There *has* to be a better word!" My student's utterance got me thinking. What nicknames do we use for the penis? We call the penis by people's names (Dick, Peter, and Johnson). By doing so, we give it legitimacy as an entity unto itself. When I realized this, Tori popped out of cli*toris* for me. And then, freed up to perceive people's names in the word "clitoris," other female names emerged, including Tara, Iris, Rita, and a variety of "cl" names: Cleo, Chloe, Claire, Clara, and Clarisse.

When I first got the idea of nicknaming the clitoris with a female name, I was really excited. My goal became to pick a word and popularize it. I started asking friends, family, colleagues, and students, "Which name do you like?" All picked either "Tori" or "Cleo." Interestingly, though, those who knew someone named Tori strongly objected to this nickname, saying they could never use it because of its association with a real person in their lives. When I pointed out that there were plenty of Dicks in the world, one student told me that no Richard she knows uses this name, and that for her generation, "dick" is not even thought of as a person's name. "Dick" has become synonymous with "penis." She also said she liked "Cleo" because it's an uncommon name and thus wouldn't be associated as frequently with the image of an actual person. "It will be a new word!" she proclaimed. And then, when I discovered that "Clio" is an alternative spelling of "Cleo," which originates from a Greek word (*kleos*) meaning glory and fame, I was sold.

I started telling more students, friends, and colleagues about the name "Clio." Many liked it, but some expressed uncertainty. A few suggested other ideas. "How about 'Doris'?" asked one student, at the same time admitting that, while rhyming with clitoris, "Doris" really didn't sound right either. Another colleague agreed wholeheartedly that we need a name for the clitoris but didn't fall in love with "Clio." Thinking of the show *Sex and the City,* she suggested "Samantha." I was convinced I had not yet found the right name—so back to Google I went.

Similar to prior searches, what I found were a couple of new names and several forums where both the lack of a name and women's hesitation in saying "clit" or "clitoris" were mentioned. I learned that in Australia, some people call the clitoris "Marcia" and that the Mexican slang word for clitoris is *pepita.*

Yet, most important, I realized the problem wasn't my word choice at all. The problem, I grasped, is the same reason I'm writing this book. There's discomfort and silence around women's most orgasmic organ. No word for the clitoris sounded just right to everyone I talked to, and no other word has made it into popular culture, because language is a reflection of culture.

> ## Tomato, Tomahto
>
> Perhaps you're wondering how to pronounce "clitoris." Some people say "**clit**-or-is," and others say "cli-**tor**-is." Either pronunciation is correct.

Until we solve this cultural problem, "penis" will remain a commonplace term. On the other hand, similar to Voldemort in the infamous Harry Potter series, the clitoris will remain She-Who-Must-Not-Be-Named.

THE DEEPER CULTURAL PROBLEM AND SOLUTION

We label "sex" as the act through which most men reach orgasm. We label women's genitals by the one part (the vagina) through which most men reach orgasm. We elevate men's sexual organ (the penis) with countless nicknames that no longer seem strange to us, but we have no word with which to comfortably name the clitoris.

Just what is the deeper, cultural root of this problem? It's cultural privileging of the male experience. To illustrate the covert and insidious nature of this cultural privileging, one feminist writer discussed the last

The Meaning of Sex for the Rest of Becoming Cliterate!

As you read on and see the word "sex," while it will take some getting used to, imagine a whole sexual encounter, which might or might not include intercourse (e.g., giving and receiving oral sex). When I want you to think of any specific sexual act, I'll make it simple and use just that word (e.g., intercourse, oral sex).

names of married couples. She pointed out that most people don't take notice when a husband and wife share the same last name, also simply assuming it's the man's family name. Likewise, few even think to ask the wife how she felt giving up something that's been part of her identity since birth. On the other hand, when a wife doesn't share the same last name as her husband, people take notice. They might ask the woman why she made that choice, or even critique her for doing so. They might ask the man how he feels about his wife's choice. The astute feminist writer who gave this example used it to define cultural privileging of the male experience. It's when society prioritizes men's interests and feelings over women's—putting this forth as the natural way for things to be. Taking this a step further, it's when society advantages men's experiences as the default normal human experience, with anything else being considered a deviation from this normal. We do this with sex. We culturally privilege male sexual pleasure with the view that sex begins with penetration and ends with male ejaculation. We assume that the male way of reaching orgasm (penetration) is the normal way for both women and men to reach orgasm. Our language reflects (and at the same time further perpetuates) such privileging. As this chapter illustrated, we name everything in relation to male pleasure (e.g., equating sex and intercourse; labelling all of female genitals a vagina), whereas if we culturally privileged female sexual pleasure, we'd name everything in relation to female pleasure (e.g., we'd call foreplay sex; we'd call intercourse "post-play"). But, we shouldn't be culturally privileging the sexual pleasure of *either* women or men. When it comes to sexual pleasure, we need sexual equality.

> There can't be true quality without equality.

That phrase comes from Dr. Peter Slavin, when talking about racial disparities in our health-care system. It applies here as well. Quality sex—for both women and men—is only possible with true sexual equality. Quality sex will come from holding women's most reliable way of reaching orgasm, clitoral stimulation, as equal to men's most reliable way of reaching orgasm, penile penetration. If we do this, a language change will most certainly follow.

While language reflects culture, language also shapes culture. Together, let's stop calling intercourse "sex," let's stop calling everything "down there" a vagina, and perhaps most important of all, let's place the clitoris in the public eye.

Start talking about your clitoris, your clit, your clitty. Start referring to your Pepita, your Samantha, your Doris, your Tori, your Clio. After all, calling the clitoris Tori, Doris, or Pepita is no stranger than calling the penis Tom, Dick, or Peter. Calling her Samantha is no more nonsensical than calling him Johnson. If my dream comes true, all these names will become commonplace. If my hopes are realized, when entering "names for the clitoris" in a Google search, someday people will find as many terms as when they enter "names for the penis." Let's make history with a linguistic sexual revolution!

Speaking of history, the next chapter will put our cultural views of women's orgasms into a long-standing context. You'll learn how the lie about the superiority of penile penetration started, and what our ancestors thought about the clitoris and women's ways of orgasming. We'll discuss the current-day landscape, including how women's orgasms are falsely portrayed in porn and how the clitoris is ignored in hookup sex. Hopefully, you'll be further inspired to become part of the cultural change to make your orgasm one quiver in a revolutionary shift in valuing the way we women come.

3.

IT'S BEEN GOING ON TOO LONG!

Cliteracy Through the Ages

If you don't know history, you are a leaf
that doesn't know it is part of a tree.

—adapted from Michael Crichton, *Timeline*

I'm not a history buff. I never took an elective history course in college, and I found my required History of Psychology course to be the least interesting of all my graduate school classes. Still, I believe that understanding the past is essential to creating a better future. To close the orgasm gap and eradicate that number one lie about getting laid, we have to look in our cultural rearview mirror. To bring the clitoris and female orgasms into the cultural limelight, we have to understand how they've been viewed historically. I'm guessing that some of you are like me and don't find ancient history all that captivating. That's why I've distilled the writings of some brilliant feminist authors (most notably Naomi Wolf in *Promiscuities* and Rebecca Chalker in *The Clitoral Truth*) to provide you with a CliffsNotes version for the early history of the clitoris and women's orgasms. Then, starting with the invention of the first vibrator, I provide more details. I think you'll find the information from then on more relevant to modern times, including your own life.

CLISTORY—THE CLIFFSNOTES VERSION

- The Greeks and Romans knew about the clitoris, even the inside part that you'll learn about in the next chapter. But they thought the clitoris was inferior to the penis. One famous doctor from the Roman Empire said the clitoris was **a failed attempt at a penis**.

- In the Dark and Middle Ages, women's sexuality was viewed as evil. In the ultimate witch-hunting manual of this era, **the aroused clitoris was evidence of contact with the devil!**

- During the Renaissance era, the clitoris reemerged as a legitimate body part. **Midwives encouraged female orgasms** to promote pregnancy. **Anatomists started including the clitoris on drawings of the female body.** Some of these anatomists said accurate, affirming things about the clitoris (one called it "the seat of women's delight"), but others had less favorable views (one called it "women's shameful member").

- Things took a turn for the worse in the eighteenth and nineteenth centuries. In anatomical drawings, **the clitoris went from being depicted as an extensive organ system to a meaningless bump**.

- By the Victorian era, women were encouraged to have intercourse for their husband's sake but were thought of as weak, asexual creatures. **Female orgasms were considered unnecessary, inappropriate, and unhealthy.** But out of this bad era came something good: the vibrator was invented!

Pooey for Pudendum!

The Renaissance-era anatomist who called the clitoris "women's shameful member" used the term "pudendum" to refer to the vulva. This term comes from a Latin word that means "to be ashamed." And this term is still widely used in Western culture, especially in medical writings. Shame on us for retaining such a shameful name!

There's More than Western History

While we'll focus on Western history, there are other important histories and present-day realities to consider. For example, the *Kamasutra* is an ancient Indian text with a wealth of information on enhancing sex. On the other hand, a horrific current reality is that female genital mutilation still occurs. Over 160 million women alive today have had some part of their clitoris removed. Many groups are working to put an end to this, including Clitoraid—an organization that provides funds and trains doctors so that female genital mutilation victims can have their clitorises surgically rebuilt.

THE FIRST VIBRATOR

Given that Victorian women were told having an orgasm was a *bad* thing, there were many sexually frustrated women. Countless numbers started exhibiting physical symptoms. They complained to doctors of anxiety, irritability, insomnia, erotic fantasies, feelings of heaviness in their lower abdomens, and an odd wetness between their legs. This syndrome was labeled "hysteria," and to treat it, doctors applied vegetable oil to their hands, put a couple of fingers inside their patients' vaginas, pressed the heel of their hands against the clitoris, and rubbed. And not surprisingly, the women had orgasms (although they were called "paroxysms" since women were viewed as inherently non-orgasmic). No surprise, there were lots of repeat customers for this "treatment."

The problem, however, was that doctors' hands started cramping up from giving so many "treatments." So they began experimenting with other ways to give Victorian women their symptom-relieving orgasms (including water-based massagers, something many women use today to orgasm in the tub). Still, nothing was as reliable as the doctors' hands—until electricity entered the picture. And now let's give a shout-out to Dr. Granville for patenting the first plug-in vibrator to relieve his cramping hands!

These early plug-in (and later battery-powered) vibrators were a big hit. They started being advertised in women's magazines, where they were called "personal massagers." Women started "curing their hysteria" at home. But when, in about 1920, these devices showed up in pornographic films and their erotic use was exposed, they became unacceptable for women to buy. From then until the 1970s, when feminists brought attention to the clitoris and Hitachi introduced the Magic Wand, vibrators were almost impossible to come by (but not *cum* by). To make matters worse, a couple of decades later, Freud dealt the clitoris a really bad blow.

FREUD'S FOUL

While Rebecca Chalker calls Freud "the hit man who delivered the final blow to the . . . clitoris," my view is that Freud did something worse than finish a job that had already been started. Despite knowing that the clitoris was central to female orgasms, he started that number one lie that we're still struggling with today. In Freud's own words, he said that once girls hit puberty, "the clitoris should . . . hand over its sensitivity, and . . . its importance, to the vagina." In essence, he said that grown women who need clitoral stimulation to reach orgasm are defective. Indeed, due to Freud's influence, women who couldn't orgasm from intercourse were labeled as having the disease of "frigidity." The one positive of this era, however, was that (unlike the era preceding it) women were at least supposed to orgasm.

SEXUAL SCIENCE SETS THE RECORD STRAIGHT (SORT OF)

A huge step toward healing the damage done by Freud and his frigid—err, rigid—followers came in the form of sexology, the scientific study of sex. While some brave researchers had been studying sex in secret for a long time, Alfred Kinsey brought it into the public eye. He interviewed thousands of Americans about their sex lives and published two books, one on male sexuality and one on female sexuality. Both were bestsellers—although he got more criticism for his book about women than he did for his book about men. One of the statements made in his book about women was especially attention grabbing: "Intercourse is not the best means of pleasure for women . . . the clitoris is the center of female pleasure." Three cheers for Alfred! Oops, hold on. Not so fast. He also wrote that once a woman has been married long enough and thus has more sexual experience, she should be able to achieve orgasm through intercourse. Darn.

Speaking of intercourse, our next two sexual scientists, William Masters (a gynecologist) and Virginia Johnson (a psychology student), also had a major intercourse bias in their research. They wanted to know what happened to the body during excitement and orgasm. So they recruited women and men for a study and then recorded what happened to their bodies while having sexual relations in the laboratory. As one example, they inserted a sex toy with a camera into women's vaginas and took pictures as the women got excited and orgasmed. But here's the rub (pun intended): the only women they let participate in their studies were those who said they could orgasm during intercourse!

Despite this flawed subject recruitment, Masters and Johnson did give us information that helped raise clitoral awareness. The book they published about their research had a whole chapter on the clitoris and another on the female orgasm. And in the clitoris chapter, they proclaimed:

> The clitoris is a unique organ in the
> total of human anatomy.

They said its uniqueness lies in the fact that it's the only human organ whose sole function is sexual pleasure. They also emphasized that only women have this one-of-a-kind organ and that it's at the center of their sexual response. And Masters and Johnson proclaimed Freud incorrect: they concluded that clitoral and vaginal orgasms are *not* two separate entities, and that no matter where a woman is being stimulated (e.g., her breasts, her clitoris, or her vagina), all orgasms are physiologically the same. They even pointed out that orgasms during intercourse are caused by indirect clitoral stimulation.

A few years later, feminists amped up this message by declaring that *all orgasms are clitoral* and by educating women that it's a hell of a lot easier to orgasm from direct clitoral stimulation (Touch it! Lick it!) than from indirect stimulation (Have your penis sort of come in contact with it). This was the only point in history when clitoral stimulation was considered by some to be equal to penile penetration. Let's take a closer look at this era when women started exploring themselves and proclaiming the clitoris as queen.

HEYDAY FOR THE CLITORIS!

While many dedicated feminist writers and researchers worked to bring attention to the clitoris, I want to focus on just a few central figures.

First is Shere Hite. In 1976, she rocked the world with a survey of over three thousand women in which she found that most weren't having orgasms during intercourse. *The Hite Report* told women that it was *normal* to not orgasm during intercourse and that, instead, the vast majority of women need direct clitoral stimulation to orgasm.

In 1981, the Federation of Feminist Women's Health Centers produced a truly radical book: *A New View of a Woman's Body*. Some versions came wrapped with a plastic speculum so women could follow the instructions to examine themselves. In the chapter "The Clitoris: A Feminist Perspective," readers were told how to locate different parts of their clitorises. This book also expanded the view of the clitoris to include parts most had previously considered separate, such as the inner lips, and parts most women had never heard of, such as the clitoral bulbs (you'll learn about these in the next chapter). Most important, the authors stated loud and clear that we need to eradicate the myth of the vaginal orgasm and to consider clitoral stimulation just as important as penile penetration.

The final feminist I want to mention is Betty Dodson, who wrote the book *Sex for One*. In a nutshell, this book teaches women to "self-love" (aka masturbate), with a major focus on the clitoris. Betty also held—and still holds—both private masturbation lessons and workshops during which small groups of naked women talk, explore their own bodies, and masturbate together. In my class, I show a video of Betty teaching a woman to masturbate to orgasm by touching her clitoris, with both her hand and a vibrator. Every time I show this video, the majority of my female students say either it taught them a new way of masturbating or it made them feel normal about the way they already masturbate. Some express sadness or anger that no one had told them this information before. (No need to go searching for this Betty Dodson video now. I will give you detailed instructions on accessing and watching it in chapter 6.)

Why don't the women in my class already have this information? Why, more than thirty years after reading *A New View of a Woman's Body* and learning about my clitoris, do I feel compelled to write a book for you about the clitoris? Why isn't this knowledge still widely known? How did it get lost?

THE G-SPOT HYPE SET US BACK

In 1982, three scientists wrote a book—*The G-Spot*—about an area in the vagina that, when stimulated, can lead to orgasm in some women. They also wrote about female ejaculation. (They weren't the first to write about this; it was in Roman writings but then went into cultural hibernation

Are There Different Types of Orgasms?

Scientists are still debating exactly what the G-spot is, as well as if there are distinct types of orgasms. The next chapter will clear up this confusion and debate.

for thousands of years.) *The G-Spot* authors provided evidence of different types of female orgasms—clitoral, vaginal, or a combination of the two called a "blended orgasm"—while also emphasizing that there is no one right way for a woman to orgasm.

However, the message picked up by the media was that if you aren't having G-spot orgasms with accompanying female ejaculation, you are *seriously* missing out. G-spot orgasms became big business (e.g., books, movies, and sex toys to help find it). One physician even developed a G-shot: collagen injected into the vagina to make the spot more pronounced. This is not a one-shot deal, however. The collagen breaks down after about four months and needs to be reinjected. Beverly Whipple, one of the scientists who wrote the original book, has expressed serious concern about this procedure, pointing out that it has no research behind it. She's tried to remind the public that she never wanted G-spot orgasms to be a goal to achieve. But her voice seems to have been lost—replaced by the message that if a woman can find her G-spot, her sex life will be dramatically improved. Both Betty Dodson and Shere Hite, two of our feminist clitoral

G-What?

Maybe you're wondering what the G stands for? While for many it stands for "Gee, I can't find that spot!" it's actually a short version of the official name: the Gräfenberg Spot. Ernst Gräfenberg was the first modern physician to write about the spot in 1951. Whipple and her colleagues honored him with a namesake.

heroines, say that these exaggerated claims about the G-spot have set us back to a Freudian era of women searching in vain for vaginal orgasms—leaving them feeling inadequate and unsatisfied.

TODAY'S TRENDS

This brings us to today's era—the one you're trying to navigate. Let's talk about two aspects of today's sexual landscape: porn and hookup sex. If you're like the students in my class, most of you have watched porn and have had at least some form of casual sex.

In my most recent class, 86 percent of the men and 77 percent of the women said they have watched porn. While there's a ton of research on the effects of porn, there's only one really definitive conclusion. Quoting the text I use in my class:

> There is one area in which porn can have an undeniably negative effect. Through porn, people may walk away with inappropriate conclusions about what is "normal."

The Dick's Not a Fix

Porn isn't the only way the number one lie is being perpetuated. It's in music too. A great example is the rapper Nelly's song "The Fix" (a remix of the old classic "Sexual Healing") in which he sings, "So come and get this dick. When you need that fix (yeah), that medicine." Nelly sure could learn a thing from those Victorian docs who knew the *real fix* for women's sexual frustration: stimulating the *clit*! And, certainly, Nelly isn't the only one singing about the power of men's dicks to please women. As you continue reading this book, just look and listen—this misguided idea is all around you.

One of the false ideas I'm hoping to wipe out is that the bigger the penis and the harder the thrusting, the better the female orgasm. While I'm at it, as I mentioned before, I'd like to wipe out the notion that women's main role is to give men pleasure—substituting it with the idea of women and men equally giving and receiving pleasure.

You've probably also heard a lot of misguided ideas in the media about hookup sex. Just so we're all on the same page, I'm defining hookups like the psychological research does: "Brief uncommitted sexual encounters between individuals who are not romantic partners or dating each other." So, basically, anything from kissing to having oral sex to having intercourse, without a commitment. Research shows that about 60 to 80 percent of you have had a hookup. You've probably heard that they're on the rise and that they're taking the place of relationships. Maybe you've read that guys never want a relationship after hooking up, but girls always do, and that hookups will make you feel bad about yourself.

The truth is that while the term "hookup" is relatively new, the behavior isn't novel. Women and men in my era were having them too (we called them one-night stands). One study shows that people graduating from college between 1988 and 1996 had about the same number of sexual partners as those graduating between 2002 and 2010, although the recent grads were *slightly* more likely to have had a sexual experience with a casual acquaintance. A new epidemic? Hardly. Just a rose by a different name.

What about the idea that hookups are taking the place of relationships—those pesky things women now don't want because they're too busy pursuing their careers and men don't want because sex is readily available without all that hassle? Strike that too:

> In one study, 63 percent of men and 84 percent of women said they'd prefer a committed sexual relationship.

In my class, the numbers were even higher: 81 percent of men and 93 percent of women said they'd rather have a relationship than a hookup.

Okay, then how about the notion that someone is always going to end up wanting more, and it's always the woman? Well, it turns out there's a grain of truth to this, but only a grain. In one study, 65 percent of women and 45 percent of men reported wishing their hookup would become a committed sexual relationship. Strike the rampant sex differences in relationship yearning.

What about the idea that hooking up leads women to feel bad about themselves—regret, shame, self-loathing? After hooking up, women and men both report a mix of positive (e.g., happy) and negative (e.g., regretful) emotions. Still, studies do find emotional gaps between the sexes. Some pretty telling findings:

> The morning after hooking up, 82 percent of men and 57 percent of women were glad they'd done it.

Now, this still means that *more than half* of women *and* men feel glad the morning after. But men feel happier about it than women.

Why? There are probably two reasons: the sexual double standard and women's lack of pleasure during hookups.

We still have a sexual double standard that judges women more harshly than men for the same sexual behaviors. In my most recent class:

> 78 percent of the men and 83 percent of the women said they'd engaged in "slut shaming."

How sad. Let's stop this. Women aren't going to fully enjoy sex that they're called a slut for having.

Speaking of enjoyment, along with slut shaming, I believe women feel worse the next morning simply because they didn't have as much fun. As you'll remember from chapter 1, the orgasm disparity is *huge* in hookup sex. (In my class, 55 percent of men versus 4 percent of women had orgasms during first-time hookup sex.) Recalling what you already know, the reason for this disparity is the lack of clitoral stimulation in hookups.

Get Me a Glass of Water, Girl

In conducting interviews with high school and college females for her book *Girls and Sex: Navigating the Complicated New Landscape*, Peggy Orenstein got frustrated by all the stories she heard of non-reciprocal oral sex. She thus asked a high school senior how she'd feel if a guy expected her to "fetch a glass of water from the kitchen whenever they were together yet never (or only grudgingly) offered to do so in return." Peggy says the young woman got the point; I hope you do too.

One of my students told me that the first time she hooked up with her now long-term boyfriend, he focused all on her. They made out and he gave her oral sex. When she offered to go down on him, he said no. He said he wanted it to be all about her. I'm guessing this story sounds crazy unusual to you. Yet the opposite story—where the hookup is all about his pleasure and orgasm—doesn't sound unfamiliar at all.

While, again, I'm not suggesting we flip things around and start having all hookups be completely about female orgasms, I am suggesting that in hookups involving genital stimulation, both parties get the gender-specific stimulation (penis for him, clitoris for her) that most reliably results in orgasms. I think if this happened, women's morning-after gladness level would be closer to men's. Indeed, in one study on hookups, better quality sex reduced regret.

Quality sex means orgasm equality. Orgasm equality means regarding clitoral stimulation and penile penetration as equal. Starting with the Greeks and Romans, and continuing through today's cultural landscape, we've never had this type of equality. We've never—at any point in Western history—had a time when the majority of the population valued women's ways of reaching an orgasm as equal to a man's. Way back in 1966, Masters and Johnson said the female orgasm "has never achieved the undeniable status afforded the male ejaculation." They also wrote that while the male orgasm has the purpose of procreation in its favor, this doesn't account for the "force with which the female orgasmic experience . . . is negated." Writing recently, Shere Hite says we've not yet overturned centuries of belief about the supremacy of intercourse. And in her keen historical analysis that she calls "Lost and Found: The Story of the Clitoris" in her book *Promiscuities,* Naomi Wolf points out that throughout history, writers have given us "*groundbreaking* instructions about exactly what to do to please women," and yet somehow we keep forgetting these messages. Wolf points out a cultural cycle in which clitoral knowledge is provided and forgotten, provided and forgotten—including overlooking the fact that the message was given in prior generations. Let's not repeat this history.

Instead, it's time to change history. Borrowing the words of Dr. Cornel West, when talking about racial injustice:

> **It's time to stop being so well adjusted to the injustice.**

Being well adjusted to orgasm injustice means not knowing enough about your clitoris. Adjusting to the injustice means going down on him and consistently getting nothing in return. Adjusting to the injustice means prioritizing his penetration-based orgasm and maybe even faking yours alongside it. Revolution comes after a long history of mistreatment. It comes from not wanting to be adjusted to the injustice any longer.

It's time for a cultural and personal orgasm revolution. It's time to *become cliterate*!

INCREASE YOUR CLITERACY

4.

LET'S LOOK UNDER THE HOOD

When we don't know what's there, we don't know
how to play with it thoroughly or well, and neither
do our partners. And, of course, we can't teach
them if we don't know how to do it ourselves.

—Sheri Winston, *Women's Anatomy of Arousal*

Remember me telling you that I found history a little dull yet I truly believe that understanding the past is the key to a better future? Well, the same is true when it comes to anatomy. I find anatomy to be a dry topic, and at the same time, I know that understanding one's genital anatomy is the key to getting wet! You can't put your lady bits to good use until you know a good bit about them. Warning: this chapter requires more than reading. I'm going to ask for audience participation. Materials needed include your vulva, a mirror, and maybe even a cell phone and a selfie stick. Here we go!

NAVIGATING TO NIRVANA

Before cell phone apps gave us directions, people needed road maps to get from one place to another. Think of this chapter as your road map

Redirecting, Redirecting, Redirecting!

Have you ever used a GPS device and taken a wrong turn, and it keeps telling you that it's redirecting you—leaving you lost but now also frustrated at the device itself? That's how making this orgasm road map was for me. Even though I lecture on female anatomy in my classes, when doing additional research for this chapter, several times I found myself more and more uncertain. I kept discovering inconsistencies in information, even across reliable sources. For example, two sources pointed out that the clitoris attaches in two places to the inner lips (parts you will soon learn about in detail), a third source presented this as an either-or choice (i.e., it attaches in one or the other place), and a fourth source (the one I trusted the most) said it attaches in one place. Trying to gain some clarity, my awesome research assistant and I looked at ours (independently, not together!) multiple times (it's a hoot to be my assistant!). We both found two attachments. So I wrote the author of my most trusted source and the reply was something along the lines of "You're right! I didn't know it attached in two places." Wow! Here was a world-renowned authority on sex who was still sometimes confused and trying to figure out accurate information on women's sexual anatomy. I was floored, but relieved to get an answer to this anatomy puzzle. Yet things

to orgasm. Once you know the ins and outs (another pun intended) of your genitals, you'll have a much easier time letting your fingers do the walking. Indeed, you'll make good use of this road map in a later chapter when you take matters into your own hands to reach orgasm. You'll also need this road map to give orgasm directions to a partner—something else we'll focus on in a later chapter.

Speaking of road maps, there are a few things I want to tell you about this one. Because I want this chapter to be your road map to having orgasms, rather than a tedious biology lesson, I've highlighted the main roads and left off some side streets. I've also used common, instead of proper or medical, names. For example, I use the term "lips" instead of got even more confusing when I tried to direct my talented illustrator to draw the clitoral bulbs (another important part you'll soon learn about). In some illustrations they looked like floppy rabbit ears and in others they looked like inflated balloons. Initially, I figured some were engorged and some weren't (you'll learn about this too), but the sources were generally unclear about if my assumption was true. Also, sometimes the bulbs ended above the vagina, sometimes below. I again wrote a trusted colleague who had a picture in their source, and they sent me the MRI image they'd used to create their picture. But the image and their illustration looked totally different to me! In the end, for the pictures in this book, I opted for a combination of aesthetics and a compilation of other pictures. When I somewhat fearfully confessed this to my brilliant editor—telling her I knew my facts were accurate but I wasn't sure if my pictures were 100 percent correct—she pointed out that this confusion and inconsistency was the reason for this book. She said it was a perfect illustration of our societal *illcliteracy*! To achieve cliteracy, we need a GPS unit that doesn't keep redirecting. So while this road map might not be perfect, I hope it provides more clarity than questions. Plus, I hope it will give you directions that are straightforward enough to get you where you need to go (or need to come, as the case may be).

"labia." Also, please know that this road map takes you on a long journey (it's a long chapter). I thought about dividing it into two separate trips (two chapters), but in the end I kept it as one. That's because every stop on this journey is related to every other stop and it all leads to the same place: an understanding of your anatomy that will enhance your pleasure. Still, akin to a long road trip, please don't keep driving when bleary eyed and tired. Take some breaks. To facilitate this, just like a good highway sign, I'll point out rest stops along the way.

Also, I didn't create this road map all by myself. Because I know a whole lot more about psychology than biology, I used several trusted sources. Most of the information in this chapter (including inspiration for some of the pictures) comes from anatomical chapters in the following books: *Women's Anatomy of Arousal, The Guide to Getting It On,* and *A New View of a Woman's Body.* So if you want additional maps, check out these sources. But for now, put on your seat belt and enjoy the ride to an exquisite and fun-filled destination!

THE ERECTION CONNECTION

Have you ever heard the riddle about what a Rubik's Cube and a penis have in common? The answer is that the longer you play with them, the harder they get. Well, guess what? The same is true for women. That's right—just like men, our genitals are chock-full of erectile tissue. And your erectile tissue works the same way a guy's does.

Erectile tissue contains capillaries with a unique feature. When you're not aroused, the blood flows freely in and out, but when you are aroused, the blood goes in but not out. Erectile tissue filling with blood is called "engorgement," and it makes the tissue feel fuller and firmer. It's your female version of a male erection. Later I'll explain what happens to all this blood at the point of orgasm. But first, as we go through your anatomy, I'll point out the places where this erectile tissue is most abundant.

PRETTY AS A PICTURE!

Have you ever taken a look "down there"? If yes, hooray for you! If not, you're in good company. A high percentage of women have never taken the time to look at their own vulvas. That's at least in part because taking a peek requires concerted effort. Most guys know what their penis looks like in intimate detail—it's right there for viewing, touching, and wrapping one's hands around while urinating and masturbating. Women, on the other hand, can go to the bathroom and have sexual relations, all without ever looking at their own genitals. Along the same lines, men have countless opportunities to look at other men's penises in locker rooms and bathrooms (and, according to both research and men I talk to, they definitely do check each other out!). All women see of one another in locker rooms is a very unrevealing frontal view (basically a hairy or hairless triangle between the legs). Unless women are having sexual relationships with other women, porn images are about the only way women see a close-up of one another's genitals. However, porn images of women's vulvas are unrealistic and even digitally altered, especially the inner lips—a part that is incredibly sexually responsive.

Speaking of the inner lips—and how they are both sexually responsive and often altered in porn—let's make sure we're all on the same page. I don't want to start talking about the inner lips or any other part "down there" until I'm sure you know what's what. So here's a very simple picture of a vulva with the most important parts labeled.

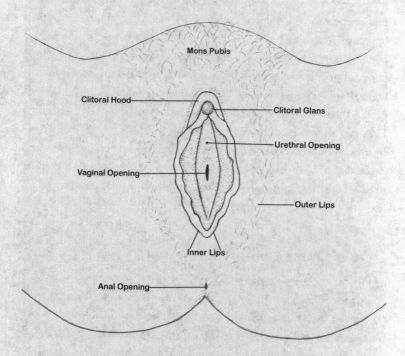

Now let's go through each labeled part one by one.

Outer Lips. As stated by Sheri Winston, author of *Women's Anatomy of Arousal*, these folds of tissue "form two fleshy parentheses to . . . enclose

Bare or Hair Down There?

Check out appendix A, "Cool Tidbits for Your Lady Bits," for information to help you decide what to do with your hair down there.

the delicate parts within." They come in a variety of sizes (thin to thick) and are covered with hair (unless you remove the hair, something Western women are increasingly doing). While it definitely feels good to have them caressed, kissed, or pushed on to stimulate what's beneath them, their main purpose is simply to protect what's underneath. In the previous picture, the outer lips have been pulled apart to reveal what they're protecting.

Urethral Opening. There is a short tube that leads to your bladder, and its opening is where your urine comes out. It's located just above the vaginal opening. Even though you can see it on the diagram, the actual urethral opening is a tiny slit hidden between folds of tissue. Even up close and personal, it may not be visible. So when you have a chance to look at yourself in a few minutes, the urethral opening might be difficult to locate. Truth be told, I couldn't find mine the last time I looked . . . but then I gave up and stopped trying because I got (er, um, cough) "distracted" by my clit! But some of you may persist in looking longer than I did, and if you do, make sure to look for a small circle of firm tissue around the urethral opening—some women find this area pleasurable to touch.

Your Outer Lips = His Scrotum

Your outer lips are made from the same tissue as a man's scrotum. In male fetuses, what starts as the outer lips are then fused to make the sac that encases their balls. In female fetuses, the opening between the lips remains and the lips fill with fat. In short, we all start out the same and our differences don't disappear. Both men and women have delicate parts that need protection.

Hey, Asshole!

No, I'm not calling anyone a nasty name. I'm reminding you that there's a third opening "down there" that leads to another canal—that is, your anus. The anal opening is where your poop comes out. It has a lot of nerve endings, so some people like to be stimulated there (e.g., touching, kissing) during partnered sex. While anal intercourse (putting a penis in the anus) is generally associated with gay men, the truth is that a lot of heterosexual couples practice it. In one recent survey, one-third of women had tried anal sex at least once. If anal sex is something you want to try, please read up on it first, because specific precautions are necessary to prevent the spread of diseases (anal sex carries the highest risk of disease transmission among all sexual activity) and painful anal tearing (unlike the vagina, the anus doesn't lubricate naturally). If you're anally curious, an especially good source is chapter 24, "Anal Sex: Up Your Bum," in the eighth edition of *The Guide to Getting It On*.

Vaginal Opening. This is the opening to a canal inside your body—the vagina. It's not a hole but more like a crevice or crack. It has touch receptors, which is why some women enjoy stimulation here. Some women who have sex with men say they enjoy their partner teasing them with his penis at the opening. Also, as a woman gets excited, the vaginal opening constricts a bit, which is why when a man first puts his penis inside, it can feel as if it's being snugly held. It's also why many women who enjoy intercourse say that the first thrust is the best one.

As long as we're talking about changes in the vaginal opening with excitement, let's talk about the changes inside the vagina with excitement. The vagina is a hollow canal whose walls are made of tissue, nerves, and blood vessels. When a woman isn't aroused, the two walls of her vagina lie flat against each other. But when a woman is aroused, her vagina does two things. First, it lubricates, or gets wet. Second, it changes size and

A Wet Tent

Vaginal lubrication and tenting make intercourse more pleasurable. Conversely, having intercourse before these two things occur can cause pain. Also, some women get wetter than others. We'll talk more about all of this in chapter 7.

shape. It narrows in the front but also gets wider in the back and elongates. The vagina expands from about 3 to 4 inches in length to about 5 to 6 inches—long enough to accommodate fingers, a dildo, or a penis. This miraculous change is called "vaginal tenting."

There are important differences between the front and back of the vagina. To understand these differences, first know that different types of nerve endings sense different things. For example, some sense touch and some sense pressure. Like the vaginal opening, the first third of the vaginal canal has a lot of touch-sensitive nerve endings. On the other hand, the inner two-thirds of the vagina has almost no touch-sensitive nerve endings and, instead, has a lot of pressure-sensitive nerve endings. In fact, there are so few touch-sensitive nerve endings in the innermost two-thirds of the vagina that one older source says that minor surgery can be performed there without anesthetic (although I wouldn't want to try this!). In one study, unaroused women couldn't even detect when they were being touched with a probe in this part of their vaginas. This lack of touch-sensitive vaginal nerve endings is also why we can generally wear tampons without discomfort. But again, the back part of the vagina is not insensitive—it's just sensitive to pressure, not touch. And, as explained by Paul Joannides, the author of *Guide to Getting It On,* these pressure-sensitive nerve endings are why some women find that "having a thicker object like a penis or dildo in the back of their vagina can feel . . . good . . . when her clitoris is being stimulated."

Mons Pubis. This is a mound of fatty tissue that sits on top of the pubic bone. Like the outer lips, if it's not shaved or waxed, it's covered in pubic hair. While a mound of fat covered in hair doesn't sound erotic, it actually

Your Vagina = His Degenerated Tissue

The embryonic tissue that becomes the vagina develops from the Müllerian ducts, tissue that disappears in the male body. So much for the vagina and penis being equivalent sex organs.

is! Some women like the feeling of their own (or their partner's) fingers pushing, pulling upward, or making a circular motion on the mons. The reason this feels good is because the mons is full of nerve endings and because it covers part of the clitoris that you can't see. We'll talk about this internal part of the clitoris a little later. Now let's talk about the parts of the clit that you can see and touch.

Clitoral Glans and Hood. And now the star of our sexual show: the clitoris! The only part of it that you can see is the glans, or tip, and the hood that covers it.

The hood provides a loose covering for the clitoral glans. In our picture of the vulva (page 57), the hood is pulled back to expose the glans. In some women, the hood totally covers the glans, and in others, it partially covers the glans. Indeed, there's a huge variety in the shapes of hoods and in the ways they cover the glans. Hoods also vary in size and color. Although some are bonded to the clitoris (and this doesn't create sexual problems), in most women, the hood glides over the glans. When pleasuring themselves, it's common for women to lightly press their fingertip against the hood and rub small circles, round and round, thereby stimulating the glans that lies beneath the hood.

Spoiler Alert!

In chapter 6, when you "take matters into your own hands" and pleasure yourself, you'll get specific instructions for playing with your mons in this way (as well as for touching yourself in other ways mentioned in this chapter).

Your Hood = His Foreskin

The clitoral hood is analogous to the male foreskin. The hood provides a covering for the clitoral glans, and the foreskin provides a covering for the head of the penis. Just like some women pleasure themselves by rubbing their clitoral hood in circles to stimulate the glans below, some men who haven't been circumcised move their foreskin back and forth over the head of their penis.

The clitoral glans is a smooth, round bump that is jam-packed with nerves. Many sex educators and researchers claim that the glans of the clitoris has more nerve endings than anywhere else on the human body—male or female—with anywhere from six to eight thousand nerve endings. But pickier scientists point out that there are about the same number of nerve endings on the glans of the clitoris as the head of the penis—it's just that they're packed more tightly together (they all fit into an area about the size of a pea). However, quoting one scientist, we know this for sure:

> **Both the clitoris and the penis function similarly as sensory organs.**

Thus, to emphasize a main message of this book, while the penis is the key to men's orgasms, the clitoris (*not* the vagina!) holds the key to women's orgasms.

The part of the clit that can be seen by peeking under the hood—the glans—is an exquisitely sensitive sexual organ. In fact, it's so sensitive that most women cannot touch it directly without discomfort, even pain. Instead, many women get intense pleasure by rubbing the hood that covers it. But some women find even touching the hood to be too intense and need more indirect stimulation, perhaps even liking to touch themselves through their panties. The sensitivity of a woman's clitoral glans

I'm So Sensitive!

Some women say that their clits change sensitivity with their menstrual cycle, and research confirms that women's level of sexual desire and ease of being aroused changes with the time of the month. This helps explain why women can vary in terms of how they like to be touched at different times.

has nothing to do with its size. Some women have a glans that is so large it resembles a small penis, while others have a glans that can hardly be seen. The average glans is about the size of a pencil eraser. But, once again, women vary. So in a minute, when you look at yours, please remember that, as wisely stated by Paul Joannides:

> There's no limit to the enjoyment a woman can have with her clitoris regardless of how big or small it is.

Inner Lips. The inner lips are *very* sexually reactive. Also filled with erectile tissue, they get engorged with blood and can double or triple in size when a woman is aroused. They also deepen in color when aroused. And guess what? Some experts say that the inner lips should be considered part of the clitoris because of their physical connection to it. The inner lips connect to both the glans and the hood of the clitoris. In fact, the hood is formed in part by the top area of the inner lips. Because there's a lot of diversity in hood sizes and shapes, there's also a lot of variety in just how the hood attaches to the inner lips. Regardless of this variety, here's the most useful and important take-away point: because the lips and clitoris are physically connected, a lot of women find that caressing or gently tugging on their inner lips is a great way to indirectly stimulate their clit.

Not only are the inner lips erotic in their own right and a great way to indirectly stimulate the clitoris but also, according to Paul Joannides:

> The . . . inner lips give vulvas their unique personality.

The inner lips fan out in different ways and shapes across women. They can be between ¼ inch and 2 inches wide and between ¾ inch and 4 inches long. They're usually asymmetrical, and it's normal for one lip to be as much as double the size of the other. Many women have an inner lip or lips that protrude from their outer lips. Full disclosure: I am one of those women with uneven inner lips, with one larger than the other and extending beyond my outer lips. Importantly, I had my sexual coming-of-age during an era not only when we all knew about the clitoris but also before media images instilled genital shame among women. My big lip never concerned me—but today, a young woman with a similar genital profile might feel self-conscious and even consider surgery.

Today, labiaplasty—surgery in which the size of the inner lips is reduced—is becoming increasingly common. Sex educators and therapists attribute this rise in genital cosmetic surgery to unrealistic porn images

The Nerve of Her!

Women also vary in how their nerves are positioned in their genitals. For example, one woman can have as many as fourteen times more nerve receptors on the glans of her clitoris than another woman—a finding that helps explain why some women find rubbing their clitoral hood to be too intense, even painful, and others find it intensely pleasurable. Also, while most women have the majority of touch-sensitive nerve endings on the glans of their clitoris, some women have more on their inner lips. Additionally, some women's nerve endings are highly concentrated in one area (e.g., to the right or left of their clitoral hood), while others have nerve endings that are more evenly spread out. These differences clearly illustrate why women vary in the type of genital stimulation they need to orgasm.

Your Inner Lips = Head of His Penis

The inner lips are made of the same tissue as the head of the penis, except that they're thinner. They're hairless and their edges are jam-packed with nerves. That's right—your inner lips are analogous to what many men say is the most sensitive part of their penis. No doubt if more women and men knew about the inner lips, more women would orgasm.

of women's inner lips. Just like men in porn are chosen for having larger than average penises, women in porn are often chosen for having especially small and symmetrical inner lips, with some porn actresses achieving this look through surgery. And when it comes to still photographs of women's vulvas, most are digitally altered. In fact, in the last few decades the inner lips of *Playboy* centerfolds have become almost invisible, and one study found that even minor exposure to such altered images influenced a woman's perception of what a normal vulva looks like. Another really telling (and sad) study found that almost all women undergoing surgery to decrease the size of their inner lips actually had normal-size ones to begin with.

Plot Twist: Pussy Perceptions

Many women feel self-conscious about how their vulva looks (or lubricates, smells, or tastes). Because self-conscious self-chatter interferes with women's ability to relax and orgasm, we'll work on eliminating this in the next chapter. For now, though, here's an interesting plot twist: research shows that men have more positive attitudes toward women's genitals than women do! As stated by a man in one of my classes, "I've never heard a guy talk shit about a woman's genitals. We're just happy to get near them!"

To counteract unrealistic porn images, several online sites and blogs have been created to show the diversity—*and beauty*—of women's genitals. On many of these online sites, real women provide pictures of their vulvas. The following picture is from one such wonderful site, Gynodiversity.

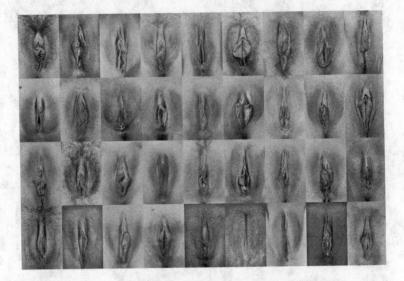

If you've never seen so many real vulvas before, looking at this picture might make you a little uncomfortable. It might surprise or even astonish you. But please take the time to look and appreciate the picture, noticing how each vulva is unique. Notice not only the huge variety in the shapes and symmetry of the inner lips but also how some clitoral hoods are larger than others, and how some totally cover and some partially cover the glans. Because of their individuality, vulvas have been compared by many writers to beautiful snowflakes. Even identical twins don't have identical vulvas. The size, symmetry or asymmetry, and color of the inner lips give each woman's vulva a distinctive look.

Now that you hopefully appreciate the unique beauty of vulvas, it's time to take a look at your own magnificence.

Stop at the Store

At some point during your journey, stop at the store and get some lubricant. You'll need it for pleasuring yourself in chapter 6. You can read about the different types available in appendix A, "Cool Tidbits for Your Lady Bits." Because of all the choices available, I asked a gynecologist specializing in sexual medicine, "If you could recommend just one lube, which would it be?" She recommended Uberlube. I tried it and agree it's awesome. Because it's made of silicone, it needs to be spot tested before use with silicone sex toys. Great options that don't need to be spot tested are hybrid lubes, such as Sliquid Silk, BabeLube Silk available at Babeland (Babeland.com), or Please Cream Lube available at Good Vibrations (GoodVibes .com). Another fun option is to get a sampler pack of different lubes at Babeland or Good Vibrations. In case you're wondering, I don't have stock in either company—I'm recommending them based on the clear information they have on choosing lubes.

GET OUT A MIRROR!

Now comes the part you might feel a bit hesitant about if you've never taken the time to examine yourself. Some initial shyness with your own body is perfectly normal. However, I lovingly encourage you to push through your hesitation and look at your vulva. And as you do, I sincerely hope you can put aside any unrealistic images of women's vulvas that you've seen. Instead, hold in mind the real vulvas you just saw, realizing that your own is also a unique, one-of-a-kind snowflake. Loving your vulva, knowing what it looks like and how it likes to be touched, is part of becoming cliterate—it's essential to your personal orgasm revolution.

So please find some quiet time when you have privacy. Make sure your room is at a comfortable temperature. Make sure the lighting is good enough for you to really see yourself. Lay this book next to you, opened to the picture of the labeled vulva (page 57). Get out a mirror. If you have one, a magnifying mirror is especially useful. Your cell phone in selfie mode, along with a selfie stick, is another great way to see yourself. Also, you'll want to moisten your fingers, since your genitals are not meant to be touched when dry. While spit isn't a good lubricant for extended touching, because it dries up quickly, you can use it now. Or, if you happen to have some *pure* coconut oil in your pantry, use that instead—it works great for touching yourself. (Other types of oils are not recommended.) Of course, if you already have some personal lubricant, that's a great choice too.

Sit on your couch or bed, prop yourself up with some pillows behind your neck and back, and spread your legs apart. You can bend one knee up or leave both legs down. With one hand, hold your mirror or your cell phone camera in selfie mode, and with the other hand, gently pull your outer lips aside. Then take the time to slowly look and identify your mons, your vaginal opening, and, if you can find it, your urethral opening. The easiest way to find your urethral opening is to put a finger inside your vagina and pull downward (toward your anus); the urethral opening will often then appear from within the folds of skin. After you've located your urethral opening, if you did, take a look at your inner lips. Follow them

upward to find where they form and connect to your clitoral hood. Then gently pull back the hood and see your exquisitely sensitive glans. Also notice how the upper part of your inner lips is attached to the bottom of the glans. Because the glans can be small, it may be hard to find, but it's definitely worth the effort. When I first saw mine, I was filled with the excitement of discovery ("There *she* is!"). Take time to look and appreciate her! Say, "Hello, Clio!"

If you're so inclined, and again with moistened fingers, begin to touch in some of the ways I've described (e.g., pull or press on your mons, caress your inner lips, rub your clitoral hood in circles, touch around your vaginal opening). As you do, you'll feel your tissue engorge and you'll see your skin change color. You might get wet. But if you just want to look for now, that's okay too! We'll get into the touching part in a later chapter. For now, the important thing is to see yourself. And as you finish looking (and perhaps touching), I'd love it if you would say to yourself **"I am beautiful"**—because you truly are!

Now's a good time to take one of those short rest-stop breaks. And as you do, I hope you'll revel at how much you've just learned about your wonderful, one-of-a-kind vulva!

BEYOND THE LOOKING GLASS

Now that you've seen your visible parts, it's time to learn about those parts you can't see, which are central to your arousal and orgasm. Let's start with the internal clitoris:

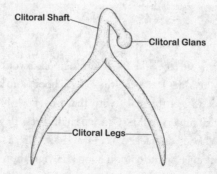

Clitoral Shaft

Clitoral Glans

Clitoral Legs

The only part of the clitoris you can see is the glans, or tip. The two parts you can't see—the shaft and legs—are inside your pelvis. And it's important to know that these inside parts are made of erectile tissue. In fact, when you're aroused, your clitoris will get anywhere from 50 to 300 percent larger! This is your female version of a male erection. But, whereas a man's erection happens on the outside of his body, where it can be seen, most of yours happens on the inside. In terms of just where inside your body your clitoris is located, the legs—which are wishbone shaped—sit underneath your lips and the shaft sits underneath your mons. You can actually feel the shaft with a little effort. Yep, that's right: time to touch yourself again!

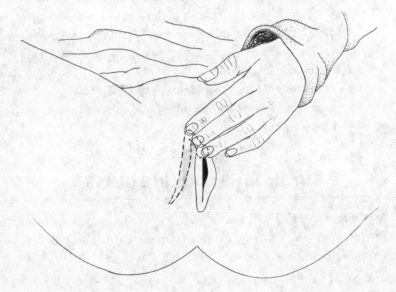

Sit on a firm surface, like the floor; then place your ring finger at the point where the inner lips meet (the clitoral hood) and gently press down. You'll be able to feel the glans with that finger while your middle and index (pointer) fingers will rest on the shaft. Press down with these two fingers as well and you'll feel the clitoral shaft. Alternatively, you can put your pointer finger on the clitoral hood and your thumb above the hood, and squeeze. You'll likely then be able to feel the shaft move; it might feel a little like a round rubber cord. And because you're touching a part of your clit, this is likely to feel good!

Now that you hopefully have both a visual and tactile sense of your internal clitoris, it's time to see another central part of your internal sexual anatomy: the clitoral bulbs.

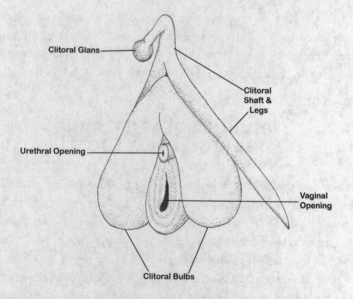

You've probably never heard of these internal bulbs before, yet they are *very* important for your arousal and orgasm. Like the clitoris, they have no other function than sexual pleasure. Some consider them part of the clitoris and others consider them a separate organ. They're two big wads of erectile tissue, shaped sort of like teardrops, that swell perhaps even more than the rest of the clitoris (or the penis) when aroused. They surround the vaginal canal. They're also nestled beneath the lips and connect at the top to the shaft of the clitoris. Knowing this anatomy helps explain why some women masturbate by putting their fingers underneath their lips and rubbing, sometimes even pushing deeply inward (kind of like a deep-tissue massage). Doing this might stimulate the inner lips, the legs of the clitoris, and the clitoral bulbs all at once. This is the best three-for-the-price-of-one deal I've ever heard of! Or, think of these three parts as:

> # A trio called Clio!

A trio is a group of three people or things. Often this word is associated with the making of music (e.g., a jazz trio). You can think of the inner lips, the clitoris, and the clitoral bulbs as a trio of musicians who work in harmony to create the beautiful music of your arousal and orgasm.

WHY NOT A QUARTET? CAN THE VAGINA PLAY TOO?

Where does the vagina fit into this musical group? After all, many women enjoy being touched at the vaginal opening and the feeling of pressure inside the vagina. Plus, like the other members of our musical group, the vagina gets engorged during arousal, and it lubricates. So why not consider it part of the symphony and make it a quartet?

Because for the vast majority of women, beautiful music can be made (i.e., an orgasm reached) with *just* the trio, yet the same is not true of the vagina. Very few women can reach an orgasm with just this instrument *alone*—and for most women, the music can be made without the vagina coming to band practice at all! It's not that this instrument can't add beautiful sounds to the music; it's just that it's not *necessary* to make the music.

Take another look at the picture of the internal clitoris and clitoral bulbs (page 71). As you can see, the bulbs are the only part of our trio that is adjacent to the vagina. They straddle the vagina. Do you also see the distance between the vaginal opening and the glans of the clitoris? In essence, this picture provides a clear visual of why penetration is generally insignificant for an orgasm to occur: penetration is happening too far

A Rule of Thumb

Some research finds that those women who can orgasm from the stimulation of just a thrusting penis may have less distance between their clitoral glans and vaginal opening than those who don't orgasm this way. There's even what's been referred to as the "rule of thumb": women who have less than 2.5 centimeters (a little shy of an inch) between the tip of their clitoris and their vaginal opening are more likely to orgasm from just a thrusting penis. Take out a tape measure and see for yourself! (I did. As suspected, the distance was way more than an inch!) Or use your thumb to measure: 2.5 centimeters is from about the tip of your thumb to your first knuckle. (Warning: if you measure this way, the tip of your thumb on the tip of your clitoris may be a little distracting!) To sum up this critically important point: if your clit tip and vaginal opening are more than about an inch apart, the penis moving in the vagina during intercourse is probably not close enough to where the stimulation needs to be. Stated even more strongly, trying to have an orgasm from a thrusting penis alone when your body isn't built that way is trying to attain something that's biologically impossible. But, no need to worry—all you need to do is stop relying on intercourse to stimulate your clit, and give her the direct attention she deserves!

away from where women's most sexually responsive organs are. A thrusting penis alone is not likely to stimulate all the parts of female anatomy (i.e., our trio) that work together for female orgasm.

What about women who do orgasm from intercourse alone? Some say it's because the bulbs surround the vaginal canal, and a thrusting penis could potentially stimulate them. Alternatively, as explained by Shere Hite, for some women under some circumstances, a thrusting penis can pull the inner lips and clitoral hood in just the right way as to stimulate the clitoral glans for an orgasm to occur. But, using an apt metaphor also provided by Hite:

> Pulling your ear slightly back and forth can also pull the skin on your cheek.

Continuing this metaphor, if you really want your cheek to move, why not just move it directly rather than rely on the adjacent ears to get it moving? Stated non-metaphorically, why rely on the vagina to stimulate the clit when you can do it directly?

BUT WHAT ABOUT THAT INTRAVAGINAL SPOT?

Perhaps you're wondering about the G-spot and how it fits into the idea that most women orgasm from clitoral versus vaginal stimulation—since, after all, the G-spot is inside the vagina. Once again, in this case, a picture is worth a thousand words.

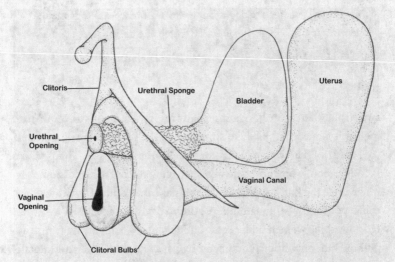

Tell Me More About That Spot, Baby

Putting pressure on the G-spot substantially increases a woman's pain threshold—it causes her to be able to tolerate more pain. Likewise, during childbirth, women experience a significant increase in their pain threshold. Several scientists have put two and two together and speculated that the G-spot may have an evolutionary purpose. As a baby exits through the birth canal, his or her head exerts pressure on the G-spot area, thereby reducing the pain of the birthing process. Some go as far as to guess that this reduction in pain is probably also helpful to mother–child bonding. (I wonder if it also makes women more likely to be willing to go through childbirth again.) Adding more weight to the idea that the G-spot is related to childbirth is the fact that the uterus pulls upward during an orgasm from clitoral stimulation and pushes downward into the vagina during an orgasm from G-spot stimulation. Indeed, one woman— quoted in the book *The G-Spot*—talked about having a similar urge to push during childbirth as during sexual G-spot stimulation.

When looking at this picture, you'll notice that the G-spot isn't labeled. This is because it isn't actually a specific thing that can be seen. In fact, the G-spot isn't a *spot* on the vaginal wall at all—it's an *area* that can be *felt through* the front (belly side) wall of the vagina. It's made up of a number of distinct anatomical parts, including—but not limited to—the vaginal wall, the urethra, a spongy area of erectile tissue that surrounds the urethra, and parts of the internal clitoris. Many scientists now call this area the clitoris-urethra-vagina (CUV) complex.

Let's talk a little more about the urethra part of this CUV complex. A spongy area of erectile tissue surrounds the urethra. This spongy area is called the urethral sponge, the paraurethral gland, or the "female prostate gland"—a name given to it in 2001 by a group of world-renowned experts who set the world standards for anatomical terms (clearly a big deal). Since the urethra and vagina are in close proximity, some speculate that the function of this sponge is to protect the urethra during sexual intercourse, acting as a buffer between the penis and the urethra. Regardless of its function, for the purpose of understanding where the CUV complex is located, the important point to remember is that this sponge runs along the roof of the vagina and can be felt through the vaginal wall. As you can see in the picture, it's near the vagina and parts of the internal clitoris and clitoral bulbs—hopefully giving you a clear visual of the fact that the G-spot is a complex area consisting of many structures— including our beloved clitoris!

Boiling down a lot of scientific debate on the G-spot, here's what we know. First, not all women can find this area. Second—*very important*— some women find it sexually arousing to stimulate this area and some don't. And, interestingly, a recent group of researchers reported that the thickness of this area is related to how pleasurable a woman finds stimulating it to be. When I asked the women in my most recent class about their G-spot, their answers reflected this diversity. Of those who had tried to find their G-spot, 37 percent couldn't find it, 17 percent found it but it gave them no pleasure, and 46 percent found it and it gave them pleasure and led to an orgasm. Yet—really interesting—the majority of the women in my class (about 60 percent) said they hadn't even tried to find it. Truth be told, I'm in this camp. Because of what I do for a living, people often ask me if I've found my G-spot—and I tell them I haven't even looked. I *know* about a very reliable, easily accessible "spot" (okay,

G-Spot Stimulation for Her = Prostate Stimulation for Him

The authors of the book that popularized the G-spot contend that women and men have two parallel erotic areas: the clitoris and the G-spot, and the penis and the prostate. They point out that the clitoris and the penis are similarly easy to find, while the G-spot (felt through the anterior wall of the vagina) and the prostate (felt through the anterior wall of the rectum) are both more difficult to locate.

In Search of G (and A too)

If you want to see if you can find this complex area—inaccurately called a spot—it's easiest when lying on your back. Insert one or two fingers into your vagina, about 2 inches past the vaginal opening. Keep your palm up and make a "come here" motion with your fingers. When you do this, your paraurethral glands might start to swell and you might feel like you have to urinate. If you keep rubbing and exerting pressure on this area, you might feel a pleasurable sensation. But you might also dislike this sensation. Experts say this area is hard to find on your own and it's easiest to find by having a partner follow these directions or with a sex toy designed for this purpose, usually something firm but soft with a curve at the end (I'll tell you where to shop for sex toys in chapter 6). Also, some women find they like stimulation even higher up in the vagina—specifically, about 5 to 6 inches inside the vaginal canal. This area has been called the AFE (anterior fornix erogenous) zone, or the A-spot. Since it's deeper than most fingers can reach, you'd need a long sex toy to reach there. Finally, some women say they can best feel pleasurable areas inside the vagina during specific intercourse positions (e.g., rear entry, woman-on-top, sitting on a partner's lap while facing him). Some women say they can only feel such good sensations with a male partner with whom they "fit just right." But don't worry about finding such a guy, because—as you'll learn later—fingers or a vibrator can always be the right fit for your clit.

a trio) that gets me there every time. So I figure why go looking for one that's hard to find and that I might not even find if I look? To me it's akin to searching for buried treasure when my ATM card is handy and my bank account is full.

My goal here is not to diminish the way any woman experiences orgasm. Indeed, becoming cliterate is all about learning what brings you pleasure and believing that you have the right to such pleasure. So if G-spot stimulation or penile penetration is your thing, go for it. But if they're not, please stop buying into the cultural myth that they should be.

Speaking of cultural myths—and while the picture of the urethral sponge is hopefully still fresh in your mind—let's clear up the confusion about female ejaculation and squirting.

FEMALE EJACULATION AND SQUIRTING

Lately, a lot of porn shows women squirting fluid during an orgasm. Many women (and their partners) are starting to think they "should" do this too. Here's the truth.

Female ejaculation is when fluid is expelled from the urethra, and it does happen to some women. Some women expel this fluid during sexual arousal and some do so during orgasm. While female ejaculation is usually thought of as related to G-spot orgasm, it can happen without G-spot stimulation, and G-spot stimulation can happen without ejaculation. Female ejaculate does, however, seem to be created in those paraurethral glands. The fluid—usually only about a teaspoonful—is often described as looking like watered-down fat-free milk. It tastes sweet. Some women who secrete this fluid know it's happening. Others don't. And what about the gushing, squirting type? The most recent evidence indicates that's probably the milky fluid plus diluted urine.

But here's the bottom line. Female ejaculation is nothing to be ashamed of. It's also not a goal to strive for. It's just another beautiful variation

Porn Squirting: Fill Her Up!

A lot of the squirting in porn is fake, accomplished by filling the porn actresses' vaginas with liquid using either oral syringes or douches. As stated by one actress, "The director filled up a bunch of douches with water and had me lie on my back and started filling me up! Then as soon as he thought there was enough he threw the bottle out of sight and hit record."

Wait. Back Up.

There's evidence that all women do have some female ejaculate (i.e., the teaspoon or so of milky white fluid), but in some women it travels back into the bladder rather than out of the urethra. This is called retrograde ejaculation.

among women. However, sex therapists say that if you're not a natural gusher/squirter, trying to become one can harm pelvic muscles that are essential to reaching an orgasm (and which we'll talk about in a moment). *Aha!* Another endorsement for not considering porn the ideal and instead finding out how *your* body most naturally orgasms.

We've now arrived at Destination Orgasm! But before we get into this topic, if you're bleary eyed, now's a good time for another rest-stop break. When you return, we'll answer a question you may have been wondering about.

ARE THERE DIFFERENT KINDS OF ORGASMS?

Hopefully, you're convinced that an orgasm resulting from something inside your vagina isn't the ultimate goal. This prompts the question: Are there different types of orgasms, and if so, what are they?

Before answering, I first need to say that a lot of sex therapists and educators take issue with even asking this question. They point out that we live in a "difference equals deficit" culture, in which whenever we say two things are different, we automatically brand one as superior to the other. Sex therapists and educators also point out that some rare women can orgasm from just fantasizing or from their breasts being stimulated, but we don't talk about breast orgasms or fantasy orgasms—in this case, we don't label the orgasm based on the point of the stimulation. Likewise, when men orgasm from oral sex versus from penile-vaginal intercourse, we don't call these mouth and vagina orgasms! Equally striking, we don't talk about male prostate versus penis orgasms, even though some scientists say these are analogous to women's G-spot and clitoral orgasms. Indeed, it's only when it comes to the clitoris, the vagina, and the G-spot that we label the orgasm by where the woman was being stimulated when it happened—and we use this differentiation to declare one type of orgasm a superior goal to strive for.

But assuming you want more than a picking apart of the question itself, here's the less than satisfying but honest answer: at this point, scientists are still arguing.

One camp says there are different kinds of female orgasms. They talk about vaginal, clitoral, and blended orgasms (those resulting from stimulation of the clitoris and the vagina at the same time), and they point out that many women say these orgasms *feel* different from each other. They also tell us the vagina follows a different nerve pathway to the brain than does the clitoris—explaining why women with spinal cord injuries cutting off communication between their clitoris and brain can still have orgasms with vaginal stimulation. This camp points out, too, that different areas of the brain are activated during different types of orgasms. They refer as well to the uterus doing something different during G-spot and clitoral orgasms. In short, these scientists use biological evidence to support their claim that different types of orgasms exist.

Blended, Best, Bullshit!

A lot of recent writings tout blended orgasms as the best, claiming that a combination of vaginal and clitoral stimulation (i.e., penetration plus clitoral stimulation) *uniformly* produces the most satisfying orgasm. Well, I call bullshit. Some women prefer to get their clit stimulated without penetration and some like it with penetration. While it's certainly a step in the right direction to include clitoral stimulation as part of a "best orgasm" formula, declaring that pairing it with penetration is better than clitoral stimulation alone still perpetuates that number one lie we're trying to eradicate.

Another camp, however, points out that no matter where the stimulation is that finally leads to orgasm, engorgement of the clitoris (and the lips and bulbs) is involved in all female orgasms. They note that the front wall of the vagina is inextricably linked with the internal parts of the clitoris, and so stimulating the vagina without also stimulating the internal clitoris and clitoral bulbs is impossible. Thus, they claim all female orgasms are clitoral—even those resulting only from stimulation inside the vagina.

A third camp says this is an irrelevant question. But they don't say this based on the philosophical arguments provided earlier. Instead, they use biological reasoning, claiming that it's time we start thinking of women's entire sexual anatomy as one functional, connected unit. They point out that no matter where stimulation resulting in an orgasm occurs, all female orgasms manifest themselves in the genital region and involve the same muscle contractions (which you'll learn about in the next section). One urologist even says we should consider calling the whole cluster of erectile tissue involved in female orgasms—including not only the clitoris and clitoral bulbs but also parts of the vagina and the G-spot area—a clitoris. As you might recall, earlier feminists said the same thing (and they included the inner lips). Both this recent urologist and earlier feminists pointed out that such an inclusive name would help us to finally stop the frivolous debate about clitoral versus vaginal orgasms.

C Is for Cervix

Those who say there are different kinds of orgasms include mention of a third type: cervical orgasms. Some women find cervical stimulation orgasmic; others *hate* it and find it painful. Another lesson in how all women's bodies are different.

Maybe you're wondering what camp I'm in. I'd like to say all orgasms are clitoral (after all, I want everyone to become cliterate!), yet I think the other two camps make valid arguments as well. In the end, my most genuine answer is "Why does it matter?" Unless you're a scientist or a doctor who wants to help women with spinal cord injuries orgasm, this question is irrelevant. Most important, I think attention to this debate contributes to women doubting their own most reliable route to reaching an orgasm. It's time to stop engaging in this argument and instead focus on something that almost everyone agrees on. That is, as stated by Sheri Winston:

> There's a lot of variety in what gets women off, but it's safe to generalize that . . . clitoral play will be the easiest and most essential orgasmic trigger.

So now let's talk about something that *does* matter to most women: What is an orgasm and what does it feel like?

ORGASMS EXPLAINED!

Many people say that if you don't know if you've had an orgasm, you probably haven't. While true, this isn't especially useful for those of you wanting to experience one. Still, as stated by Paul Joannides:

> The best way to define orgasm is to put your hand in your pants and give yourself one.

You may have already started this process in this chapter; you will definitely do so later. Still, I'd like to give you a little more sense of what an orgasm is and feels like.

To understand orgasms, remember engorgement, which is when those special capillaries in erectile tissue let the blood in but not out. All that blood going into your erectile tissue creates tension that builds up to a very high point. An orgasm is when powerful, rhythmic muscle contractions release that tension. These muscles are called pelvic floor muscles and their contractions prevent additional blood from coming into your

The (Yawn!) Sexual Response Cycle

Often when you hear about orgasm, it's in relation to the sexual response cycle: excitement, arousal, plateau, orgasm, and resolution. While I teach this in my human sexuality class, it's the most boring lecture I give. So I'll spare you the details and just say that there are a lot of physiological changes that happen in stages, leading to orgasm. Still, here's one change that's useful to know about: As you approach orgasm, the tip of your clitoris disappears. This might cause you (or your partner) to worry about where it's gone. But there's no need for concern—just keep the stimulation going. The clitoris still responds to stimulation where the tip used to be visible.

erectile tissue. When the contractions cease, blood flows in and out again, rather than just in, and your erectile tissue shrinks back to its original size and color. An orgasm is also accompanied by fast breathing and, oftentimes, flushed skin on your chest and stomach. And, stating the obvious, having an orgasm feels good. Here's a description by one woman, as quoted in a widely used human sexuality textbook:

> It feels like all the tension that has been building and building is released with an explosion. It is the most pleasurable thing in the whole world.

What's really important is that how women experience this buildup of tension and release varies—as does the experience of orgasm from one encounter to another. Many women feel the intense, pulsing muscle contractions of orgasm, yet others feel a general buildup of muscle tension followed by a very pleasurable feeling of overall release. Some orgasms

Is Female Orgasm Functional or Does It Just Feel Good?

There's debate about why women orgasm. Over twenty evolutionary theories have been proposed, all focused on the adaptive value of female orgasms. Some focus on how orgasms may cause a woman to feel bonded with her partner, and others focus on how orgasms may promote conception. One careful theorist, Elisabeth Lloyd, wrote a book debunking all these theories, concluding that the female orgasm serves no purpose at all and is just a fantastic bonus of fetal development. This scholar pointed out a faulty assumption underlying all theories about orgasms and conception: if an orgasm were needed for conception, most women wouldn't conceive since they don't orgasm during intercourse. In short, this scholar convincingly argued that there is no *current* function of the female orgasm for conception. But a really exciting new theory proposes the *past* function of female orgasm. Two scientists discovered that some other female mammals release the same hormones (oxytocin and prolactin) during mating that female humans release during orgasm—and that in these other species, eggs are released only during mating. This discovery led these scientists to speculate that

feel intense and some feel diffuse. An orgasm can feel like riding a series of waves or like being part of one huge tidal wave. Some people experience orgasms as a loud bang, others as a whisper. Using an earthquake metaphor, women may rate their orgasms as a 1 on the Richter scale or as a 10. No matter how big or small your orgasm feels, it's an orgasm that's yours to enjoy. (But here's something cool—you can make your orgasms feel bigger by exercising your pelvic floor muscles. Check out appendix A, "Cool Tidbits for Your Lady Bits," for exercise instructions.)

Also, both when you're close to and having an orgasm, you cannot think about anything. The latest brain research confirms that parts of the clitoris *used* to be located inside the vagina—causing our ancestors to orgasm during intercourse in order to send hormonal signals to the brain to release an egg. This worked well when we rarely encountered males, as it helped us to make the most out of each mating encounter. But when mating started occurring more regularly (due to our ancestors spending more time in social groups), it was no longer adaptive to release an egg each time one mated. So, our female ancestors evolved a new system of releasing eggs in a regular, monthly cycle instead of each time they had intercourse. And, so as not to confuse the old and new signals for ovulation, the clitoris moved away from its original position inside the vagina. In short, this theory speculates that the clitoris used to be in the vagina so that we could orgasm and therefore get pregnant from intercourse. Now, we still get pregnant from intercourse, but we don't orgasm this way. And, in fact, another theory (my all-time favorite one) proposes that women's *inability* to orgasm during intercourse is adaptive because it helps women pick out mates that will be attentive to their needs. In other words, a mate who is concerned about his female partner's clitoral-based sexual pleasure is going to be a good mate overall. Now there's one for cliteracy!

your conscious brain turn off leading up to and during orgasm. You truly do enter into another state of being.

By the time you finish reading this book, you'll be able to get into this state. And, while knowing where and how you like to be touched is essential, the path to satisfying, knock-your-socks-off sex begins in the mind. Letting go of critical self-chatter and turning off your thinking brain enough to relax into the sensations of your orgasm is what the next sextion is all about. If you're anything like me (and most of my students and clients), these techniques might be the most important skills to master on your way to becoming completely and utterly cliterate.

Male Orgasm = Female Orgasm

In one study, women and men wrote out a description of their orgasms; expert judges were asked to guess the sex of the writer, and they couldn't. Both men and women talked about tension building up to a point of intensity, followed by a very pleasurable release of that tension (e.g., "A great release of tensions that have built up that is extremely pleasant and exciting.") So while the type of stimulation that gets men and women there is different, in the end, our orgasms are all the same.

Viva la Variation!

You've probably noticed several mentions in this chapter of how women vary. To recap:

- Some women have clits farther from their vaginal opening than other women do.

- The pattern of women's genital nerve endings differs.

- G-spot areas vary in thickness.

- Some women squirt and others don't.

These aren't random, irrelevant differences. They relate to how a woman likes to be touched. To top it off—and perhaps partially explaining why women experience orgasms differently—scientists say women's brains vary in how they interpret the sensations of genital touch. So, here's the major take-to-bed point: **No two women get off sexually in exactly the same way.** Every woman needs to explore what she likes—and a partner won't know what this is without being told. You'll figure out what you like and how to tell your partner this in subsequent chapters.

THE TIME HAS COME FOR YOU TO CUM

5.

TRAINING THE SEX ORGAN BETWEEN YOUR EARS

A woman's orgasm is . . . dependent as much
upon her mind as on her clitoris.

—Megan Hart, *Dirty*

You just learned all about the clitoris and your other sexually responsive parts. You looked at your beautiful genitals and I foreshadowed
the fact that you'd soon be touching yourself (if you didn't already get
a head start while looking!). I told you that every woman's nerve endings are positioned differently and that you'd figure out how yours are
set up. I promise that I'll help you find your sensitive spots and bring
yourself to orgasm in the next chapter—but we have an essential step to
accomplish first. Before you can revel in the sensations of touching the
head of your clitoris, you have to clear some pesky, pleasure-draining
thoughts from your other head. This means observing and shifting
your thoughts when you *aren't* having sex and not thinking at all when
you *are* having sex.

WHEN YOU AREN'T HAVING SEX:
SEX-POSITIVE THINKING

The comedian Amy Schumer told *Glamour* magazine:

> Do what you feel you want to do while also considering how you'll feel the next day. Don't not have an orgasm. . . . *Make sure he knows that you're entitled to an orgasm.* . . . I'll be like, "Oh my God, have you met my clit?" Don't be self-conscious.

When I first heard this, I thought, *Wow. She summed up* Becoming Cliterate *in a few sentences!* Then, as I further contemplated her words, I realized she'd pinpointed three mind-sets that can hinder—or enhance—women's orgasms. Let's break them down.

Optional Versus Entitled Sexual Pleasure. Hopefully, you've now rejected the idea that women should orgasm during intercourse and that women's orgasms are less important than men's. But rejecting deeply rooted cultural messages on principle doesn't mean they no longer have the power to affect you personally. As one example, research finds that even women who reject unrealistic standards for female appearance have at least part of their self-esteem dependent on their weight. We'll deal with these damaging cultural pressures for women's appearance later. The message we're talking about now—*that women's orgasms are less important than men's*—is also so deeply entrenched in the fabric of our culture that it can subconsciously affect even women who consciously reject it. Let's do a little thought experiment to see if it's still affecting you.

Have you ever had a sexual encounter with a man when he had an orgasm and you didn't? If you have sex with men—and remember, I mean sex broadly, not just intercourse—it's likely you'll be able to recall several such incidents. Replay one in your mind. Really, truly take a few concentrated moments to think about how you felt (e.g., unsurprised, unperturbed, neutral, disappointed, worried, upset) and why you think you felt that way. Now reverse the scenario. Have you ever had sex with a man when you had an orgasm and he didn't? If not, imagine one. Either way, real or imagined, take another few moments to genuinely examine how you felt and why you think you felt this way. If you felt more negative about his lack of an orgasm than your lack of an orgasm, you're still at least somewhat buying into the insidious cultural message about men's orgasms being more important than women's. Likewise, if you imagined a scene in which you didn't orgasm during intercourse and felt concerned about your male partner's ego, you're likely still negatively affected by the cultural lies about the importance of women's intercourse-based pleasure.

So what's the solution? Truly believing that your sexual pleasure is of utmost importance. Like Amy said, it means feeling *entitled* to pleasure.

I know some of you might be having a negative reaction to the word "entitled." It's gotten a bad rap lately. Urban Dictionary associates this word with being rude, demanding, and spoiled, but I'm not using "entitled" this way. Among psychologists, "feeling entitled to pleasure" means believing that it's essential a partner cares about your pleasure. To me, it also means that if you're having sex with a man, you and he both genuinely believe that your pleasure is as important as his. This means that you consider—and expect him to consider—stimulating your clitoris to be as central to sex as stimulating his penis. In other words, entitlement could simply be another way of saying *equality*.

Entitled to Orgasm Too?

Maybe you noticed I'm saying you're entitled to *pleasure* instead of saying (as Amy does) that you're entitled to *an orgasm*. This is because goal-oriented sex is way less likely to be satisfying sex. Setting up orgasm as a goal to achieve ("I want to come! Am I going to come yet?") makes having an orgasm less likely. So when it comes to the attitudes needed to orgasm, we ironically need to stay away from anything that makes an orgasm something you *must* have and focus exclusively on your sexual *pleasure* instead.

How do you get this feeling of entitlement to pleasure? By talking to yourself. Tell yourself, "I'm entitled to pleasure!" or something else that gives this same message. Go ahead and steal my "The time has come to cum" line, if you'd like, but personalize it: "The time has come for *me* to cum!"

To make sure you have lots of entitlement messages to choose from, two students and I brainstormed several other self-talk options for you. Some are straightforward and some are full of alliterations and slang words. Whether you want a mantra or a motto or a slogan that could sell T-shirts, the important thing is to find a message that resonates with you.

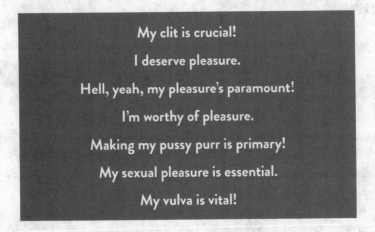

My clit is crucial!

I deserve pleasure.

Hell, yeah, my pleasure's paramount!

I'm worthy of pleasure.

Making my pussy purr is primary!

My sexual pleasure is essential.

My vulva is vital!

Or how about talking to yourself metaphorically? Remember in chapter 3 where non-reciprocal oral sex was likened to you getting him a glass of water whenever you were together and him never doing the same for you? Well, tell yourself, "I deserve water too" or "I need my thirst quenched too." Pick whatever thought or thoughts work for you or create one of your own. The bottom line is to embrace your entitlement to pleasure.

In case you're not yet convinced of the importance of believing you're entitled to pleasure, researchers have found that holding this attitude is related to experiencing more orgasms, having higher self-esteem, and even being happier in general! They've also found that feeling entitled to pleasure is related to being able to reject the sexual double standard—the next sex-negative attitude we're going to attack.

Is Self-Talk Silly?

Some people feel silly talking to themselves. However, psychologists recommend consciously and purposefully replacing negative thoughts—even subconscious ones—with positive thoughts. Research proves that positive self-talk leads to positive behavioral and emotional change. Changing your thinking is also harder than it sounds. But it starts with noticing the conversation inside your head—first tuning in to what's already being said and then flipping the script if necessary. It takes effort to change your internal chatter, but it's essential, and definitely worth it!

Double Versus Equal Standards. Recall that Amy advised to "Do what you feel you want to do while also considering how you'll feel the next day." While this is really good advice, it's often tricky for women to separate how they'll "feel the next day" from the slut shaming that's ingrained in our culture. This can be another one of those instances when you reject an idea yet still have it mess with you personally. You can think that the sexual double standard is a bunch of sexist crap yet still have messages like "Good girls don't . . ." and "Don't be a slut" subconsciously interfere with your enjoyment of sex, especially casual sex.

Here's my advice—based on both research and talking to my female students and clients who struggle with this: To enjoy casual sex, you have to *consciously* work to wholeheartedly reject the sexual double standard. You have to believe that you have *as much right* to enjoy casual sex as any partner you have casual sex with. You have to stop slut shaming other women—and yourself.

How? With that same self-examination and self-talk I recommended to help you counteract the idea that men's pleasure is most important. If you find yourself feeling ashamed or guilty after a hookup, ask yourself if this is due to believing, even to a small degree, that women who enjoy casual sex are slutty. Obvious research finds that women with positive attitudes toward hookups (and approving attitudes toward all kinds of sex) have the most positive feelings after hooking up. So give yourself the approval that society—and maybe your mother, father, grandmother, grandfather, sisters, brothers, aunts, uncles, and even some peers—have denied you. Talk to yourself, saying "I approve of my sexuality!" or something along these lines that resonates for you. This self-approval is likely to have a positive domino effect. The less guilty a woman feels about sex, the more likely she is to orgasm. And the better the sex, the less the hookup regret. Win-win.

But here's a really important caveat. If you can't get past feeling bad the next day, it could be that hooking up just isn't for you—and that's 100 percent okay too. Some women need more intimacy to enjoy sex than other women, and this is neither good nor bad—it's just another wonderful way women vary. And if you're a woman who needs to feel genuinely connected with a partner before getting sexual—even if you truly reject the sexual double standard—you're not likely to enjoy casually hooking up. My goal here isn't to tell you what type of sex to have or not to have; it's to have you deeply examine your sexual attitudes and reject any that are interfering with your pleasure. Choose the sex you want to have—casual or not—and whatever you choose, make it pleasurable.

Speaking of casual sex, it's really common for women (and men) to hope that a hookup will turn into a relationship. Recall that study I mentioned in an earlier chapter that found that 65 percent of women and 45 percent of men reported wishing their hookup would turn into something more serious. One of my closest friends, a therapist at a university counseling center, tells me that almost every client—male and female—who talks to her about hooking up reveals a secret part in the back of their mind that hopes this hookup partner will actually be "the one." She also told me the same was true for her in her hookup days—and I admit the same was true for me. One of my students recently told me a story about "finding a quick, no strings attached, fuck buddy on good ol' Tinder." She swiped right and chatted with some lawyer dude for a while. They met up for drinks and dinner, which, despite including a pretty unsatisfactory conversation, ended in an evening of pretty satisfying sex. She said that "even as a strong feminist, preaching to decrease the orgasm gap, as much as I wanted this to be a casual fling, a very tiny part of me still longed for

Really Better in Relationships?

Research consistently shows that women emphasize relationships as a context for sexuality more than men do. Even in sexual fantasies, women tend to imagine intimacy, connection, and a familiar, committed partner more than men do. One scholar who reviewed decades of research concluded that "women's sexuality tends to be strongly linked to a close relationship. For women, an important goal of sex is intimacy; the best context for sex is a committed relationship. This is less true of men." While I can't dispute years of research, I can add two caveats. First, research reports averages, so there are always exceptions to the rule (e.g., men who need intimacy to enjoy sex and women who prefer casual sex). Second, it's not clear if these findings are due to nature or nurture—in other words, if they're due to inherent sex differences with an evolutionary or adaptive function or if they're due to cultural messages about the proper context for women's sexuality. Still, what *is* clear to me after talking to thousands of young women is that some need emotional intimacy plus clitoral stimulation, and some just need clitoral stimulation. In short, no matter the intimacy needs a woman has, her clitoris still needs its proper stimulation!

it to go further." She said that for three days after the hookup, she got excited every time her phone rang, thinking it might be him.

What's the moral of her story (which I'm guessing many of you might relate to)? Casual sex can sometimes end up feeling more confusing than you anticipate. As Lonnie Barbach, author of *For Yourself,* wrote:

> Many women find themselves sexually experienced but not experiencing sex as the comfortable, carefree experience it is billed to be.

Indeed, research tells us that most women feel a mix of positive and negative feelings the morning after hooking up. (But I'm guessing we don't need research to tell us that.)

I'm here to "normalize" these mixed feelings—and to help you get rid of (or at least diminish) any of the negative feelings that are rooted in sex-negative slut shaming. I want you to believe that you have an equal right to casual sex without judgment. I want to help you detangle any hookup regret you feel from the sexual double standard. And I want you to understand that this detangling may involve some trial and error. As one of my students told me:

> "I used to feel guilty about having casual sex, because of stuff I'd learned about good girls and all that. But the more casual sex I had, the less guilty I felt. This definitely took some time. It was a process I had to go through."

Conversely, another student told me:

> "I honestly don't think there's anything wrong with a woman having casual sex, but I always feel bad about it anyway. It took me a long time to figure out that I need more intimacy. Casual sex just doesn't work for me."

The ultimate goal is to have sex you feel good about having, whether or not you decide casual sex is for you.

Remember earlier when I told you that it's time to start approving of the sex you're having? Well, here's a really important first step in that direction: start approving of the sex other women are having. When I teach this in my class, I show a video of Amber Rose doing the "Walk of No Shame" (you can find it on YouTube). It shows Amber leaving a house in her dress from the night before, carrying a pair of high heels. As she walks home, people stop and congratulate her. One older woman says, "It looks like you haven't been home all night." Amber says, "I sure haven't," and the woman replies, "Congratulations." Another older woman tells her, "Nothing I haven't done. In my day, I was no stranger to the walk of shame," and Amber replies, "No shame here." A man honks at her and says, "Hey! You're an inspiration to my daughter!" and another man, this one a construction worker she walks past, tells her, "I respect that you enjoyed yourself last night. I think we can all agree that having sex is fun," and Amber says, "Oh, yes it is." Take a look at this two-minute video. Maybe even watch it a few times. Then, the next time you think about slut shaming another woman, think of Amber. Indeed, it's only when you truly stop slut shaming other women that you'll be able to disentangle any hookup regret you have from your perhaps subconscious slut shaming of yourself. You'll then be able to more clearly decide if casual sex is for you or not. If it is, enjoy it and walk proudly the next day, just like Amber. And to fully enjoy any type of sex, there's one more thing you're going to have to learn: to appreciate your body.

Body Shame Versus Body Love. Countless women in our culture hate their bodies—or at least dislike some of their body parts. Much of this is a reaction to the unrealistic cultural expectations of what women are supposed to look like.

False images of small and symmetrical inner lips are causing some women to feel self-conscious about the way their vulvas look. And advertisements for "feminine hygiene products" lead some women to believe their genitals are dirty and smell bad (more on that in appendix A, "Cool Tidbits for Your Lady Bits"). Obviously, women who think their genitals look, smell, or taste bad are not going to be able to relax during sex.

The dislike women feel for their bodies isn't limited to their genitals. Women hate their stomachs, their thighs, their boobs, their hips, their asses, and the list goes on. Basically, if there's a body part, there's a woman out there who dislikes hers. Along with disliking specific body parts, countless women feel disdain for their overall size and shape—and, of course, their weight.

Just by virtue of being a woman in our culture, there's a good chance that some amount of body dislike is part of your reality. And disliking your body will interfere with your sexual comfort and satisfaction. Research has found that the worse a woman's body image is, the more likely she is to avoid sexual situations and, when in them, to be more hesitant to tell a partner what she wants. On the positive side, research has found that the more a woman likes her body, the more she initiates sex, the more sex she has, and the more orgasms she enjoys.

How much a woman dislikes her body and how much this interferes with her sex life is more about her body perceptions than about her actual body size or shape. I've worked with women who have the type of body our culture worships who feel too self-conscious to enjoy sex. I've also worked with women who have the type of body our culture ostracizes who are comfortable with their bodies during sex. Letting yourself relax during sex isn't about how much you weigh; it's about your feelings and thoughts about your body. And, unlike the thoughts we attacked earlier, negative body thoughts are usually quite conscious.

When I lecture on this topic in my class, I read items from a scale measuring how much women are distracted during sex by self-consciousness about their bodies. Whenever I do this, a palpable heaviness and sadness falls over the room. Here are a few sentences from that scale that might sadden you too if you relate to this all-too-familiar experience:

> "The idea of having sex without any covers over my body causes me anxiety."
>
> "The worst part of having sex is being nude in front of another person."
>
> "During sexual activity, I am (or would be) concerned about how my body looks to my partner."

These are just a few illustrative sentences. Others focus on women preferring to have sex in the dark, liking a certain sexual position because it covers up a body part they consider fat, and thinking about how a partner can feel their fat when touching them. If you relate, you're definitely not alone. This was something I struggled with for a long time and I'm happy to say that I no longer do.

Exercise = Medication

Exercise has been found not only to enhance sexual function but also to be an effective treatment for depression and anxiety. Some studies have found that exercise is equivalent to antidepressant medications but without the side effects, including sexual ones, such as diminished orgasms. The exercise doesn't have to be extreme. Even walking fast for thirty-five minutes a day five times a week or sixty minutes a day three times a week has been found to improve mood.

You too can overcome your negative body image. Some women benefit from reminding themselves that their partner appreciates their body. While this can be truly helpful, it's ultimately more powerful if you can learn to love yourself. To do so, one effective strategy is, again, self-talk. Say things like "I love myself. I love my body." Or if this feels like too much of a stretch, say something about appreciating your body's various amazing abilities, including its ability to enjoy sexual pleasure. Say to yourself, "I love how my body is able to feel luscious sexual sensations." Or appreciate your physical stamina, energy level, or coordination—because high esteem for these aspects of your body has been found to increase sexual satisfaction. And if you don't already exercise, I strongly recommend you start. I'm not recommending this so that you lose weight or better live up to our cultural ideal. I'm recommending it because physical fitness has been shown to increase sexual satisfaction. As you exercise and see the amazing things your body is capable of doing (walking, running, lifting weights, climbing stairs), you'll also have an opportunity to appreciate what your body can do.

One type of exercise, yoga, has been found to be especially related to good sex. This may be because yoga teaches you to be fully immersed in the present moment. As we'll talk about in a minute, a complete focus on the present is the most effective way to decrease cognitive distractions

Religion and Sexual Shame

I've had a lot of students and clients over the years tell me that their religion instilled negative feelings, especially shame and guilt, about sexual pleasure. However, upon learning that the only function of the clitoris is sexual pleasure, one of my very religious clients exclaimed that "the clitoris must be God's gift to women!" She further reasoned that God must have intended her to have sexual pleasure. She had her first orgasm. I share this story with you so that if sex-negative religious messages are a problem for you, perhaps you too will find comfort.

during sex. But before turning to this, I want to point out that the three cognitive distractions we just attacked are not the only ones that can mess with your sexual enjoyment. Unfortunately, there are countless more. Plus, some sex-negative messages you received might have been so indirect (e.g., an awkward silence that fell across your family when a sexual scene came on television) that you end up having vague, uncomfortable feelings about sex that you can't trace back to a specific message or incident. That's okay: the skills taught in this chapter can still help. Tell yourself global, sex-positive messages (e.g., "Sex is a wonderful part of life that I deserve to enjoy!").

Here's an essential sex-positive "homework" for you. Please take a minute to think about the sex-positive thoughts we've just gone over. Which resonated most for you? Was it about your entitlement to sex, loving your body, the final global sex-positive message, or a combination of these? Now choose up to four messages and write them down. Tape them somewhere you'll see them (e.g., the mirror, your computer, the back of a door), or put them somewhere you'll be aware of their presence (e.g., written on a small piece of paper folded in your wallet). Then say them to yourself several times a day—as you wake up, as you go to sleep, as you walk out the door for the day. This is what psychologists recommend when trying to replace negative thoughts with new, positive ones.

It may sound hokey, but it works! Practicing sex-positive thinking when you *aren't* having sex will increase your enjoyment when you *are* having sex—which leads us to our next topic.

WHEN YOU'RE HAVING SEX: STOP THINKING!

When you're engaged in sex with a partner, monitoring and evaluating yourself will diminish your sexual pleasure and orgasms. Psychologists call this "spectatoring." Women's most common form of spectatoring involves evaluating and worrying about their bodies, but women—and men—also have "performance" worries (worries about whether they're "doing it right," being a good lover, taking too long to orgasm, etc.). Again, it's impossible to have an orgasm if you're thinking about such concerns. To have an orgasm, you need to switch your brain to "off mode."

Turning off your brain during sex can be accomplished with mindfulness, which is a simple but very potent remedy for a lot of psychological problems. Mindfulness increases happiness, decreases depression, diminishes anxiety, and even helps people deal with chronic illness and pain. Most important for our purposes: it leads to better sex and more orgasms.

What is this powerful thing called mindfulness? In a nutshell, it's simply focusing completely on what's happening in the present moment. When I teach my students and clients about mindfulness, I tell them that being mindful is akin to riding a roller coaster, whether you like riding them or not. As you climb upward, you might be thinking *This is fun!* or *Why did I get on this thing?! I want off!* But as the roller coaster descends, you become too immersed in the sensations to think any thoughts at all (*Aaaahhhh!!!*). This *not* thinking—just feeling what's happening—is mindfulness. And it's sex's best friend.

Another way I've heard mindfulness described is it's putting your mind and body in the same place. Recall that roller coaster: As you fly downhill, your mind and body are focused on the same sensations. But in daily life, your body may do one thing while your mind is somewhere

Mindful, Mind-Empty

To help me remember that mindfulness is the opposite of thinking one thing while doing another—it's fully immersing your mind and your body in the same moment in time—I have a cute cartoon taped to my computer with the title "Mind Full, or Mindful?" It shows a person and a dog in a park. Thought bubbles depict the person pondering all kinds of stuff (except what's right in front of them) while the dog is thinking about only what is right in front of them: the beautiful trees. Mindfulness means having your mind full of only what's right in front of you, not other junk. (If you put the title of this cartoon into a search engine, you can find it and tape it someplace as a reminder too.)

else. Your body can be in the midst of being touched by a sexual partner while your mind is thinking about an e-mail you need to respond to. Or, as a client recently told me, while receiving oral sex, instead of focusing on the sensations, you could be fretting about whether your partner is getting bored.

Being mindful takes practice. By practice, I don't mean it has to take a lot of time! Despite what you may have heard, you don't have to set aside time for long daily meditations to learn mindfulness. You can practice it just by living your life. Even brushing your teeth can be a mindful, present-moment experience—all you need to do is completely immerse yourself in the feel of the toothbrush against your teeth and the toothpaste and water in your mouth. The same goes for washing dishes and eating. When washing dishes, fully immerse in the warm, sudsy water on your hands, and when eating, totally focus on the taste and feel of the food as you chew it. A state of total immersion and present-focus can be invoked while doing anything: walking, working out, showering, talking with friends, and even going to the bathroom. Any moment can be a mindful one.

What do you do about distracting thoughts during such mindful moments? Some of my clients develop a saying that reminds them to come back to the present. One of my clients takes a deep breath and tells herself, "Center," then refocuses on being mindful. Another client developed the saying "Bed not head" to move herself back to the moment whenever she has distracting thoughts during sex. Still, most mindfulness teachers recommend that when a distracting thought occurs, simply notice it. Don't get stuck on it and don't judge it. Don't try to force it to go away either. In mindfulness, distracting thoughts are noticed and observed, then released without judgment. For me, it's helpful to imagine whatever particular thought is bothersome being taken away by a gently moving conveyer belt. Taking a really deep breath is also one of the most useful strategies to bring yourself back to the present moment. While taking this breath, it's important to breathe deep into your gut and to focus on feeling the air going in and out of your nose. When bringing yourself back to the moment during sex, combining deep breathing with scent perception helps some people. For example, I have a client who likes to nuzzle her partner's neck and breathe in his scent as a way to signal herself to get back to the moment.

More Mindfulness

You have all you need to learn mindfulness right in these few pages. But if you want more, see appendix B, "Additional Resources." There you will find books, online resources, and apps for learning mindfulness and meditation.

I hope you can now clearly see how mindfulness can be applied during sex. **Mindful sex is when you're totally and completely immersed in the physical sensations of your body.** Mindful sex doesn't mean you'll never have distracting thoughts (e.g., about your body, about whether you're going to come soon). It means that you're able to let these distracting thoughts go without getting stuck on them. It means you use the strategies described in this chapter to lead you fully back to your body's ecstatic physical reactions.

Here's something else that's super important: before applying mindfulness to your sex life, it's best to get into the groove of it in your daily life. The better you are at getting into an in-the-moment state in life in general, the easier it will be for you to achieve this same state during sex.

In the next chapter, you're going to invoke a mindful state while touching yourself and bringing yourself to orgasm. While I'm guessing you're eager to get started—excited to get excited—this will go much better if you first take a couple of days to be mindful in your daily life. Learning to immerse in your sensations while doing daily activities will enable you to better do so during sex (including the solo sex you'll have in the next chapter).

Shopping Reminder

If you didn't buy lubricant already, as recommended in chapter 4, now's the time. You'll need it in the next chapter.

It's not a coincidence that the term "mind blowing" is associated with sex. Mind-blowing sex means that your mind is not working; only your body is reacting. Do you remember in the previous chapter where I said that leading up to and during an orgasm a part of the conscious mind turns off? This is exactly what mindfulness helps you do. Having an orgasm requires letting go of control and not thinking at all. That's why studies have unequivocally shown that teaching women to be mindful leads them to be more sexually responsive and satisfied. Busy brains are not for the bedroom. So start practicing mindfulness today. Then, as you read further, you'll be ready to have mind-blowing sex—first with yourself and then with a partner!

6.

TAKING MATTERS INTO YOUR OWN HANDS

Don't knock masturbation. It's sex with someone I love.

—*Annie Hall*

"Masturbation"—even the word conjures up discomfort for many people, maybe you included. Perhaps that's why, as the quote above illustrates, it's the butt of a lot of jokes. While I laugh at masturbation humor as much as the next person, I'm also a serious fan of self-love. By the time you finish reading this chapter, I hope you're a masturbation enthusiast too.

SELF-LOVE 101: LET'S GET COMFORTABLE

As stated by Lonnie Barbach:

> The guilt, fear, anxiety . . . that surrounds masturbation is astounding, especially when one realizes . . . how pervasive it is among human beings.

Do you relate? If you've never pleasured yourself, do you feel apprehensive to do so? Or do you already pleasure yourself but feel guilty or embarrassed about it? If you answered yes to either of these questions, you're not alone. When I polled my most recent class, 11 percent of the women had never masturbated. Of the 89 percent who had, about a third felt guilty about it.

Where does all this guilt come from? For some women, it's due to a lack of information. The majority of the women in my class say that when growing up, no one ever talked to them about self-pleasure. However, a good percentage says they got something worse than the silent treatment. Authority figures told them masturbation was bad and to be avoided. Many were told it was unhealthy or sinful.

The idea that masturbation is sinful isn't surprising since many religions condemn it. A lot of them point to a Bible story in which a guy named Onan is supposed to have intercourse with his brother's widow to make a baby. He refuses, "spills his seed," and is struck dead. But here's a twist: modern Bible experts aren't sure if he's struck dead for not making a baby with his dead brother's wife or for masturbating—and some think he didn't even masturbate at all but pulled out so as not to ejaculate inside her! These experts also point out that aside from this one ambiguous story, the Bible says little about masturbation in general and almost nothing about female masturbation. That's why these experts disagree about whether or not the Bible is against masturbation. It's also why a lot

Thanks, Mom!

A big shout-out to my mother. When I was about seven, I knocked on the bathroom door while she was soaking in the tub and fearfully confessed that I'd been "touching myself down there." "Oh, is that all you're worried about?" she matter-of-factly replied. "Everyone does that. Just keep your bedroom door closed. Now please get out, so I can take my bath." Thanks to her, I've never felt guilty about pleasuring myself. If you did not receive such an affirming message, channel my mom and pretend she's saying this to you!

of respected religious leaders from diverse faiths say masturbation is actually acceptable. Here's an affirming masturbation quote from the book *Mirror of Intimacy* by Alexandra Katehakis and Tom Bliss:

> Masturbation is . . . an inherent gift. The design of the human body gives us free access to our genitals. . . . It's clear this function was granted for our enjoyment.

Clearly, some new-age spiritual writers give self-pleasure a thumbs-up. But religion isn't the only source of guilt. Sometimes women feel guilty because they've been told that masturbation is harmful. This is a relic of the past. In the eighteenth century, people were warned that if they masturbated, their hands would get covered in warts and hair. Yikes! People were also told that masturbation would cause blindness, acne, and infertility. Also, doctors in mental hospitals observed patients masturbating and concluded that this was the source of the patients' mental disorders. In reality, the patients were just doing what most of us do—although with less privacy and at more frequency since they were cooped up with little else to do. The bottom line is that in previous generations, medical experts told people that masturbation was the root of a lot of illnesses.

Now we know that just the opposite is true. As Jenny Block, author of *O Wow,* writes:

> Have a migraine? Masturbate. Feeling stuck creatively? Masturbate. Feeling blue? Masturbate. Can't sleep? Masturbate. Mired in stress? Low self-esteem? Sex drive in low gear? Chronic pain? Masturbation is good for what ails you.

All of this is true—indeed, it's backed up by research. And there's more. As just two additional examples, pleasuring yourself burns calories and enhances your immune system (so you get sick less often). There's absolutely no doubt that solo sex has enormous psychological and health benefits. But it's not the masturbation that's causing all these benefits. It's the self-induced orgasms!

Let's talk about self-induced orgasms. First, as you may recall from an earlier chapter, women are way more likely to orgasm by themselves than with a partner. Many women also say the orgasms they have by themselves are more intense than those they have with a partner. Plus, self-induced orgasms happen faster (on average, about four minutes of clitoral stimulation) than the orgasms women have with partners (on average, about twenty minutes of clitoral stimulation). This is because during masturbation, the majority of women are able to touch their clits exactly the way they like. It's also because without a partner in the picture, there are fewer of those pleasure-sucking cognitive distractions we talked about in the previous chapter (*Do I look okay? Am I taking too long?*). Obvious, but still aptly stated by Lonnie Barbach in *For Yourself*:

> The reason self-stimulation works so well . . .
> is that you are the only one involved.

This ability to focus completely on oneself is the reason pleasuring oneself is always the first step in helping a woman have her first orgasm. It's also an essential step in all sex therapy aimed at helping women learn to orgasm with partners.

In terms of our Self-Love 101 lesson, we also need to debunk a major myth, and that is the notion that solo sex is just for women who don't have partners. Just the opposite is true. Women who pleasure themselves have more—not less—sex with partners. That's because the more sex you have, including with yourself, the more sex you want. And the more orgasms you have by any method, including by giving yourself one, the more sexually responsive you'll be. Research shows that women who pleasure themselves have more orgasms with partners as well.

I'm hoping you're now convinced of the benefits of self-love and able to let go of any anxiety or guilt you may have had. Still, you may be wondering just what female masturbation looks like, or if other women do it the way you do.

SELF-LOVE 102: HOW WOMEN DO IT

There's endless possibilities when it comes to female masturbation—legs spread apart, legs held tightly together, knees up, knees down, silent, loud, laying still, wiggling around, touching only one's genitals, touching other parts of one's body, direct genital touch, indirect touch through one's panties. While no two women have identical ways of pleasuring themselves, there are commonalities across women. In her landmark study, Shere Hite categorized the way women masturbate. And, no surprise, she found out that women stimulate what she called the "clitoral/vulva area." In the study, most women—73 percent—did this while lying on their backs; about 5.5 percent while lying on their tummies; 4 percent by rubbing up against a soft object; 2 percent by massaging their genitals with running water (e.g., placing their vulvas under the bathtub faucet or using a handheld shower attachment); and 3 percent by simply pressing their thighs together rhythmically. Another 11 percent of women didn't just stick to one way or position; while they had a favored method, they sometimes switched it up. Hite also found that the vast majority of women focused completely on external stimulation, but around 12 percent always or sometimes simultaneously put something inside their vaginas. Consistent with cliteracy and the notion that it's rare for women to orgasm from just penetration, only 1.5 percent masturbated solely by putting something inside their vaginas.

What do all these statistics mean for you? Well, first off, if you've never masturbated, they explain why I'm going to start you off on your back. And if you already masturbate, I hope you've found your general style in that previous list. No matter how you masturbate, I want you to know there are other women out there using a similar style.

If your style is one that few women use, perhaps you're wondering if this is a concern. Absolutely not. However you masturbate is right for you. Also, while many women think what they do when they pleasure themselves is separate or different from what they do with a partner, just the opposite is true. The more you incorporate your solo-sex methods into partnered sex, the more satisfying and orgasmic your sex will

Cushion Pushin'

Many young girls discover masturbation through unplanned, extremely pleasurable encounters with pillows or stuffed animals. Clearly, young girls intuitively know that the route to orgasm is something that rubs them on the outside—not something that goes on the inside!

be. However, some styles are easier to transfer to partnered sex than others. Stating the obvious, those (rare) women who masturbate solely by putting something inside their vaginas aren't going to have a problem transferring this to heterosexual sex. On the other hand, women who can reach orgasm only by running water on their clitorises would have a harder time transferring this to partnered sex—they'd need to find a partner who is always willing to take a shower or bath with them. Most masturbation styles can be transferred to partnered sex with creativity and communication.

If you already have a masturbation style that consistently leads to orgasms, take a moment to think of how you might transfer this to sex with a partner. If you orgasm from touching yourself with your hand or a vibrator while on your back, for example, you could show your partner how to do the same. If you have sex with men and want to combine intercourse and clitoral stimulation, you could touch yourself with your hands or your vibrator during intercourse. Indeed, if you're already reliably orgasming while pleasuring yourself and just need help transferring your method to partnered sex, you can simply skip to the next chapter. Still, I'd love for you to read on and learn fun new ways to pleasure yourself. On the other hand, if you're currently pleasuring yourself with a style that you'd find difficult, impossible, or uncomfortable to transfer to partnered sex, the next lesson is for you.

Of course, if you've never pleasured yourself or never had an orgasm while doing so, come on, cum on, let's go!

A Note to Women with an Abuse History

If you've suffered sexual abuse in your past, touching yourself can be triggering. Be gentle with yourself. If a certain touch triggers bad memories or feelings, stop and take a break. Resume when you feel calmer. And when you do, feel free to try the triggering touch again or simply skip over it. Talk to yourself—tell yourself that you're in charge and safe. Work to separate past abusive touch from this new sexual touch. Give sex a new meaning, one that includes control and pleasure.

ADVANCED SELF-LOVE (AKA PRIVATE) LESSONS

You just learned some general ways women masturbate. Now let's get more specific about how and where women touch themselves. Some use vibrators. Some use their fingers to rub, caress, or tap. Some touch lightly, some touch vigorously, and some start out light and work up to a harder touch. Some use one finger; some use several. Some use their palm or wrist, either alone or combined with finger action. A lot of women touch on or around their clitoral hood, stimulating the glans below. Some rub under their outer lips, thereby stimulating the inner lips, clitoral bulbs, and clitoral legs all at once. And because how the nerves are positioned varies between women, some like to touch to the right of their clit and inner lips, while others favor the left side. These are just a few common examples—it's not an inclusive list. In fact, if you put everything we've talked about together—positions, where to touch, how to touch, etc.—the combinations are almost limitless, which may leave beginning masturbators feeling a little overwhelmed. Don't worry. Some women and some sex experts have detailed common ways women touch themselves. That's where we're going to start.

A few more thoughts before we get going: First, if you've previously been fearful or ashamed of masturbation, allow me to again reassure you that touching yourself is totally okay. My clients who are especially hesitant like to remind themselves that I'm a health-care professional, and thus think of my instructions to pleasure themselves as a prescription. If it helps, please think of the rest of this chapter in the same way. Also, as you follow the directions for touching in Lesson 1 below, if anything feels physically uncomfortable, stop and make some adjustments. You might want to add more lubricant. Or you might try the motion but with more or less pressure. You can also adjust by moving your fingers to a slightly different angle or nearby place; a tiny adjustment can make a huge difference to what you feel. If you find yourself saying "Ouch" to any of the movements I'm about to suggest—especially those near your clit—you could be pulling your hood up and touching your glans directly; most of us are *way too sensitive* for this. Similarly, if anything feels at all uncomfortable while you're touching any part of your clitoris (e.g., rubbing your clitoral hood), you could be a woman who finds even this to be too intense. So try something else, such as stimulating your lips or touching yourself through your panties. Do a lot of experimenting to see what you like and what you don't like. I'm genuinely excited for you to find out about yourself!

Lesson 1: Let's Touch. Take this book to a private place. You'll need about ten minutes (although you certainly can linger longer if you like). Lie on your back, take a deep breath, and get into your now hopefully practiced mindful state. Put some lubricant on your fingers, and as you read each description, give it a try, lingering in each movement for as long as it feels good or until you feel like trying the next one. If a description isn't clear, don't get hung up on trying to get it right. Instead, just do anything that seems close to what's being described. The goal of this lesson isn't for you to stimulate yourself to orgasm but simply to play with yourself. Just have fun!

- Using your pointer and middle finger, squeeze your outer lips together, around your clit area. Then move your fingers (e.g., squeeze and release, move up and down). The writers on a website called OMGYes (which you'll learn about in the next lesson) call this "making a clit sandwich" and explain how this finger placement gives your clit soft, indirect pressure.

- Softly—or, if needed and as you get aroused, more vigorously—rub small circles on the hood of your clitoris. Try using your pointer finger, middle finger, or both.

- Tap, tap, tap—lightly or more vigorously—on your clitoral hood. Again, use your pointer finger, middle finger, or both.

- Rub, pull, pinch, tap, or caress your inner lips.

- Rub to the side of your clitoral hood, using your pointer finger, middle finger, or both. Try touching both to the right and to the left to see if you have a favorite side.

- Put three or four fingers close together, side by side, and place them on your clitoral hood and its surrounding area. Massage circles on and around the clitoris.

- Separate your outer lips with your pointer finger and ring finger and use your middle finger to stimulate your clitoral hood and glans.

- Make large figure-eight circles on your genitals. Go over the clit, under the clit, and around the vaginal opening.

- Position your hand so that you make a V with your ring and middle fingers (or your pointer and middle fingers). Put this V inside your outer lips, with the space in between these fingers around your clitoral hood. Then lay your other fingers on each side of your outer lips. Rub up and down with your whole hand. You might even want to exert some pressure on your mons with the base of your palm or wrist as you do this.

Again, these are just a few starter movements. Maybe you found one, or a couple, you liked. If so, that's great! If not, spend a few more minutes simply playing around with different fingers, different motions, different pressures, different rhythms, and different parts of your vulva. For example, you might want to explore the vaginal opening with your fingers. The aim of this lesson is for you to find one or more touches that feel good. Then take a break—a video break, to be exact.

Lesson 2: Let's Watch. This is when I find myself wishing this book could temporarily morph into a video. Learning to pleasure yourself is easiest to do when you have a model to look at first, and there are two outstanding models I want to recommend.

The first is the website OMGYes.com, created by women who paired up with researchers from Indiana University. They interviewed over two thousand women to see how they masturbated, uncovering twelve common ways. Not surprisingly, all methods focused on external stimulation—with the clitoris being the main focus. The researchers gave the techniques names, some of which you'll find in this chapter (e.g., "edging"). They then made videos of women talking about and demonstrating—up close and personal—these twelve clitoral-focused masturbation techniques. You can go to this website and see a sample of the videos covering one of the techniques, as well as a general introductory video. If you like what you see and want more, you can buy access to what the creators call Season One. Season One includes fifty videos covering the twelve masturbation techniques and eleven touchable videos (i.e., touch-screen technology) to help you practice techniques on a virtual vulva and to get feedback as you do.

While I may show some OMGYes clips the next time I teach my human sexuality class, the film I've shown in the past to teach about masturbation is a video by Betty Dodson called "Celebrating Orgasm: Carol." The video (which costs a few dollars for all-day viewing) focuses on Betty teaching a woman, Carol, to both appreciate her beautiful vulva and masturbate to orgasm using her hands and a vibrator. My women students love this video. Most say that it either normalizes the way they masturbate or teaches them a new way to masturbate. Still, some women students tell me they feel sad or angry that no one ever taught them this before.

The first time I showed this video, I forgot to tell my students that most women get aroused watching it, and a woman who strongly identified

Betty's Group and Private Lessons

If you watch the Carol video, you will also notice a brief, somewhat surprising scene from the feminist era in which Betty Dodson teaches a bunch of naked women standing in a circle to use vibrators. Dodson has long been giving women both group and private masturbation lessons. She did it in the 1960s and she does it today!

as heterosexual came to me after class to express worry that she got so wet watching another woman masturbate. This is perfectly normal! Research shows that arousal in women isn't related to sexual orientation. Women who identify as lesbian get excited watching both lesbian and heterosexual sex; women who identify as heterosexual get excited watching both heterosexual and lesbian sex. In fact, women are quite easily visually aroused, and so, in a moment, when you hopefully watch the Carol or OMGYes videos, please expect some arousal. Additionally, as you watch these videos, please notice where the women touch themselves and try to put this together with the anatomy learned in chapter 4. For example, see how a lot of the women in OMGYes videos touch their clitoral hood, or notice how Carol gives herself a somewhat deep two-finger massage, likely stimulating her inner lips, clitoral bulbs, and clitoral legs all together.

What's That Barbell?

If you watch the Carol video, the "vaginal barbell" you'll see portrays clitoral stimulation coupled with penetration. This doesn't work for everyone. Some women like clitoral stimulation alone, and some like it coupled with penetration. One way is not better than the other. It's personal preference. Still, the barbell does point to the importance of pelvic floor strength; see appendix A, "Cool Tidbits for Your Lady Bits," for more details and exercise instructions.

Please now go to OMGYes.com, watch the introduction video, and sign up for the sampler video (and maybe for all of Season One—I promise I don't get paid for referrals). Or put "Celebrating Orgasm: Carol" into any search engine and you'll find the Carol video. Alternatively, go to Betty Dodson's website (DodsonandRoss.com) and click on "Video." You'll be taken to a number of videos, including the one I'm recommending. See you when you get back from the movies!

Lesson 3: Extended Touch Time. Now we're going to take your masturbation lesson up a notch. Rather than going through the list of touch types one at a time, you'll linger on one type or a few types you like best. If you need a refresher, feel free to redo Lesson 1 to find the type or types of touch you prefer.

Some women strongly prefer one type of touch, and others like several types. Women who prefer one type of touch generally just use this type but increase its intensity as they get more aroused. Among women who like two or more different methods of touch, some use them in a reliable pattern, while others use them all but not in any specific pattern. Still others begin with one type of touch and switch to another type as they get more aroused. Now you'll find out what *you* like!

For this lesson, set aside at least thirty minutes of privacy. It will be impossible to relax if you're worried that someone will walk in on you. Make sure your space is comfortable, including being warm or cool enough, depending on the season and your location. If you prefer, make the space partially or totally dark. You may also wish to do some extra preparation

There's More, but Beware!

While OMGYes and "Celebrating Orgasm: Carol" are great masturbation models, they aren't the only ones. Once you make it to Dodson's website, for example, you'll find many other videos of women masturbating. However, please don't use porn and YouTube masturbation videos as models. They're generally for male entertainment rather than for helping women learn to pleasure themselves!

of your space (e.g., light some candles, play some music), but don't if you find this cheesy or distracting. Either way, make sure your personal lubricant is nearby, take a few deep breaths, and get into your mindful state. Also, in terms of your mind-state, just focus on enjoying yourself, not on having an orgasm. This is supposed to be fun, not work! While I've written this chapter as a series of lessons, there's no exam to pass. And as Vivienne Cass, author of *The Elusive Orgasm,* says:

> If you're feeling a little awkward or self-conscious, remember there's no one to judge you except yourself. And you've probably done enough of that.

So please go ahead and take at least thirty minutes to touch yourself. You might want to set an alarm so you don't have to look at the clock. Then just relax, touch, and pay close attention to your sensations. Allow yourself to flow with the touch. Change the rhythm and pressure, and maybe the location, of the touch as you go by tuning into your body's sensations. As you get more and more aroused, your body may crave different types of touch. Or you may find a specific type of touch you like to do consistently in the exact same way. Experiment. See what your body wants. While an orgasm isn't the goal, if you end up having one before the thirty minutes are

It's Okay to Hit Snooze!

If your alarm goes off after thirty minutes and you want to keep going, by all means do so.

up—no matter if that means two or twenty-five minutes in—you can either keep touching yourself or stop. While many women say that clitoral stimulation can be painful if it occurs too soon after an orgasm, some like to resume touching themselves but in a different way from what just led to the orgasm. Some even like to start over from the beginning of their sequence or routine. Again, the point is to find out what's best for you.

The point of this lesson is to revel in your own sensations for a half hour. Have fun and then return for the next lesson.

Lesson 4 and Forward: Assessment and Adding On. How was it? Did you figure out how you liked to be touched? Whether you answered yes or no, continue to do this exercise as often as you can. I recommend either daily or a few times a week—whatever your schedule allows. Do this until you're truly comfortable with touching yourself. At some point, you will naturally orgasm. If not, you'll find several pointers and add-ons below that will help you to do so. In fact, there are so many options, I strongly suggest first reading through the list below and then seeing what you want to try. You can try them one at a time or a few at once. Please be patient and take your time to work through these suggestions. There's no need to rush your pleasure!

And for those of you who've already orgasmed, I still strongly suggest that you read through this list. While some of the tips will be irrelevant, I'm sure you'll find others that you'll want to try just for fun and to enhance your orgasm.

- Check in with yourself. If you still feel guilty about pleasuring yourself, reread the first part of this chapter.

- If you didn't actually watch the videos, or use lubricant, or follow all the previous steps, please do so now. Or invest in a few more Betty Dodson videos or in Season One of OMGYes to see real women masturbate. Again, sometimes a picture (or, in this case, a video) is worth a thousand words.

- Take out your mirror and look at yourself again. Relocate your inner lips and clitoral hood. Retake Lesson 1 while looking at yourself in the mirror.

- Try working more on your mindful state, both in daily life and while pleasuring yourself. Close your eyes and focus fully on the sensations. Make sure you're not trying too hard to have an orgasm and instead you're just enjoying the feelings.

- If mindfulness isn't working for you, try fantasizing. You may want to fantasize the whole time or move from fantasy to mindfulness once you're aroused. For fantasy, anything goes—

even something you'd never want to do in your real life. Some women like what Lonnie Barbach calls the "most patient lover" fantasy. This is when you imagine that you're making love to someone who is willing to take as long as you need and do anything and everything just for you. On the flip side, some women enjoy forced sex fantasies. This doesn't mean a woman wants to be forced; it's just a fantasy that allows some women to let go. Try any fantasy that appeals to you.

- Try reading or watching some erotica before or while you touch yourself. If you've never watched erotica before, a great way to start is by putting "feminist porn" into a search engine and looking around. If you've never read erotica before, check out *Passion: Erotic Romance for Women,* since one study found that women who read it increased their desire, arousal, lubrication, and orgasms. This collection of short stories is mostly about heterosexual sex, so you may want to use it just as a starting point for a search. Or search for "best women's erotic literature" to locate online erotic stories.

Medications Messing with Masturbation

Some medications, such as antidepressants, can diminish your sensations and make reaching an orgasm less likely. Birth control pills and other medications can also diminish your sex drive. Antihistamines can dry more than your runny nose; they can decrease your vaginal lubrication. The same is true of some diseases—some diminish your sex drive, some decrease your sensations, some lessen your lubrication, and some do all three. If you think this could be an issue for you, make an appointment with your doctor. The good news is that if there's a physical or medication-related cause for your missing orgasm, it's usually easily fixed (e.g., by switching to a different medication). Also, even if you discover there's a medication or medical cause, working through the suggestions in this lesson can still be useful in enhancing your orgasm!

- Have a glass of wine, a beer, or another alcoholic beverage to lower your inhibitions before pleasuring yourself.

- Take a bubble bath first. This might help you relax and get in a more body-focused, mindful state.

- Go for a run, watch an adventure movie, or read an adventure novel. This might key you up enough to get you in a more body-focused state.

- If you used candles and/or music, don't. If you didn't, give it a try.

- Increase the time of your self-pleasure sessions. Set your alarm for forty-five minutes or an hour instead of thirty minutes, or don't set your alarm at all.

- If you've been pleasuring yourself while naked, try doing so partially clothed—and vice versa.

- If you've been touching yourself through your panties, take them off. If you've been pleasuring yourself with your panties off, put them on and try touching yourself through them.

- Try moaning and groaning. Let your sexual feelings out verbally as you arouse yourself.

- Maybe you need more of a warm-up. Caress your breasts, nipples, and inner thighs before touching your vulva. Or start off by rubbing your entire vulva slowly and luxuriously, using lubricant. Then very, very slowly move to your clit and inner lips and perhaps your vaginal opening as well. If desired, continue your breast stimulation as you touch your vulva.

- It may be helpful to work with your breath as you get aroused, especially if you find yourself getting tense about whether or not you're going to orgasm. This type of worry can cause you to hold your whole body tight like a spring without even realizing it. Experiment with the following suggestions as you pleasure yourself—it'll help you to achieve the balance of muscle tension and muscle relaxation needed to orgasm.

- Inhale as you rock your pelvis up and exhale as you rock your pelvis down.

- Breathe deeply. Try this through both your nose and your mouth. Some women like to breathe deeply in and then imagine that they're exhaling the air through their genitals.

- Pant in short rhythmic gasps.

- Hold your breath for several seconds at a time or for as long as you can as your orgasm approaches.

• Work your pelvic floor muscles as you touch yourself (see appendix A, "Cool Tidbits for Your Lady Bits," for instructions on how to do this). Alternatively, try purposefully relaxing your pelvic floor muscles.

• Rock your hips while you pleasure yourself. Alternatively, if you've been moving around, see what happens when you lie still.

- Combine working your pelvic floor muscles with rocking your hips. Specifically, rock your pelvis forward as you squeeze your pelvic floor muscles, then relax your pelvis as you release your pelvic floor muscles. (This is something that Betty Dodson routinely recommends, and it's even called "Betty's Rock 'n Roll" orgasm technique. One article describing this technique instructs readers to "move your pelvis like Elvis.")

• Switch up your leg positions. If your legs were closed, open them, and vice versa.

• If your knees were up, put them down, and vice versa.

• Change the angle of your body by putting a pillow under your bottom.

- Just as you did with Lesson 1, experiment with different types and ways to touch, but this time while lying on your stomach instead of on your back. Also experiment with angles by putting a pillow under your tummy.

- Try any other position that's comfortable, such as lying on your side or sitting up, perhaps against pillows.

- Tease yourself to build arousal. Move toward a sensitive spot over and over, yet only occasionally touch it. Tease your clit, or tease the touch-sensitive nerves near the opening of your vagina—grazing but not going in. Build up intensity by getting close to your sensitive spots and then backing off, over and over, until you finally go in for more intensive touching.

- When you feel like an orgasm is inevitable, back off. This is sometimes called "edging." The folks at OMGYes describe three ways to edge. One is to completely stop touching yourself until the feeling of an impending orgasm is gone and then start touching again (you can do this over and over). Another way is to move your touch away from your clit as your orgasm approaches (e.g., instead of circling your clit, tap your inner lips); again, do this over and over. Or you can back off by continuing to touch your clit but not in the way that's about to result in an orgasm. When edging in any of these ways, most women like to lighten their touch. No matter how you edge, the goal is to do so until you can't take it anymore, finally giving in to the touch that will result in an orgasm.

- Instead of edging, when you feel like an orgasm is inevitable, keep doing exactly what you're doing and don't change a thing.

- If you feel like your orgasm is "stuck"—you keep touching and touching but no orgasm comes—get up and take a break. Take a thirty-second walk or do something else (e.g., brush your teeth while you mindfully focus on the feel of the toothpaste in your mouth; take a sip of wine, really focusing on the taste and feeling on your tongue). Then go back and resume. I promise the excited feelings won't go away—but you may relax enough to flow more calmly into your orgasm. If you feel like you're at a really high state of arousal but the orgasm won't come, just enjoy these feelings instead. This stage is a lot of fun, with or without an orgasm following it.

- Maybe you're one of those women who likes simultaneous clitoral stimulation and penetration or who craves the feeling of something in her vagina when she's really excited. Try putting your finger into your vagina after you're very aroused. Or keep your finger in your vagina the whole time. Or put your finger into your vagina just as you think you might orgasm; this pushes some women over the edge into orgasm. Whatever you do, remember to lube up your fingers first. You could also use a sex toy in place of your finger. (The next lesson will tell you about two great websites where you can purchase vibrators.)

- Try pleasuring yourself by lying on your stomach and rubbing up against a soft object, like a pillow. Don't worry about the transfer to partnered sex here. The goal is just to feel pleasure and perhaps orgasm.

- Try pleasuring yourself with water. Lie in a bathtub full of water, with your genitals directly under the faucet of running water. Or direct a handheld faucet attachment onto your genitals. There are even waterproof vibrators you can purchase. Again, don't worry about the transfer to partnered sex—just enjoy yourself!

Lesson 5: Special Topic—Good Vibrations. A great number of young women I've worked with don't have their first orgasm until they try using a vibrator. If you've sampled the many suggestions in the previous list and you still aren't having an orgasm, get yourself a vibrator. (Even if you're orgasming with your hands, a vibrator can be a really fun addition to your sex life.) As stated on one sex toy website, "If you have never tried a vibrator before, you are in for an amazing experience! Many women find that vibrators can help them achieve orgasm more easily than a hand or a lover's tongue."

She's Gotten So Nervy!

A recent study found that vibrations on rabbit's clitorises increased the number of clitoral nerve endings. Since, apparently, rabbits and women have similarly structured clits, some scientists have speculated that this could apply to humans as well. So much for the "Fucking like rabbits" saying. It's more like "Vibrating like bunnies"!

Unless you know that you like pairing clitoral stimulation with penetration, I strongly recommend that you start with a vibrator specifically designed for clitoral stimulation. If you can afford to do so, also get one with a range of speeds so you can experiment with the vibration intensity level and find what suits you best. Since there are so many vibrators to choose from, I'd also recommend getting your first one by browsing at either Babeland (Babeland.com) or Good Vibrations (GoodVibes.com). Both have online chats for help as well as customer service lines. Both sites also have special sections for anyone purchasing a vibrator for the first time—with current prices starting as low as eight dollars. (Do I sound like an advertisement?)

Very Often Vibrating

A recent study of over two thousand women in the Unites States, ranging in age from eighteen to sixty and including women who identified as heterosexual, lesbian, and bisexual, showed that many use vibrators. Specifically, 46 percent had used one during solo sex, 41 percent had used one during partnered sex play/foreplay, and 37 percent had used one during intercourse. We'll talk about introducing vibrators into partnered sex in the upcoming chapters. For now, just know that very many of us are vibrating, alone and with partners.

Let's talk a little bit more about using your first vibrator. If you have one with multiple speeds, start off slow and then experiment with increasing the intensity. If it feels too intense, you might want to put a washcloth between your vulva and the vibrator, or keep your undies on. Just like you did with your fingers, play around with different places and pressures with your vibrator.

If you come for the first time with a vibrator, please don't worry about vibrator addiction or your vibrator "ruining" you for sex with a partner! Research shows that women who use vibrators actually have easier and more frequent orgasms, both alone and with partners. Despite many women's fears that male partners will be threatened or turned off by the idea of incorporating a vibrator into their sex routine, in a study of over two thousand women, the vast majority who used vibrators said their partners knew—and liked—that they did so. When I asked the college men in my class, 95 percent said they either had incorporated or would be interested in a female partner incorporating a vibrator into their sexual encounter. So please have no fear. Buy that vibrator and enjoy! You might get used to having an orgasm with your vibrator and simply include it in your partnered sex, or you might use a vibrator to lead you to the type of finger stimulation you need to orgasm. Either way is okay! An orgasm is an orgasm is an orgasm.

Hopefully, now as you finish this chapter, you'll have either had your first orgasm or learned new ways to come. Congratulations! But this isn't the end. Keep masturbating! It's a gift to enjoy for life. As Lonnie Barbach says:

> Lie down and enjoy the time; one of
> your favorite lovers can be you.

And remember, masturbation isn't fun and healthy for just you alone. The more orgasms you have by yourself, the easier it will be to orgasm with a partner. And that's our next step: transferring your masturbation skills to sex with a partner. Look to the next chapter to find out how!

7.

EQUAL OPPORTUNITY ORGASMS

> It is very clear by now that the pattern of sexual relations
> predominant in our culture . . . [t]he sequence of "foreplay,"
> "penetration," and "intercourse" (defined as thrusting),
> followed by male orgasm as the climax and end of the
> sequence, gives very little chance for female orgasm. . . .
> But we can change this pattern, and redefine our sexual
> relations with others. . . . [W]e can take control over
> our own orgasms. We *know* how to have orgasms in
> masturbation. How strange it is . . . that we don't use
> this knowledge during . . . the sex we have with men.
>
> —Shere Hite, *The Hite Report*

Hopefully, you now have firsthand (i.e., your own hand) knowledge of what you need to orgasm when pleasuring yourself. This chapter is about transferring that understanding to the sex you have with a partner. The first step involves what you think inside your head. The second step concerns what you do between your legs.

In terms of your thinking, we've already focused a lot on the attitudes necessary to orgasm—including believing that your pleasure is as essential as your partner's pleasure. And if you're having sex with a man,

CVS: Not Just a Drugstore

From here on, I use "clitoral stimulation" and "touching your clit" to mean any external stimulation you like—including, for example, touching your clitoral hood or your inner lips. In order to stay true to my message of using correct anatomical terms, I tried to come up with a better term. I thought of abbreviating clitoral-vulva stimulation as "CVS," but this reminded me of the drugstore. So I decided to use the less than anatomically inclusive "clitoral stimulation." Still, after the earlier stance I took about calling a vulva a vulva, I apologize for being a little hypoclitical.

this means considering clitoral stimulation to be as important as penile penetration.

However, since we're now at the crucial juncture where you'll put these attitudes into action, please allow me to give you a quick refresher pep talk. Using the words of Elisabeth Lloyd, author of *The Case of the Female Orgasm*:

> The most striking thing about female masturbation is how likely it is to produce orgasm and how little it resembles, mechanically, the stimulation received from intercourse.

The stimulation that a man receives through masturbation and intercourse (as well as blow jobs and hand jobs) are all similar: they focus on his most sexually sensitive organ, his penis. In fact, lots of masturbation advice for men tells them to touch themselves in ways that make it feel like their penis is inside a vagina. Conversely, the stimulation a woman receives through masturbation and intercourse is quite different: only masturbation focuses on her most erotic external sexual organs. When with men, women often shortchange themselves, prioritizing intercourse instead. But it doesn't have to be this way. The first step to *orgasm equality* is genuinely believing that the clitoral stimulation you need is *just as central to sex* as the penile stimulation he needs. The next step is translating this attitude into action.

THE MOST IMPORTANT ACTION STEP FOR ORGASM

You can't touch your clit one way during solo sex and then ignore this during partnered sex. **The most crucial action needed to orgasm with a partner is to get the same type of stimulation you use when pleasuring yourself.**

There are two general ways to transfer your self-pleasure techniques to sex with someone else. One is teaching your partner what you like, and the other is doing it yourself.

Teaching a partner will sometimes entail introducing them to your vibrator. It may involve showing them your favorite finger motions, or explaining what feels good while they're giving you oral sex. In the next chapter (on communication), you'll learn strategies for telling a partner what you like. For now, the take-to-bed message is that one way to get clitoral stimulation is for your partner to give it to you.

Another way is to do it yourself. You can use your hands or vibrator on yourself during intercourse. An equally good example is to bring yourself to orgasm before or after intercourse while your partner holds, kisses, and caresses you. One more example is to touch yourself while giving a partner oral sex.

And, here's something really important about touching yourself during sex with a partner: it's *not* a lesser form of sex than having your partner stimulate you. For some women, this is the most—or only—reliable way to reach orgasm with a partner. This may be especially true for women who prefer a type of stimulation that's difficult, or even impossible, for someone else to provide. As just one example, a woman who can reach orgasm only by lying facedown and rubbing on pillows is going to have to do this herself—although her partner can be part of the action

It's Not Me—It's You

I had a student tell me that she could only reach orgasm using a vibrator with her legs held tightly together. However, when she tried to teach her first long-term partner to stimulate her this way, he said she was "weird." For a long time, she believed him and considered herself freakish. Eventually, however, she realized that it wasn't her masturbation style that needed to change but her partner. Happily, she found a new partner who wanted her to orgasm in the way that worked for her. Now after intercourse with her new boyfriend, she uses her vibrator on herself. He holds and kisses her while she does. They're now living happily (actually, blissfully) ever after!

(e.g., entering her from behind for intercourse while she does this or lying next to her and touching her in other erotic areas). On the other hand, a woman who reaches orgasm by rubbing circles on her clitoral hood can more easily teach a partner to do this with his or her hands.

Of course, touching yourself and having your partner touch you are not mutually exclusive. You can do both during a sexual encounter. Let's go over how this could play out during sex with a partner.

CLITERACY IN ACTION: CREATING NEW SEXUAL SCRIPTS

We're now at the point where things get real in terms of sex with a partner. In other words, the time's come to stop engaging in what academics call the "traditional sexual script"—you know, the one in which "foreplay" is followed by intercourse (during which the man comes) and then "sex" ends. In this traditional script, the man is responsible for the woman's orgasm and he "gives" her one by lasting long and thrusting hard. The woman's role is to protect the man's ego by pretending to orgasm that way—instead of having an orgasm for real.

It's time to rework this entire escapade. Continuing the metaphor of a sexual script, it's time to create modern plays in which his orgasm is not the only climax of the show. It's time to write scripts in which the word "foreplay" is never uttered and "sex" is not used as a synonym for intercourse. Most important, the storyline for these plays all center on women taking ownership and responsibility for their own orgasms. And to reflect all of this, the titles of these four modern-age plays feature your orgasm:

You Come First

You Come Second

You Come Together

Only You Come

You could also perform the first three plays all in a row, coming multiple times. Likewise, you could orgasm multiple times in one play (e.g., you could come three times before your partner's first orgasm). Still, while women's bodies are capable of multiple orgasms, that's not a goal to strive for—it's just a lovely bonus when it happens.

And, now, onto the four plays in more detail. Oops, wait, not so fast. Akin to the instructions you hear at the beginning of a live play on stage, there are some instructions for attending our new sexual plays as well.

The Delicate Balance

Throughout this book, I've tried to strike a balance between the fact that I'm committed to giving you the attitudes, knowledge, and skills to orgasm and the fact that pressure to orgasm is going to interfere with actually having an orgasm. But since this book is intended to fix the cultural problem of men having *way more* orgasms than women, I've created plays that revolve around female orgasms. This doesn't mean you *have to* orgasm every time you have sex with a partner; it just means that in these new-age plays, your orgasm is as central as your partner's.

SOME DIRECTIONS FOR
ATTENDING THE PLAYS

First, just like any show, turn off your cell phone (unless it doubles as a remote-control vibrator—for real, these exist and are great for long-distance couples!). This way you won't be distracted and, instead, can approach sex mindfully. You can't immerse in the pleasure of the play if your mind is somewhere other than your body. Other equally essential instructions for understanding and making the most of the four plays follow.

Inclusive Plays. The plays are written so that everyone can find a way to enjoy them, including those of you who have sex with men, those of you who have sex with women, as well as those of you who pleasure yourself in common ways (e.g., rub your clitoral hood) and less common ways (e.g., run water on your clitoris). I've also included male and female partners who like to be stimulated in common ways (e.g., oral sex, intercourse) and less common ways (e.g., women and men who like female partners to penetrate them, vaginally or anally, with a strap-on). What this means is that you'll read about ideas that sound awesome to you and others that sound unappealing or outlandish. Please just skip over the ones that you'd never want to try, knowing that another reader may be hearing about something that sounds great to her.

Partner Preferences for Attending the Play. While the following plays involve two people, you're the only one reading them and figuring out what sounds good to you. Certainly, any partner you're with will have his or her own ideas of what they like to do. I find it helpful to think of what two people do together sexually as two overlapping circles. You're willing to do some stuff and you're not willing to do other stuff, and your partner has their own limits. What you do together is where the circles overlap.

At this point, you may be thinking, *Hey, what about if I love something and my partner doesn't like this same activity?* This is where communication and compromise come in. Perhaps you'll find satisfaction through your partner pleasuring you in other ways. Or, out of a desire to please

More than Two and Anal Sex for You

While I tried to be inclusive, I didn't include everything. (If I did, this chapter would be as long as my favorite all-time sex guide, *The Guide to Getting It On,* whose eighth edition is over a thousand pages long.) Although a couple of women I've quoted talk about receiving anal touching and one talks about engaging in kinky sexual activities (i.e., blindfolds and mild restraints), I've mostly left these out of the plays. Likewise, I've limited the plays to two people acting. If you want to learn about threesomes, kinky sex, or anal intercourse, check out the *Guide.* After a little reading, you'll have no trouble introducing these into the structure of the plays that follow.

you, perhaps he or she will engage in (and maybe even learn to like) the previously disliked activity. On the other hand, if your desire and your partner's dislike are both especially strong, you might break up, knowing that the two of you are sexually incompatible. For example, I worked with a gay male couple and one partner detested anal intercourse (he found it aversive) while the other loved it (it was the only way he could orgasm). They couldn't work it out and ended the relationship, although they remained good friends.

But please remember this: there's a difference between a partner who is not into a sexual act (totally legitimate, we all have preferences) and a partner who doesn't give a rat's ass about your pleasure. If you're dealing with the latter, my not-so-subtle advice is to kick them to the curb. Same goes for men who simply won't put in the effort to become cliterate and stubbornly hold on to the notion that their penis is paramount to your pleasure. Happily, though, I think this is a very small minority of men; the vast majority of men in my classes care about women's pleasure. In fact, in one research study, about two hundred men in long-term relationships said that the number one thing they wanted out of sex was to pleasure their partner. But first we have to learn how to pleasure ourselves and then we can tell our partners how.

Directions for Your Pleasure. In several of the plays, you'll read the line "Your partner pleasures you *for as long as it takes you to orgasm*! He or she uses a tongue, hands, a vibrator, his penis, water, or a combination—*whatever and however you prefer!*" The reason I don't give more directions for what your partner should do is because I want to honor the fact that while most of you need clitoral stimulation, just what type you need (e.g., with panties off or on, type of pressure, type of rhythm) is individualistic. So while these modern-age plays give you a new sequence of events to replace the traditional scripted sequence that isn't working for women, just what you do during your part of the play is for you to decide.

"As Long as It Takes"

You may be wondering just how much time "as long as it takes" is. As you've read before, it's a whole lot quicker when you're by yourself (about four minutes) than when you're with a partner (anywhere from fifteen to forty-five minutes, with an average of twenty minutes). Indeed, if a partner spends twenty or more minutes on clitoral stimulation, about 92 percent of women will orgasm. While that might sound like a long time, here's what Ian Kerner says when he compares this rate of orgasm to our usual rate of female orgasm in heterosexual sex:

> That's a shift of tectonic proportions—from two out of three women not *being able to reach climax to nine out of ten achieving satisfaction*—all because of a matter of minutes. Few, if any, of the world's problems can be solved with a mere twenty minutes of attention, and yet here, in the complex sociopolitical landscape of the bedroom, we have an opportunity to create bilateral satisfaction.

Two Types of Women. To help understand how I came up with the four plays, let me underscore something I've mentioned before. Some women say their most reliable orgasms are from penetration and clitoral stimulation at the same time; others say they're from clitoral stimulation alone. And, importantly, some of the women who prefer clitoral stimulation alone also say that the feeling of a penis in their vagina while their clit is being stimulated makes it impossible for them to reach orgasm. Clearly, these women would need a totally different play than the women who like to pair clitoral stimulation and penetration.

Can I Change My Style? At this point, you may be wondering if you can change your style. Or—continuing the metaphor—perhaps you think you've been assigned a role in which you only orgasm with full-on clitoral stimulation but you wish you'd been cast as the woman who likes to pair clitoral stimulation with penetration. Well, sometimes women do start pleasuring themselves in new ways and end up reconditioning their body to enjoy a different type of stimulation. For some, this includes touching their clits in new ways, and for some, it does entail conditioning themselves to like penetration paired with clitoral stimulation rather than clitoral stimulation alone. One of my clients did this after she bought a vibrator that had a clitoral stimulator and vaginal penetrator in one (called a "rabbit" vibrator). One of my students did this by starting to put her finger in her vagina at the point of orgasm. But other women have told me they tried reconditioning their body and it didn't work. I suspect some women's preferred styles are more malleable than others.

But, here's the really vital thing. If a woman wants to change her self-pleasure style, my first question is "Why?" Sometimes it's just to mix things up, but most times the answer I hear is that she wants to train her body to prefer vaginal penetration. And underlying this desire is the deeply ingrained cultural attitude that a woman's orgasm is better if penetration is involved. It's like there's a female orgasm hierarchy, with orgasming from thrusting alone at the top, followed by penetration plus clitoral stimulation, with full-on clitoral stimulation in last place. Hogwash! Getting exclusive clitoral stimulation is just as legitimate as penetration plus clitoral stimulation.

The Voices You'll Hear. You'll find quotes from real women throughout the plays that follow; they're either things women have told me or are taken from previously published studies and books that asked women to write about how they reach orgasm (i.e., *The Hite Report* and a survey conducted by the author of *The Guide to Getting It On*). You'll hear women talking about sex with other women and sex with men. Please use their voices as role models while modifying each play to fit your particular wants and needs. Also, like these role models, learn to use your own body as a guide.

And now the moment you've been waiting for: our climactic new plays! Each of the four plays starts with the same first act.

ACT I: "FOOLING AROUND FOR TWENTY MINUTES"

Most of the action in our modern-age plays center on what you and your partner do between your legs. But most women require about twenty minutes of fooling around (making out, caressing, etc.) before a partner should even reach between her legs. It takes most women that long to get aroused and thus for their genitals to be lubricated enough to be comfortably touched. Yet, strikingly, in one survey about heterosexual sex, men and women said the average amount of time spent on such warming up was only five minutes. Using the metaphor of scripted plays, please don't cut yourself short and instead, include a sufficiently long Act I (a full body warm-up) in all your plays. On the next page, you'll find a sampling of things you can do to get warmed up in the first act.

Sometimes It's a Quick First Act

While the first act usually takes about twenty minutes, sometimes you'll feel like cutting it short. In the words of one woman, "Sometimes I can go from kissing to clitoral stimulation to orgasm."

- Kiss each other on the lips—in the limitless ways that people kiss (lightly, heavily, with tongue, without tongue).

- Kiss each other on the neck and ears and other parts of the face with clothes on.

- Stroke and caress each other's bodies through your clothes.

- Grind and roll around together with your clothes on.

- Take your own or each other's clothes off.

- Have your partner stroke, kiss, and caress your breasts.

- Have your partner play with your nipples, maybe rolling them gently between his or her fingers, sucking on them, tugging on them, or giving them a little pinch if that turns you on.

- Stroke and kiss each other's naked bodies, focusing mostly on all-over body caressing but slowly moving to Act II—the scene set between your legs. (Many women say they like it when their partner touches their genitals and then returns to another area of the body and teases back and forth for a while like this.)

For Some, the First Act Is Orgasmic

Throughout this book, I've focused on women who need clitoral stimulation to orgasm, since that's the vast majority of women. Still, recall that there are some women who orgasm most reliably in other ways. For example, I mentioned in chapter 1 that 4 percent of my students consistently orgasm from vaginal penetration alone. I've also known a few women whose most orgasmic areas are not in their genitals. One woman I know reaches orgasm when a partner nibbles on her ears—so for her the first act is the orgasmic one. All of these women are still cliterate, because cliteracy is about knowing what you need and feeling empowered to express this need to your sexual partners!

Act I can also include showering and bathing together, as well as laughing and joking with each other. Yes, these modern-age sex scripts include playfulness!

I hope I've given you some good ideas to start with, but please know it's impossible to make an exhaustive list of warm-up acts. Be creative and make up your own. And, then, when you've fully enjoyed Act I, move on to the place where the plays diverge—what you do between your and your partner's legs. In all four plays, we'll call this Act II—and name the plays after your orgasms!

PLAY 1: YOU COME FIRST

In this play, you and your partner *take turns* having orgasms and you take your turn first. This is going to work great for women who orgasm most reliably from clitoral stimulation without penetration. This also works well for women who like to combine the two—but with the penetration involving fingers or a vibrator rather than a penis. After the first act of "Fooling Around for Twenty Minutes," try either of the following two versions for this orgasmic Act II.

Act II—Version 1. Your partner pleasures you *for as long as it takes you to orgasm.* He or she uses a tongue, hands, a vibrator, his penis, water, or a combination—*whatever and however you prefer.*

> "I lie on my back and my partner lies to my right—her left hand under my buttocks with her middle finger inserted in my vagina, stimulating my clitoris with her right hand."
>
> "I like him to grip my ass hard, suck on my clitoris, and just let me move!"
>
> "I lie on my stomach and he's on my back, reaching up under me, and he makes me come and come, and he won't stop and he won't let me up. Wow!"

> "I lie on my back with my partner between my legs,
> flicking his tongue very gently, over and over. I like
> not doing anything else except concentrating on the
> sensations until I orgasm."

Act II—Version 2. You stimulate yourself to orgasm (just like you do when you pleasure yourself—with your hands or a vibrator or pillows or water) while your partner watches, holds you, or touches another erotic part of your body.

> "The best thing we've found so far is for me to bring
> myself to orgasm directly before fucking. This lubricates
> and prepares my vagina for intercourse, which I then
> enjoy very much. And my husband enjoys watching
> me do this. So it works."

> "I do most of the clitoral massaging while my lover plays
> with the other parts of my cunt, runs her hands gently
> between my legs, plays with and sucks my breasts, and
> talks to me softly all the time about coming."

Act II Continued. It's your partner's turn, and what you do will depend on your partner and what they like.

If you're with a man, you could

- have intercourse.

- give him oral sex.

- stimulate him with your hands.

- combine these activities (e.g., give him oral sex and then have intercourse).

- hold him, kiss him, or caress other parts of his body while he pleasures himself.

- use sex toys designed for male pleasure, such as a prostate massager (check out men's toys at Babeland or Good Vibrations).

- wear a strap-on or use a dildo and penetrate his anus.

> "After years of trial and error, my lover and I finally found a foolproof way for me to orgasm. We have intercourse and then before he has an orgasm, he pulls out and uses his penis to stimulate my clitoris. I guide him with my hand. I invariably orgasm this way, and while I am in the throes of it, he enters, we fuck, and he orgasms."
>
> "He puts a blindfold on me and ties my hands and legs lightly to the bed. It's really erotic because I can focus on what I'm feeling and not worry about what I should do for him. He uses his hands and one or two of my vibrators, switching it up all the time to surprise me. He also pinches and plays with my nipples, which I love. I always have at least one orgasm, often more, this way. Then, at some point when I'm squirming and really wet and ready, he gets on top and fucks me. He usually comes after a minute or two, which is fine by both of us."

A Five-Star Play

A woman receiving oral sex, followed by the man receiving oral sex and/or intercourse, is a favored turn-taking model for many. There's even a great book that teaches men oral sex skills: *She Comes First: The Thinking Man's Guide to Pleasuring a Woman* by Ian Kerner. I'll be sure to mention this book in the chapter for guys! Still, please remember that all women like different things, and while many women love oral sex followed by intercourse, others don't. When it comes to women's orgasms, there's no one-size-fits-all.

Why Is Lesbian Sex So Orgasmic?

Women have more orgasms when they have sex with other women than when they have sex with men. And while you might assume that this is because both people have a clit and therefore know what to do with it, this isn't wholly accurate. Since every woman needs a different kind of clitoral stimulation to orgasm, just having a clitoris—and even knowing what *yours* needs—doesn't mean you'll know what another woman needs. I think the reason lesbian sex is so orgasmic is because having a clitoris teaches you that it's important to ask a partner just how *hers* needs to be stimulated.

If you're with a woman, you could

- pleasure her for as long as it takes her to orgasm, using your tongue or hands or a vibrator or water or a combination—whatever and however she prefers.

- hold her, kiss her, or caress other parts of her body while she pleasures herself.

- penetrate her vaginally or anally with a dildo or strap-on.

- combine any or all of these activities.

> "We lie facing each other, with our legs intertwined, and fondle each other's bodies until one of us comes near orgasm, then I or she concentrates on that person until orgasm. Then it's the other's turn."

I hope this gives you an idea about how sex in which you come first would transpire. Now let's look at our second play.

PLAY 2: YOU COME SECOND

In this play, you and your partner also *take turns* having orgasms, but you take your turn second. This works well for women who need full-on clitoral stimulation and who have their most intense orgasms after a lot of stimulation—including, for example, clitoral stimulation that is arousing but not orgasmic, followed by intercourse. This play will also work best for women who can't relax and get into their own pleasure until they know their partner has had his or her orgasm.

However, when using this script with a male partner, even if you're going to come after intercourse, rushing to intercourse is almost never a good thing to do. A lot of pain during intercourse results from women prioritizing intercourse for their male partners, thus having it before they're sufficiently excited to make it pleasurable for themselves. As stated by Sheri Winston:

> Just because he's hard and ready, doesn't
> mean it's time to let him in.

Recall, from chapter 4, that when a woman is aroused her vagina becomes a "wet tent" (i.e., it lubricates and gets longer). Because the vagina getting longer in the back is due to the cervix pulling upward, if a woman has intercourse before this happens, a penis can hit her cervix and cause pain. Likewise, if a woman has intercourse before she's lubricated enough, this will hurt. Therefore, sex therapists are adamant in recommending that women pay attention to their arousal level, making sure it's high before intercourse begins.

Writers who say that women need to be highly aroused before intercourse begins are equating arousal and lubrication. But this isn't always the case. Women vary in terms of the amount of natural lubrication they produce. Some women tell me they produce so much wetness that they soak their mattress; I tell them to put a towel underneath or to invest in

Vulva and Intercourse Pain

There are also medical issues that can cause both pain during intercourse and other types of vulva pain. Some women's vaginas also contract involuntarily so that a penis can't enter (called "vaginismus"). No matter the cause of the discomfort, therapists advocate halting intercourse—or any sex act—if it starts to hurt. For more information on vulvar and intercourse pain and discomfort, see the sidebar "When *Not* to Exercise" in appendix A (page 241) as well as the resources in appendix B.

a waterproof mattress pad. Other women tell me they feel really excited but still don't produce enough lubrication on their own; I tell them to use a store-bought lubricant and put it all around their vulva. For intercourse, I also advise putting some inside the vagina with their fingers or, if that's not sufficient, with a syringe (search for "lubricant launcher" or "oral medication syringes" in online stores). Lube can be put on a partner's penis too.

Now on to more details of the *You Come Second* play. Again, after the first act of "Fooling Around for Twenty Minutes," try either of the following two versions for your second act.

Act II—Version 1. This version of Act II involves you, a male partner, and intercourse. Specifically, he pleasures you until you're ready for intercourse, which could include him touching you with his hands or your vibrator, or giving you oral sex. You could also touch yourself, with your hands or your vibrator or water or pillows.

For some men, pleasuring you is arousing enough to get them ready for intercourse. Others need you to do something for them. You can

- touch his penis with your hands.

- give him oral sex. (Bonus: Use your vibrator or hands on yourself while giving him oral sex.)

- rub his penis around your vulva, using your own or applied lubrication to get him wet. (Bonus: Don't go for full insertion immediately but instead tease at the vaginal opening awhile. Since this is where most of your vaginal nerve endings are, it'll probably feel great for you too.)

You and your partner then have intercourse. After your partner has his intercourse-based orgasm, you have your orgasm any way you want. This could include

- your partner stimulating you with his hands or a vibrator, or after a quick wipe off, giving you oral sex. You could also hop into a shower or bath and he can use your handheld shower attachment on you.

- you stimulating yourself while your partner watches, holds you, or touches another erotic part of your body. You could rub against pillows, use your hands, use your vibrator, or hop into a bath and lie back against him, with your legs positioned to have the water from the faucet massage your clitoris while he caresses your breasts.

> "We fool around until we're both ready. Then we put lube on his penis and all around my pussy and we screw. After he comes, he pulls out and I lie on my back and he uses my vibrator on my clit, sometimes playing with my nipples at the same time. I always come this way."
>
> "We both touch each other a lot, including taking turns giving each other oral sex. Then, when we're both really excited, we fuck. We do this with me lying on my stomach with pillows under me and him entering me from behind. He usually cups my breast in his hands and squeezes as he thrusts in and out. I rub against the pillows while he does this. After he comes, he pulls out and we stay in the same position. He keeps playing with my tits while I keep rubbing up and down on the pillows and then I come."

> "I have my most satisfying orgasm lying on top of my partner after he's come. He lies there exhausted and I rub my clitoris against him."

> "I need a really specific type of finger motion to orgasm and I've never been able to teach a partner to do this for me. I have to be lying on my stomach, and I rub up and down on both sides of my clit while pushing really deep and hard and rocking my hips. So with my current partner it works really well if we fool around enough to get us both ready for intercourse. We use all kinds of positions, and sometimes I also rub my clit during intercourse or use my vibrator, but I can never come that way. So after he comes, no matter what position we're in, I roll onto my tummy and finish myself off with my fingers. He lies really close to me and caresses my back and plays with my ass. Sometimes I even like him to gently slap my butt while I'm finishing myself off. It's really intense that way."

Act II—Version 2. In this version of Act II, you give your male or female partner oral sex or manual stimulation with your hands or a vibrator, during which time he or she comes. Then your partner gives you oral sex or manual stimulation, during which time you come. As an alternative to this, your partner stimulates him or herself to orgasm while you watch or hold or touch another of his or her erotic parts. Then you have your orgasm any way you want.

> "There's always a lot of touching and affection—fingers run over each other's bodies, legs entwined, and a great deal of kissing all over our bodies. Then we get into oral sex, one person at a time."

I hope this gives you an idea of how taking turns and you coming second would transpire. Now let's talk about another way to take turns.

PLAY 3: ONLY YOU COME

Our third play also includes turn taking, but only one partner reaches orgasm during this sexual encounter. Before you say this sounds strange, stop and consider that this is generally what happens in current heterosexual encounters! The unusual part is to think of this in a reverse manner: the man stimulates the woman to orgasm and gets no stimulation in return. Still, this does happen. In fact, a reader wrote about this in the comments of my *Psychology Today* blog. He said:

> It is a *shame* that the *"Love* Button" does not get attention! It is so unique, beautiful, and feminine, yet most men are oblivious to its anatomical structure and how to stimulate it. . . . Every man should find some quiet . . . time with his lover and explore her clitoris. Have her lie back and close her eyes, slowly explore and observe. Listen to her breathing, watch her chest rise with each deep breath. Hear her moans and watch her wriggle. I try to do this with my wife every Sunday morning, and it is a loving and giving experience that pays huge dividends!!

He clarified, "It is almost always an asynchronous experience and I am totally fine with that." He also asked, "How can a man be in love with a woman, sexually intimate with her, and not explore the most sensual part of her body?"

This play is all about asynchronous turn taking, which means sometimes the focus is all on one partner and sometimes it's all on the

OMing

There's a fairly new movement, called orgasmic meditation, in which a partner spends fifteen solid minutes rubbing just one portion of a woman's clitoris (called "OMing"). Author Jenny Block wrote, "I find it sad and ironic that you have to create a movement to get men to do what lesbians have been doing forever." And a student of mine pointed out, "This is also akin to what women have been doing forever—spending a lot of time giving men oral sex, with nothing in return."

other. Perhaps it's obvious—unless you find a partner who likes only to give, not receive, pleasure—this style will generally work best for a long-term couple between whom the turn taking evens out over time. I once worked with an older couple who, after much experimenting to figure out what worked best for them, settled on a total turn-taking model. Sometimes he'd spend an evening stimulating her to orgasm—usually with a combination of oral sex and finger stimulation, asking nothing in return for himself. Other evenings, she'd do the same for him, usually with oral sex. They both reported they were much more able to relax and revel in being both the giver and the receiver that way. Certainly, instead of being the mainstay of a couple's sexual life, this type of turn taking could be done in addition to encounters that involve mutual stimulation.

"I become very aroused by caressing my female lover's breasts and clitoris and vagina and get so hung up on her body that she need not do anything to me. The mere touch and taste of her body is all the stimulus I need."

PLAY 4: YOU COME TOGETHER

This play is about you coming while engaged with your partner in the same sexual act, rather than while the focus is all on you. Just as in the other plays, after Act I (the all-body fooling around, warm-up act), move on to the second act—which in this play, has three versions.

Act II—Version 1. Whether you're with a man or a woman, you could

- give each other oral sex simultaneously (often called "69").

- give each other hand and/or vibrator stimulation at the same time.

- lie near each other and do your own thing.

> "Sex is slow with long preliminaries and explorations, conversation, gentle mutual stroking, and then clitoral stimulation in unison. It's great to do and feel the same done to you."
>
> "I enjoy mutual face-to-face voyeuristic masturbation!"

Too Much Going On!

While "69" gets a fair amount of attention in the media, it doesn't work that well for many people. That's because it's hard to focus on pleasuring someone else while also being fully absorbed in your own pleasure. In essence, it can distract from mindful immersion. In the words of one woman, "It's just too much going on at once!"

Act II—Version 2. Because of our distorted cultural perceptions of what real sex is (i.e., intercourse), you don't have to look very far to see countless magazine articles touting "The Best Sex Position for Her Orgasm."

Simultaneous Orgasm: Not Part of the Script

It's key to not put pressure on yourself to orgasm while intercourse is going on—and especially not to expect some magical, mythical simultaneous orgasm. If you orgasm during intercourse, maybe it will be before he does and maybe it will be after. And if after, maybe he will stay inside or maybe he will come out. Either way, it's okay!

For example, you might have read about the "woman-on-top position" or the "coital-alignment technique" as solutions for women's "problem" of not having an orgasm during intercourse. Or maybe you've heard that it helps to put a pillow under the small of a woman's back or her rear end during missionary-style intercourse. Since this kind of advice is bountiful in the rest of the world, I'm not going to go into detail about anything like that here. Instead, I'll point out that if these tips work, they generally do so because the woman involved is getting her clitoris stimulated by rubbing or grinding it against a part of the man's body, typically his penis or pubic bone. While this does indeed work for some women, for others it provides insufficient clitoral stimulation. In fact, I'm guessing some of you have already tried these intercourse positions and found they didn't result in orgasm. Or perhaps some of you tried them but didn't realize you were supposed to be rubbing or grinding your clitoris into one of your partner's body parts. If that's the case, you can try it again with this in mind. However, those of you who need more intense or direct clitoral stimulation will likely be better off using the version that follows.

"I have an orgasm when I assume the dominant position and rub my clitoris against his belly and pubic area."

"I lie on the bottom with my legs around him, then grind my pelvis and pubic area against him."

Act II—Version 3. In this version of pairing clitoral stimulation with intercourse, you or your partner can use a hand or a vibrator. Many (but definitely not all) women who use this method say they prefer to "do it themselves," since they best know what they need at any given moment.

"
> "I have no qualms about manually stimulating myself during intercourse. . . . I deserve satisfaction as much as he does!"
>
> "I like to lie on my belly, over a pillow, and he enters me from behind. He reaches underneath me and stimulates my clitoris with his hand at the same time that he penetrates me."
>
> "He lies sort of on his back but kind of on his side. I lie on my back at a ninety-degree angle with his dick inside me from the rear. He can reach my tits and I can reach my clitoris."

There are also little-known but super-fun wearable couples vibrators that provide clitoral stimulation during intercourse. With one type, the man wears a cock ring (which will also enhance his erection) that has a vibrating clitoral extension attached to it. The ring is placed at the base of the man's penis with the clitoral vibrator facing in the direction where it will stimulate the woman's clitoris during intercourse. You can find these types of toys by looking in the couples toy section of Babeland (Babeland.com) or the wearable vibrators section of Good Vibrations (GoodVibes.com). There is variation in these toys, both in terms of how tight or stretchy the cock ring is and the style of the clitoral vibrator attached to the cock ring, so some trial and error in purchasing may be necessary. When I first discovered the existence of this type of toy (and found my personal favorite), I enthusiastically gave it to five of my friends as a holiday gift! All of them loved it and one asked me where to get more so that she could give others this gift that keeps giving!

Which Intercourse Position Is Best?

You might be wondering which position is best when you're pairing direct clitoral stimulation with intercourse. The answer I like most comes from a woman who uses this technique: "It can be done in almost any position with a little effort." But, remember: it's best if you can have intercourse that involves clitoral stimulation in a position that closely mimics the one you use when pleasuring yourself (e.g., on your back or your stomach).

While vibrating cock rings are worn by men, several hands-free wearable vibrators can be worn by women. The first popular toy of this kind was the We-Vibe (We-Vibe-Shop.com), and while it has gone through many updates, the basic principle is the same. The woman inserts part of this toy into her vagina, presumably providing G-spot stimulation (yet still leaving enough room for the man's penis) while the other part of the toy rests on her clitoris. Truth be told, I tried this toy out and it didn't work for me; however, I have a friend who swears by it. I share this to emphasize that what type of stimulation women like varies not only generally but also specifically when it comes to sex toys—including wearable, clitoral-stimulating ones. So, again, if you want to try out these types of toys, do some experimenting. You may not get your ultimate toy the first try.

Two other sex toy products worn by women are designed to provide clitoral stimulation during intercourse. First, and fairly new to the market, are crotchless vibrating panties, which make the vaginal opening accessible while holding a clitoral vibrator in place. These types of toys can be found at Adam and Eve (AdamEve.com). Second is the Eva (which can be found at Babeland), a fairly pricey clitoral vibrator that stays in place with little plastic bendable wings that fit under a woman's inner lips. But since inner lips come in all shapes and sizes, these wings won't work for everyone, and some women find that they need to hold the Eva in place. What's really interesting to me, though, is that the Eva was designed by

Equal Opportunity Routines

You have a routine when you pleasure yourself. And once you apply this to sex with a long-term partner, you two will also develop a routine for mutual pleasure. As you've seen illustrated in the quotes in this chapter, couples usually develop a consistent sexual sequence that works for them. But having a routine isn't the same thing as being in a boring rut. As one of my yoga teachers, who does the same thing in every class, tells me, "I take you through the same moves each class, but you show up different each time. Stay open to your new reactions." Still, if a routine starts to feel lackluster, it's time to add in something new. You can try an entirely different routine or you can add some spice (e.g., a new vibrator, some new lube, a little kink) to the old one.

two women—a sex therapist and a mechanical engineer—who said they wanted to close the orgasm gap in heterosexual sex! And that, my friend, was my main motivator in writing *Becoming Cliterate*.

PUTTING IT ALL TOGETHER: SEX IN A CLITERATE WORLD

I hope you now have some new, fun, and orgasmic ideas to try after reading this chapter. Indeed, I hope you found a new sexual script to replace the misguided cultural one that's at the root of the orgasm gap (i.e., foreplay, intercourse, male orgasm, sex over). Still, please remember that the four plays provided in this chapter were starter scripts. Adapt them to fit your sexual needs and preferences. Also, because these are not either-or plays, you can combine them in limitless ways. The various women quoted in this chapter illustrate the countless ways women and their partners enjoy having sex together.

> "My body achieves orgasm best by a combined effort of my lover and myself. She uses her mouth and tongue to stimulate my clitoris and then gently blows into my vagina; while she does this I masturbate. This combined effort leads me to a most terrific orgasm."

> "We go in the missionary position. He fucks me for a while, then sort of leans sideways, so I can play with my clitoris while he's still inside. When I get to a certain point, he starts fucking me again. We take turns till somebody gets tired or can't take it anymore. Sometimes I come first, and if so, I'm super sensitive inside and can feel waves of his orgasm. Sometimes he comes first and then he stays in me till the last sensations have subsided, then lies beside me, lending encouragement while I bring myself off."

The key to sex in our new cliterate world is taking responsibility for your own orgasm and making sure you get the type of stimulation you need. *Yeah, right. Sure,* you may be thinking. Maybe you're thinking this is a lot easier said than done. Perhaps you're wondering how you're going to tell your partner, especially a new one, what you need to orgasm. You're going to do it with the communication skills you'll learn in the next chapter. Read on and find out how!

8.

THE OTHER C

Communication

Many sex myths encourage us to believe that to
be great lovers we need to be mind readers, not
communicators. Communication isn't always
about talking, but I can promise you that one of
the keys to great sex is an ability to talk about it.
I can also promise that it's easier to learn to talk
about sex than it is to learn to read minds.

—Cory Silverberg, sex educator and author

We ended the previous chapter with the promise that next you'd learn the
communication skills to teach your partner what you need for pleasure
and to reach an orgasm. Because good sexual communication is an extension of good general communication, we're going to start there. In
other words, we're first going to improve your general communication
skills and then extend this to your sex life. This is the format I follow
when I lecture on communication in my class, and it works wonderfully.
Every year, several students e-mail me months after my communication
lecture, saying they've been using what they learned and it's been life altering. I want you to have this same information.

LET'S TALK!

In terms of its ability to enhance your life, communication is something I feel as passionately about as I do the clitoris. Truthfully, in over twenty-five years of counseling, I can't think of a client I've worked with whose communication style has not contributed to their problems, been part of their healing, or both. Sadly, very few of us grow up in households where effective communication and fair fighting are modeled. The ability to communicate clearly is an uncommon skill—and yet it's the key to better relationships, including sexual ones.

Good communication involves two components: beliefs and skills. Let's focus on each.

From Faulty Beliefs to Fantastic Philosophies. There are four common, but faulty, ways of thinking about communication that not only make it less likely for you to get your needs met but also can erode your relationships with others.

The first faulty belief is:

> **I shouldn't have to say what I want.**

The Importance of Intercourse

A premise of this book is that intercourse is not the *ultimate* pleasure for women. Yet, ironically, the word "intercourse" means communication—the exchanging of thoughts, feelings, and ideas. *This* type of intercourse is vital to your orgasm. Along these same lines, after learning about female anatomy, a perplexed student once asked me, "Why is the clitoris so far away from the vaginal opening?" Without thinking too much, I answered, "So that women and men can learn to communicate about sex!" In other words, it's important to have intercourse about intercourse!

I can't begin to tell you how many times, when I counsel romantic partners, one will *hint* at something they want from the other. I will then make this wish explicit, saying for example, "Julie, it sounds to me like you want Greg to stop making jokes about your sex life in front of your friends." "Well, yes, of course!" is the general reply. I then ask, "Have you told him this?" About half the time, the answer to such a question is "I shouldn't have to. He should know this!" This response is based on the mistaken belief that our partners should know what we want without us telling them.

No one can read minds, nor should they be expected to try. The belief that people should know what you want without you telling them is a surefire way to communicate ineffectively. To be angry at someone for doing something you find offensive, but you haven't told him or her you don't like, is unfounded. It's also unreasonable to be upset with someone for not doing something you never told them about in the first place. To have any chance of getting what you want, you have to learn to state your wants clearly. People can't be expected to guess your needs. To use a sexual example, your partner won't know how you like your clit to be touched—or how you don't like it to be touched—unless you tell him or her.

Perhaps you think that if you have to request something, it's less meaningful to receive it. But here's another way of thinking about this: Contemplate how wonderful it can be to directly state that something is important to you and then receive it. This means the other person listened to you and demonstrated their caring by giving you what you said you desired. Of course, you won't always get what you want, but the best way to have a shot at it is to ask!

Julie and Greg: Just a Great Example

I used a couple example—Julie and Greg—to illustrate this first faulty belief, and I'll continue to use couple examples in the rest of this chapter. But these general communication skills and beliefs apply to *all* relationships, not just sexual and romantic ones.

And what about the flip side of this equation—that is, giving people you care about what you *think* they want? This is actually related to our next faulty assumption:

I'm sure I know.

Assuming you know something can be hazardous to relationships. I've worked with a lot of couples who make faulty sexual assumptions (e.g., "He'd never want to try anything kinky") without actually checking them out. Here's a nonsexual example: One of my clients, Lucia, had been in a relationship with another woman, Olivia, for about six months. Lucia assumed their committed relationship status meant that they would reserve Friday and Saturday nights for each other. So whenever Olivia made weekend plans without letting Lucia know, Lucia would get hurt and distance herself from Olivia—unfortunately without telling her why. When they finally talked about this, Lucia learned that Olivia didn't think they had this unspoken agreement about their relationship and weekends. In other words, Lucia thought she knew something, but she was mistaken. They talked about their desires and reached an understanding.

Talking about a problem is related to the third faulty belief:

It's useless to discuss.

For most couples—whether they've been together three months or thirty years—ineffective communication leads to unresolved issues that both partners feel hurt or angry about. This is why when I counsel couples, I tell them a metaphorical story about a backpack.

We all walk around with an invisible backpack on our backs. When things bother or upset us about the significant relationship we're in, we often don't tell our partners. We may think it isn't worth it or we won't be able to solve the problem anyway. Each upset that we don't discuss is akin to a pebble. These pebbles can be about anything in the relationship, including sex (e.g., "He always gets out of bed after, even though I want to cuddle"). We walk along, picking up pebble after pebble, putting them into our backpacks. Eventually the pebbles add up and the backpack is so heavy that it hurts to carry it. Sometimes we carry it anyway but resent every difficult step we take with it on. Sometimes, in an attempt to lighten our load, we dump it out—we get rid of the whole relationship, throwing away the backpack and its pebbles. Other times, we keep the relationship but take out the stones and start throwing them at each other.

I tell the couples I counsel that we'll work on emptying the backpack. I help couples get rid of the old stones by helping them to talk through past hurts and misunderstandings, while explaining how the stones were initially put in the backpack due to a lack of communication. Most important, I teach couples new communication skills so that in the future they don't hold on to pebbles; they learn to reach an understanding by openly and calmly talking through issues.

Couples finding common ground isn't generally portrayed in our culture. Instead, we hear about couples "fighting" over issues. And this fighting attitude is our final faulty assumption:

Fights have winners and losers.

Oftentimes, we're taught to argue to prove a point. We're taught to fight to win. This is rarely constructive and can harm relationships. People who care about each other are much better off taking the attitude that the purpose of disagreeing is to get closer rather than to win.

My husband taught me this lesson—it's both a moment in time I will never forget and one of the reasons I fell in love with him. We'd been in a committed relationship for a couple of months when we had our first fight, the topic of which I can't even recall. Using my sharp tongue, I started fighting both dirty and to win. He looked at me with a perplexed expression on his face and asked, "What are you doing?" "Fighting with you, you idiot!" is what I think I replied, because I didn't even know what he was asking. He then calmly said, "Well, the purpose of fighting isn't to hurt each other; it's to resolve the issue." Lightbulb! I'd honestly never considered this option before. But he taught me this, and now I try to teach this attitude to others—including you. This lesson is inherent in *Becoming Cliterate,* which is about creating a world of orgasm equality—one in which *both* people get what they want rather than one person consistently coming out ahead (pun intended).

We've just covered four faulty beliefs about communication that can erode relationships, and hopefully the healthier attitudes were clear as well. Still, let's make these positive beliefs explicit. Here are the guiding principles of effective communication:

- **State what you want. Don't expect someone to mind read.**

- **Check out your assumptions. Don't act on beliefs about the other person without verifying their accuracy. (I promise, you'll be surprised at how often your assumptions are inaccurate.)**

- **Work out issues as they arise rather than hold on to them in your metaphorical backpack.**

- **Work to resolve issues rather than to win a fight.**

Maybe these sound like great ideas to you but you're wondering just how to implement them. The answer is with eight powerful communication skills that I believe can change lives and relationships.

The first skill is a prerequisite to all the others:

> Allow yourself to be aware of what you want and your right to express it.

Being in touch with what you want (generally and sexually), and clearly stating it, is something many women don't do. Sometimes women are so focused on trying to please others that they don't even know what they want. One of my current clients, Ashley, epitomizes this problem. She was raised with strict instructions to be considerate to others. Also, in her family, no one ever directly expressed what they wanted. The result is that she has an automatic, knee-jerk reaction of trying to assess what others want and acting on this. In therapy, she's working on slowing down her

It'll Be Okay—Take the Plunge

Imagine a child standing fearfully on the edge of the diving board, afraid to go in—but after she does, she not only is proud of herself but also discovers that the water feels good. This is how starting a hard conversation, especially about sex, can be. It's often nerve-racking to bring up a difficult sexual—or nonsexual—topic in a relationship. If you find yourself standing on the edge of the board, remind yourself that this is the person who touches your most intimate parts—so you might as well have an intimate conversation about it too. Ask yourself what's holding you back. Are you afraid your partner will get hurt or mad? If so, you can use the skills in this chapter to have an adult, productive conversation about it and hopefully work things out. Also remind yourself that your partner may not be mad or hurt but instead relieved and appreciative that you brought up a topic they've been afraid to broach. Remember too that if you don't bring it up, there's no way it'll get worked out, and the longer you stand on the edge of the board, the worse you'll feel. So go ahead. Dive off. I know you can do it!

reactions to consider what *she* wants. Once she figures that out, she can then decide whether or not she wants to express what she wants to others.

In terms of actually expressing your desires, the next three skills are my favorites. I often tell students and clients that if they master just these three, their lives will change for the better. Grandiose, but true! First:

Don't ask questions that aren't actually questions.

People often ask a question that isn't a question, consciously or unconsciously, to avoid facing their needs head-on. When I'm especially worn down, I fall prey to asking questions that are actually statements about what I want. Last night I was lying in bed, wanting to go to sleep, and my

Do You Want to Have Sex?

This question (that isn't really a question) can have many possible meanings. It can even mean one thing at one time and something totally different at another. It could mean "I'm totally horny and want to get it on" or "I hope you aren't horny because I'm exhausted and want to cuddle and get some sleep." Depending on what the asker actually meant—and their partner's reply—you can see how things could go downhill quickly.

husband was putting his laundry away. I asked, "Are you going to be done soon?" What I meant was "I want to go to bed. I would appreciate it if you could do your chores tomorrow so I can turn the light out now." I asked a question that wasn't a question because it was easier than mustering the brainpower to make a clear statement of my needs. My husband laughed and pointed out my non-question to me by saying he would be doing chores for the entire night, with the lights on. "Is this a problem for you?" he laughingly asked.

The result of asking non-questions is generally not this joking or positive. Indeed, when someone asks a question that isn't a question, they rarely get a satisfactory answer. Sometimes the receiver won't realize it isn't a real question and will provide the opposite of what the asker is hoping for. The receiver may also become defensive, mistaking the question for a criticism. Either way, asking questions that aren't questions rarely ends well.

Starting today, observe how often you ask questions that are actually statements, and work to change this pattern. Instead, use "I" statements. In fact, this is the second of the three most powerful skills I mentioned earlier:

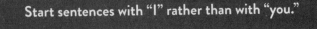

Start sentences with "I" rather than with "you."

I Feel Selfish!

Oftentimes women have concerns about coming across as self-centered or selfish when they use "I" statements or when they use direct statements rather than indirect, veiled questions. Quite the contrary, these skills are actually respectful of relationships because they allow the other person to react to a clear message rather than one that needs to be deciphered.

Starting a sentence with the word "you" is almost guaranteed to result in a nonproductive conversation. It comes across as an accusation and puts the other person on the defensive. Contrast how you would react if your partner said "You never go down on me!" with "I'd love you to go down on me more often." My guess is that the "you" statement would result in you feeling attacked, defensive, or guilty. The "I" statement, on the other hand, would hopefully be the entry into constructive dialogue.

Also, disguising a "you" statement with an "I" at the start isn't the same as making an "I" statement. To illustrate, "I think you're acting like an asshole!" is still a "you" statement. An "I" statement would be "I feel really hurt when you [insert whatever behavior prompted the 'asshole' sentiment]." So please, starting today, try to start as many of your sentences with "I" as possible. Owning your needs with "I" statements in your daily life will help you do so in your sex life.

Here's the final of the three most powerful communication skills:

Communicate about communication.

Psychologists call this meta-communication. It's especially useful when starting conversations you're worried about having. As an example, you might say something like "I have something to talk to you about, but I'm afraid you might get hurt or angry with me" or "There's something I want to talk about, and I'm afraid you're going to feel criticized

Queen of the Preface

I sometimes go overboard with my pre-conversation meta-communications—so much so that my husband calls me Queen of the Preface. Often, by the time I'm done with my start-up, people say, "Oh, is that all you wanted to say? No big deal. You scared the shit out of me."

and get defensive rather than realize that I'm bringing this up because I care about you and our relationship." Starting a conversation with meta-communication allows you to put your fears out there, and it also generally helps the other person monitor his or her reactions—as well as take loving care to avoid the reaction that you feared in the first place.

Along with being great conversation starters, meta-communications can be used in the middle of conversations. For example, you might say "I feel like I'm not getting my point across clearly. Let me try again" or "I feel like we're both getting defensive and I don't want the conversation to be like this." Meta-communications—coupled with "I" statements—are also very helpful when you notice a discrepancy between someone's verbal and nonverbal behavior. You might say something like "I hear you saying you aren't mad, but I keep seeing you scowling. I wonder if it's my imagination or if something is going on that you aren't telling me." In short, any communication about the communication is meta-communication. It generally involves putting out there what you're thinking or observing about the interaction but ordinarily would not say explicitly. I often tell my clients that whenever they're all up in their head in the middle of a conversation, it's probably time to meta-communicate.

While I truly believe the three skills I just presented have the most power to improve relationships, the next three are also extremely useful, especially for difficult conversations. The first one is:

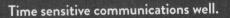

Time sensitive communications well.

What you have to say is not going to be heard if you say it at a lousy time. Have difficult conversations when both you and the other person are in the "right space" to do so—when you're both feeling calm and have some time to talk things through. Waiting to have a hard conversation at a good time is definitely better than rushing to have one at a bad time. Telling your partner you've been faking orgasms for three months is likely not a conversation you want to start five minutes before your mother comes over for dinner.

And when having a difficult conversation—about sex or anything else—here's another skill that can truly help:

Find the grain of truth.

When you're in conflict with another person, keep in mind that there's likely some truth in what this person is saying. If you can find it and acknowledge it, the disagreement will de-escalate. This technique reminds me of my late father-in-law. When he and my mother-in-law were fighting, he would say to himself, *This is the woman I love and respect. She's a smart woman. There must be some truth in what she's saying, and I will find it.* I've had several female clients struggling with low sexual desire get mad at their partners for bringing up their lack of interest. When my clients acknowledge the truth in their partners' words rather than rally against them, a productive conversation (instead of the same old fight) generally ensues.

The next time you're in the heat of battle with someone you like, respect, and/or love, take a deep breath, slow down, and remember that this person is not the enemy and likely has some valid points. Nothing will de-escalate conflict quicker than if you can say with sincerity "I see your point."

A great way to let someone know you see their point of view—and that you understand what they're saying—is with the next skill:

Reflect what you hear.

Reflect Versus Advise

Reflection is also helpful when comforting someone; people often want to know the other person understands what they feel, rather than to be given advice. For example, if a friend tells you she just found out that her boyfriend cheated on her, saying "Wow. I'm sorry. That's so upsetting" (i.e., a reflection of her feelings) is going to be more helpful than providing unsolicited advice (e.g., "I think you should tell him you're done!").

Reflection is using your own words to repeat what someone said and, if possible, to acknowledge their emotions. Whenever I work with couples in counseling, reflection is one of the first things I teach them to help de-escalate and work through conflicts. While most say it feels weird and cumbersome at first, in over twenty-five years of doing counseling, I've yet to find a couple for which reflections doesn't help diminish clashes and enrich understanding—including sexual understanding. One couple, Alex and Rebecca, told me they'd had the same conversation over and over, but they couldn't work it out. So I had them have the conversation in therapy, while using reflection. Rebecca said, "I want you to take more time during sex." Alex reflected back, "You want me to last longer" with a hurt look on his face. I asked Rebecca if this was what she meant. "No," she said, "I want him to take more time *before* we have intercourse, not during." Alex looked surprised. "I didn't get that's what you wanted. I can do that," he said. Had they not used reflection, Alex would have continued to try to last longer during intercourse, thinking that's what Rebecca wanted, and Rebecca would have continued to feel as if she didn't get something she had said was important to her.

To even further enhance relationships, here's the final skill:

Create a culture of appreciation.

Too often in long-term relationships we stop telling each other what we like and instead focus on what we don't like. Stopping this pattern and commenting on what you appreciate about someone works wonders. In fact, a famous relationship researcher, John Gottman, can predict with over 90 percent accuracy which newly married couples will stay together and which will eventually divorce—with a big predictor being the ratio of positive, appreciative comments to negative, critical ones. The ideal ratio is five compliments for every criticism! Compliments are also best when they're specific rather than general, such as "I really appreciated the way you took your time giving me oral sex" versus "I appreciate how good you are in bed." So create a culture of appreciation today, with friends, family, and sexual partners.

LET'S TALK SEX

It's time to put the finishing touches (pun intended!) on your personal orgasm revolution. For women, having good sexual communication is related to frequency of orgasms. Indeed, among women who tell their partners how they like to be touched, the vast majority have orgasms. On the flip side, not saying what you want generally has the opposite result: unsatisfying sex. As you read about in the previous chapters, many women put up with unpleasant, even painful, heterosexual sexual encounters and fake orgasms. Yet, as stated by Lonnie Barbach:

> By faking, you are training your partner to
> do precisely what doesn't work for you.

And the longer the faking goes on, the harder it is to reveal it to a partner. It's a lot cleaner to just start out *all* sexual relationships with clear communication.

Certainly, it's more difficult to say what you want the first time you're sexual with someone—putting yourself out there can feel vulnerable. Women also commonly worry that telling first-time male partners that they want clitoral stimulation will be perceived as pushy. However, just the opposite may be true. In one study, men said they're turned on by women's requests for clitoral stimulation. The men in my class say they feel relieved when a woman gives them instructions for clitoral stimulation, since they find women's bodies complicated to navigate. They also say they genuinely want to give women pleasure but are often at a loss for just how to do so. The fact that every woman needs something slightly different to reach orgasm makes it even more important to tell a new partner what you like. Even if the relationship doesn't go past one night, at least it will have been a good one!

Now let's turn more specifically to how to get your sexual needs met. Truth be told, when I first wrote this chapter, I organized it into two sections: "Skills for Any Encounter," be that a first time or a fiftieth time (e.g., guiding a partner's hands where you want them to go); and "Skills for Long-Term Partners" (e.g., talking through a sexual problem outside the bedroom). But this organization didn't work because some skills don't fit squarely into only one of these two categories. I then realized that while some skills might be more *comfortable* to use with long-term partners, they're still applicable (and often with wonderful effects) with first-time partners (e.g., an *honest* "How was that for you?" talk right after the encounter). So I decided to present sexual communication skills the way I do when I lecture to my class—by dividing them into five types of sexual talks: "Kitchen Table," "Let's Have Sex," "Provocative," "In the Midst," and "Afterglow." Then, because the main focus of this book is to get the clitoral stimulation you need, I've also included a special section called "Cliteracy Chats."

I assume many of you are most interested in the ways to get your clitoral stimulation needs met *during sex*. I promise we'll get there, but these general sexual communication skills are tremendously important too.

Kitchen-Table Sex Talks. Despite the name, these talks don't have to be held at the kitchen table; they can occur in any nonsexual location. They can be general, positive discussions of things you want to try to make good sex even better. Or they can be used to solve problems. In fact, it's best not to bring up sexual dissatisfaction or any other difficult topic in bed, because it may create a negative association with a place you want to be fun, exciting, and positive. For the same reason you don't bring stressful work with you to bed (if you do, sleep experts would tell you not to), you don't want to bring stressful conversations there either.

No matter where you have "kitchen table sex talks" (e.g., on a walk, in the car, at the actual kitchen table), when trying to problem-solve, the key is to use the general communication skills discussed earlier. Say, for example, "I think it would help me get turned on if you . . ." rather than "You don't seem to know how to turn me on." Likewise, remember to time these talks well. Having them on a five-minute car ride to a party is not a good idea. Instead, have them when there will be enough time for you to use good communication skills to work through the issues.

One topic for a kitchen-table sex talk is sexual fantasies. While many people feel embarrassed or hesitant to do this, sex therapists recommend it. When partners share sexual fantasies, it can open the door to trying fun new things together. Some new apps and websites even help you talk about your fantasies (e.g., MojoUpgrade.com). Of course, before sharing fantasies, it's important to agree to this ground rule: it's perfectly okay for either you or your partner to give a nonjudgmental "No" to trying out the other person's fantasy. Sex therapists recommend stretching your boundaries but never engaging in an act you'd find distasteful or painful, or feel averse to. Sex therapists also debunk the myth of unplanned sex, which is related to our next type of talks.

Let's Have Sex Talks. Imagine getting dressed to go out for a date or to a party where you know a hot guy you want to get with is going to be. You take a shower, put on your sexy underwear, maybe spray on perfume, and then you put your best flirt on all night long. You make eye contact, touch his arm, etc. And lo and behold, you end up having sex at the end of the night. If you think about it, this is actually well-orchestrated sex, not spur-of-the moment sex! Once you realize this and let go of the unrealistic notion that sex *should* be spontaneous, it opens the door to helpful talks that occur *before* a sexual encounter. These talks are useful because, unlike in the movies, one partner may want to have sex and the other may want to study for an exam, complete a work project, or just go to sleep. And the longer a relationship goes on—and the more responsibilities each partner has in addition to the

Sexual Consent Talks

Sex educators are increasingly teaching people to explicitly—verbally—ask for consent before a sexual encounter, as well as emphasizing that individuals have the right to revoke consent at any point in a sexual encounter. To learn more about consent skills, check out a series of four videos by Planned Parenthood called Consent 101 (you can find them all on YouTube).

relationship—the more important it becomes to be able to talk about if it's a good time to have sex or not. Once children enter the picture, this type of talking is totally necessary; in fact, sex therapists tell couples that *planning* sex is the key to not falling into the all-too-common sexless marriages that plague many couples after children are born. But if the idea of talking about sex in the context of marriage and children feels really far off to you now, please place it in the back of your mind for later use. Here's the take-home point to remember now: while the movies don't portray it as romantic, talking about both *if* and *what* you want to do before doing it is perfectly normal.

Provocative Sex Talks. While having a serious "Do you want to have sex?" talk may sound a little odd to you, texting about a future hookup or sex in general might sound more familiar. If so, you're thinking of what I call provocative sex talk. No discussion of sexual communication would be complete if I didn't mention "talking dirty" in texts, including on Tinder and other dating apps. Honestly, when I thought of writing about this, I felt overwhelmed. I called my trusted undergraduate research assistant to talk it through. "Wow, Laurie. There are so many unspoken rules about texting, Tinder, and other dating apps, that's like a whole other book." I told her that maybe she could write this book, since I wanted to write about more traditional sexual communication—with the focus on getting one's needs met. But here's what I can briefly say about sexual communication via text. It's tricky—especially with someone you've never met or a new partner. Nevertheless, provocative text messages (e.g., about the night before, about what you want to do tonight) sent between partners can be fun.

And such messages don't need to be limited to texting. When I work with long-term couples struggling to spice up their sex life, I recommend provocative sex talk outside the bedroom—by text, e-mail, phone, and in person. I applaud couples using jokes, secret references, and evocative hints at nonsexual times as a type of everyday foreplay, as well as a wonderful form of post-play (e.g., "I can't stop thinking about last night . . .").

In-the-Midst Sex Talks. Let's get to what I'm guessing many of you have been waiting for: how to communicate your desires, including for clitoral stimulation, during sex! While I call this in-the-midst sex talk, not all of it involves actual words. Instead, one way to communicate what you want is:

> ## Let your fingers do the talking.

Stated simply, you can put your partner's hand in the right place, guiding it with yours. The following quote from the book *I Love Female Orgasm* is a man talking about receiving such coaching:

> "She would take my hand, or my finger, and she would put it exactly where it was supposed to be, and she'd move it the way she wanted me to move it, and she would apply pressure to the back of my fingers, the amount of pressure she wanted, until I got the hang of it, and then she would take her hand away. If I got out of sync or something, she'd put her hand back and show me until I got it right."

In short, whether it's the first or the fiftieth time, you can guide your partner's hands to touch you the way you like.

Think this will be hard to do, particularly with a new partner? It's possible you're still falling prey to those insidious attitudes hindering sexual pleasure that we talked about in chapter 5. Remind yourself that you have as much right to pleasure and orgasm as any male partner does—and unless you provide specific instructions and feedback about the clitoral stimulation you need, you aren't likely to get it! As the authors of OMGYes say, "It's impossible to 'already know the moves' with a new partner or with the same partner on a different day." This website also points out that we need to stop thinking of giving such feedback as awkward and instead think of it as sexy and fun.

Another enjoyable, erotic way to provide feedback during a sexual encounter is:

Make some noise.

You may make noises during sex—breathe heavily, sigh, moan, or groan. These sounds tell your partner what you like. Interestingly, sex sounds may also enhance your sexual pleasure, both when you make them and when you hear them. In two separate studies, both men and women reported that sex sounds were a turn-on. So make some sex sounds to give feedback and it'll probably turn both you and your partner on as you do! Still, a problem with using sounds to give feedback is that the other person has to realize that's what you're doing and react accordingly. Not all lovers may be that in tune. Another option is to use—oh my heavens—*actual words during sex*!

Talking during sex can be one of the most effective ways to let our partners know the type of stimulation we need, yet it's something many people are hesitant to do, especially with new partners. I think this is because the media has misguided us about the importance of talk during sex. In the movies

Repetitive Reminder

Remember: men say they find it to be a turn-on when women show them how to provide clitoral stimulation. It's time for women to start considering this erotic (rather than awkward or pushy), as well!

Bonus: Combining Skills

These sexual communication skills are best when combined. For example, couple your words ("faster") with your hand coaching (put your hand on top of your partner's and demonstrate what fast means). Once your hand is removed, if they have it right, use your sex sounds and words to give positive feedback.

(with the exception of serious dirty talk in porn) there's very little talking during sex—and everyone knows what to do and does it just right, even the first time. Of course, in many of these same movies, women are having screaming orgasms from hard thrusting alone. You already know that's not happening in real life. The same goes for talking: in real-life sex sometimes people actually talk!

There are three really good reasons to talk during sex. The first is to **offer brief instructions**. As Jenny Block advises, "If you like it, say so. If you don't like it, say so. If you want more or less or harder or faster, say so." In other words, you can use words to convey your sexual desires, such as to touch here or there, harder or lighter. "More," "faster," "slower," and "harder" are words that can be quickly and efficiently used. Of course, such simple instructions can result in miscommunication. You could say "faster" and your partner could think this means "harder." So it's important to be willing to continue to give instructions. Then, when a partner hits it just right, give positive feedback, saying, for example, "That feels great," "Yeah. Just like that," or "Oooh. Keep doing that."

Along with using words to quickly convey how you like to be touched, a second, more nuanced reason to talk during sex is to **make a choice**. Having a sexual encounter involves a series of ongoing choices. For example, when it comes to intercourse, there are several positions to choose from. Going back to the general communication skills covered earlier, making choices in the midst of sex will go better if the partners use "I" statements. To illustrate, if you want to be on top, say, "I want to get on top of you." And, of course, your partner could say something to acknowledge that sounds good to him or just agree by getting into that position. Or maybe he'll disagree and suggest another position. If you're using good communication outside the bedroom, these types of in-the-midst sexual decisions can go quite quickly and smoothly.

Okay, so I'm guessing some of you are reading this thinking, *That sounds totally awkward and unromantic!* If so, please ask yourself if this is less romantic than doing something that isn't your preference. Along these same lines, let me (yet again) remind you that most of our notions about what is "normal" are based on false images. In this case, the falsehood is that two people having a sexual encounter will always want to do the exact same thing or be able to mind read, rendering talking unnecessary. This is a load of sex-myth crap. Very brief conversations can make sexual encounters better.

In terms of making sexual encounters better, a third purpose for talking during sex is to **check it out**. Let me illustrate with a true personal story. While my then-boyfriend (now-husband) and I were dating, during the midst of a stressful joint job search, he noticed that I seemed preoccupied during a sexual encounter. Being the great communicator he is, he said something like, "I notice you seem distracted. I wonder what's going on." I confessed, "I'm really sorry. But honestly I can't focus. I keep rewriting my résumé in my head." We then stopped for a few minutes and talked about what I needed to get in the zone and focus. I said a back rub would help me relax—and it did. (As a side note, whenever one of us is seeming to not be having mindful sex, we now call it résumé-writing sex.)

In my personal example, my husband was totally right about my lack of focus. But assumptions made during sex can be wrong as well. I have a friend who never had an orgasm during sex with her long-term boyfriend—despite the fact that he always wanted to please her. They had one of those kitchen-table sex talks in which he earnestly told her that he wanted her to relax and take as long as she needed to orgasm. He also encouraged her to voice her concerns in the middle of sex the next time she had them, so he could reassure her. And she did. The next time she was receiving oral sex, she said, "I'm doing it. I'm afraid you're getting bored." He told her to relax and take as long as she needed, and that he was having fun pleasuring her. She was able to relax and have an orgasm—something that wouldn't have happened without her checking out her false assumptions!

Afterglow Talks. Many couples benefit from talking immediately after sex (or soon after waking up from their post-sex nap!) in order to "process" the encounter. This is something that may be easier to do in longer-term relationships, but it can be very helpful after *any* encounter. A client of mine recently told me that after a first-time hookup, her male partner said, "I got the feeling you weren't comfortable." She replied honestly, telling him that she didn't feel at ease and that she's one of those people who require both more intimacy and a slower start-up than they had. He told her he understood and had felt uncomfortable as well. They had a really nice talk about it. They then hung out together the rest of the weekend, including having another sexual encounter. After that encounter, they agreed they both felt more comfortable this time. They also said the sex had been much better! Clearly, processing a sexual encounter after it occurs can have great benefits, even in the context of a hookup or a new relationship.

Afterglow talks can also occur in the context of long-term relationships. Routinely, after sex, my friend Patti and her partner, Amy, discuss what just occurred. They even rate their sex on a one-to-ten scale. "What was that for you?" one of them will ask. They then use this as a way to discuss what would have made it a better encounter—or sometimes they just bask in the glow of their mutually high scores. However, because they've already busted some of the myths we'll discuss in the next chapter, they expect to sometimes have mutually low scores (not all sex is great and that's totally normal). They also expect times when one of them rates the encounter a two and the other a ten (not all sex is mutually great for both partners). All of this is simply material for non-defensive and open discussion. Certainly, you don't have to go as far as a one-to-ten rating scale, but talking after sex can help you and your partner make improvements the next time—or it can help you both feel confident in continuing to do what you're doing. Of course, as per the rules set out earlier, if you run into a more serious problem during sex, it's best to get out of bed and to the kitchen table. Or agree to discuss it later when you're both in a good place to do so.

CLITERACY CHATS

And now, true to the theme of this book, let's focus specifically on communicating with a partner about the clitoral stimulation you need to orgasm. I hope it's already obvious that you can do this with the in-the-midst methods we just went over, such as letting your fingers do the talking or offering brief instructions. You can also have a kitchen-table sex talk in which this is the focus, saying something like, "I need direct clitoral stimulation to orgasm. I want to try to see if this works for me while we're having intercourse by using my vibrator on myself." As another example, you might say, "I find it impossible to orgasm during intercourse. I want to use my vibrator on myself afterward." Or use this book as a conversation opener, such as "I've been reading this book about enhancing female orgasms and I want to try some of the things the author suggests."

Additionally, if you want to teach your partner *exactly* how to stimulate your clitoris, something that works wonders is:

> ### Show not tell.

In other words, masturbate while your partner observes. While this idea initially sounds embarrassing for many people, those who've tried it mostly give it rave reviews. As stated by a man in *I Love Female Orgasm*:

> "I've watched my partner masturbate—it was very helpful to me. . . . Really watching her do it was a turn-on as well as an educational experience. And after watching, I could imitate the things she did to herself."

Clearly, showing your partner how you touch yourself can be extremely beneficial. One of my clients, Martina, was nervous to do this but then she remembered that she'd had her first self-induced orgasm after a glass of wine—so she did the same thing before showing her partner how she pleasured herself. They both said it was not only really useful for him to learn her way but a major turn-on as well.

Of course, if this feels too out there for you, another option is:

Take them to the movies.

You can watch a *realistic* (i.e., not porn) female masturbation video together. I'd specifically suggest one of the models I recommended in the solo-sex chapter: Betty Dodson's video or the many videos at OMGYes. Last week one of my clients asked me if I'd heard of OMGYes, telling me that she and her husband had watched several of the videos together. She smiled and told me it was a turn-on to watch them together. Then, with a more serious tone, she said, "Even after four years together, we both learned new things. I found new ways to touch myself, and he seemed to truly get the hang of how to touch my clit." She added, "I mean, he's always been a really great lover—he's always taken care of me. But now—*Oh my god! Yes!*" She laughed. No doubt, taking your partner to the movies—specifically the movies about clitoral stimulation—provides entertainment that lasts well beyond the show!

Last but not least, another way to open a conversation about the clitoral stimulation you need is:

Take them to the library.

In other words, give your partner something to read. I recently recommended that a student of mine and her female partner together read the lesbian sex passages from *The Hite Report*—and she reported that doing so really helped them both more comfortably and directly talk about the specific type of clitoral stimulation they each wanted. One of my other clients recently came to a therapy session very happy, reporting that her boyfriend was reading and trying out the instructions from Ian Kerner's how-to oral sex manual *She Comes First*. Of course, I also hope you'll give a male partner the "Cliteracy—For Him" chapter of *this* book, specifically designed to give him a summary of the important clitoral-focused information you've been receiving.

In fact, congratulations! You now have all the essential information you need to orgasm. Kudos to you for all the reading, contemplating, touching, and maybe even talking to others that you've done to become cliterate. I'm out here giving you a round of applause. Please give yourself a big cheer too. You deserve it.

And once we're done applauding your accomplishments, guess what? There's an encore to attend. Your learning doesn't stop here. The next sextion includes more surprising and inspiring sex education that will both help you become even more cliterate and lay a foundation for your future learning.

WAIT, THERE'S MORE (CUM AGAIN)

9.

YOUR ENDLESS
EROTIC EDUCATION

Sex education should feel like an exhilarating adventure
rather than a boring lecture. . . . We may be just beginning
our education or filling in the gaps at a late age, but
learning is always best nurtured through encouragement,
kindness, support, stability, appreciation, and healthy
boundaries that engender trust—many of the same
qualities that make for a healthy sexual relationship.

—Alexandra Katehakis and Tom Bliss, *Mirror of Intimacy*

A couple of years ago, after I lectured on the orgasm gap, about twenty
students stayed after class (for over an hour!) and continued to discuss
the topic. We had an awesome conversation, and when the students left,
they were motivated to do something to close this gap. They started a
Facebook group and made up flyers with sex facts written on them to
hand out around campus. As you might guess, the main feature of the
handouts was statistics about women's need for clitoral stimulation. They
came up with other fun facts they wanted to share too, mostly concern-
ing myths about sex that our class had busted for them. This chapter includes those same useful facts. In this (almost final!) chapter, you'll find
a compilation of simple information to enhance your sex life, both now
and in the future.

MYTHS TO MANGLE MORE

Along with calling me Queen of the Preface, my family teases me about sometimes going on about a point I've already made (i.e., "We get it!"). True to form, I want to expand on two points I made in passing in previous chapters.

Vibrator Fears. In chapter 6, I said, "If you come for the first time with a vibrator, please don't worry about vibrator addiction or your vibrator 'ruining' you for sex with a partner!" I'd like to reassure you further by quoting a blog entry from Michael Castleman about vibrators:

> Myth: Vibrators are addictive.
>
> Truth: Do carpenters become addicted to power tools? No, power tools just get the job done faster. Many women really love their vibrators, but that's a personal preference, not an addiction.

Okay, so vibrators aren't addictive. What about the replacing-men part?

> Myth: If women enjoy vibrators in partner sex, men are left out.
>
> Truth: Absolutely not. Vibrators provide only one thing, intense stimulation. They can't kiss women, embrace or massage them, warm the bed, tell jokes, say "I love you," or do anything else lovers provide to support and enjoy each other. Vibrators don't replace men. All they do is provide especially intense erotic stimulation.

Numb Down There?

Some women worry that vibrators will cause their clitoris to go numb. A small percentage of vibrator users do report occasional numbness. Still, it's not permanent—this type of numbness can last from a few minutes to a few hours. It's no different from one's rear end feeling numb after a long bike ride. There are also simple solutions, including taking a break, using a lower speed, using the vibrator through your panties, and not pressing as hard.

When you incorporate a vibrator into sex with a partner, you're still having sex with that partner, not with your vibrator. Your connection is to the person, not the object you're using with the person. This is akin to a couple swimming in a pool together: One gets on a raft to float around and the other hangs on the raft, talking, teasing, and kissing. The person on the raft is still swimming with the other person—she's just using the raft to float. She won't go home and tell her friends, "I had an awesome day swimming with my raft. Oh, and my boyfriend was there somewhere too." Instead, as she tells her friends about her day, the raft won't even come up, since it wasn't about that. Like rafts help people float (when someone else is in the pool and when they're not), vibrators provide the intense stimulation some women need to orgasm.

Once you start reaching orgasm from a vibrator, it's true that you might get used to reaching orgasm that way. But this isn't specific to vibrators; it goes for sex in general. If a person gets used to reaching orgasm one way, it can be harder to reach orgasm in other ways. The solution is to mix up your routine once in a while (e.g., hands sometimes, vibrator others). However, most heterosexual men get used to reaching orgasm from intercourse, and we don't tell them to give this up and try new ways. So there's no need to tell women to give up their vibrators if they work! Some women simply need a different kind of stimulation than a partner's hands or tongue can provide. Quoting sex educator and author Cory Silverberg:

> If you always like to have sex with your vibrator, why not always have sex with your vibrator? Many people hold this belief that "real sex" has to be somehow without any outside influence (no lubricant, no sex toys, etc.). This is a socially constructed idea whose time has passed. Real sex is precisely whatever we say it is, and good healthy sex is anything two (or more) consenting adults engage in for sexual satisfaction. There is no reason not to bring your vibrator into the bedroom and make it a regular part of your sex life.

The bottom line is that there's no evidence of vibrator addiction or of vibrators causing harm. Conversely, studies show that women who use vibrators have better sexual experiences, including more lubrication, less painful intercourse, and easier and more frequent orgasms. Happy vibrating!

Simultaneous Orgasms. Now that I've hopefully laid your vibrator fears to rest, let me address another concept I mentioned only briefly. In chapter 7, I said, "It's key to not put pressure on yourself to orgasm while intercourse is going on—and especially not to expect some magical, mythical simultaneous orgasm." The myth of simultaneous orgasms is connected to that number one lie we're trying to eradicate. Most movie scenes depicting simultaneous orgasms involve a man and a woman having intercourse when they not only orgasm at the exact same moment but both do so from penile thrusting alone. You already know this isn't going to happen for most women, but here's the other reason that simultaneous-orgasm scenes are mythical: To accomplish this goal, both partners would need to be even more tuned in to *each other's* impending orgasm than their own. Yet precisely the opposite is needed for orgasm—that is, mindfulness to stay totally tuned in to *your own* pleasurable sensations. The author of *The Guide to Getting It On* debunks the simultaneous-orgasm myth further, telling readers that it's *not* desirable for both partners to come at the same time, since it's awesome to feel or watch your partner have an orgasm.

ADDITIONAL INTRIGUE ON INTERCOURSE

Here's another myth that goes hand in hand (or penis in vagina) with the vaginal and simultaneous-orgasm myths: the longer intercourse lasts, the better. Most men typically require 2 to 10 minutes of intercourse to reach an orgasm, with a recent study finding that 5.7 minutes was the average amount of time it took hundreds of men from five different countries to orgasm—counting from the time they put their penis into a vagina until they ejaculated. Alfred Kinsey came up with a shorter time: he said the typical male lasts about 2.5 minutes. Yet one study asked men how long they thought intercourse should last and the average answer given was 30 minutes. Geez! Guys clearly feel a ton of pressure to perform the impossible (and unnecessary) with their penises.

MORE ABOUT MEN: PENIS PERCEPTION PROBLEMS

Men are not only under pressure for their penises to perform but also told that when it comes to female pleasure, size matters and bigger is better.

But what do women say? In one survey, hundreds of women were asked an open-ended question about what's most important to them during intercourse, and not one mentioned penis size. Instead, they talked about men who care about their pleasure. And in a recent online survey of over three thousand women, the overwhelming majority said that sexual communication skills were much more important than penis size. In another survey of college women, the overwhelming majority said penis size makes no difference to their pleasure.

Sadly, many men don't know this and struggle with anxiety about their penis size. In fact, only 55 percent of heterosexual men and 65 percent of gay men say they're satisfied with their penis size. Given porn images of extra-large penises and their central role in female pleasure, it's not surprising that almost all dissatisfied men want their dicks to be bigger. Yet, strikingly, 99 percent of these discontented men have normal-size

Penis Size: No Joking Matter

Many women make jokes about penis size. I was guilty of making such jokes until I realized penis size humor fuels men's anxieties, and these jokes are analogous to men talking about women's bodies in ways that fuel insecurities (e.g., breast-size jokes). Ceasing to joke about men's penis size is central to becoming cliterate: if we want men to embrace the fact that their penises are not the key to our pleasure, we need to stop making jokes that indicate that they are. Let's cut the cock jokes and instead, if we want to make jokes that are funny because they're true, let's start playfully teasing about the flexibility of men's fingers and tongues!

penises! Obviously, way too many men are falsely basing their manhood on the size of their penises.

Maybe you're wondering just how big the average penis is. There have been many studies on this, but they all suffer from flaws. In studies that entail men measuring themselves, the men tend to exaggerate. Studies that involve men being measured by experts tend to attract men whose penises are larger than average (and therefore they're happy to be in the study). Despite such flaws, one scientist reviewed a lot of the studies—including more than fifteen thousand penises—and reported the average length to be 3.6 inches when flaccid and 5.2 inches when erect. Only about three of every one hundred men have penises that are 7 inches or longer when erect (like those we see in porn). Clearly, unrealistic porn images of large penises lasting all night and creating powerful female orgasms are causing both women and men sexual difficulties.

THE TRUTH ABOUT SEXUAL TROUBLES

This book has focused on—and hopefully, as far as you're concerned, fixed—one specific type of sexual trouble: the lack of female orgasms during partnered sex. But people face many other sexual problems. In fact, most people will deal with a sexual concern at one point or another in their lives. And, importantly, the vast majority of sexual worries are easily fixed with basic information and concrete suggestions.

What's most helpful is to understand that many "problems" aren't concerns after all and instead are actually "normal" sexual functioning. You already know that women's lack of orgasming during intercourse fits this description. So do the increasing number of men calling sex therapists because they think they're orgasming too quickly—even though they're right within that two- to ten-minute range mentioned earlier. In sum, because of distorted cultural information about sex, much totally normal sexual functioning is mistaken for sexual problems.

Of course, there are genuine sexual problems. Yet here's something really cool that many people don't know: compared to most other psychological concerns, sexual problems are among the most easily alleviated! They're often resolved with simple suggestions—including those given in self-help books. (Check out appendix B, "Additional Resources," for a listing of books by sexual problem.) Therefore, if you, a friend, a relative, or a partner ever faces a sexual problem in the future, don't hesitate to seek resources.

Kinky: Not a Problem!

Being interested in "kinky" sex is not a sexual problem. In fact, it's a pretty widespread sexual interest. In one survey of over a thousand people, 50 percent said yes to the question "Are there types of non-vanilla sex you enjoy having (non-vanilla sex includes being spanked or spanking a partner, having rough sex, biting, restraining or being restrained, acting out a rape fantasy . . . finger up your rear, etc.)?" And, despite myths, research shows that people who are into *consensual* bondage-type stuff are *not* any less psychologically healthy than those who aren't.

MORE FACTS FOR YOUR FUTURE

While a major focus of this book has been your orgasms—and while orgasms are *absolutely, positively awesome*—please don't define the entirety of your sexual satisfaction by your orgasm. While I hope you have an abundance of great orgasms in your future, you can have erotic, fun, satisfying, and connected sexual encounters without orgasming. To repeat one final time, believing you *have to* orgasm is a surefire way not to orgasm. Pressure and sex simply don't mix well.

Here's a second pressure to take away: the idea that *every* sexual encounter has to be *equally great* for you and your partner. Equality sex doesn't mean that both people involved will *always* experience the exact same level of enjoyment. One famous sex therapist says that about one-fourth of all sexual encounters are good for one partner and just okay for the other. Yet he doesn't say this is something we need to fix. He says it's a reality we need to be aware of, so as not to put unrealistic pressure on ourselves. He calls it the "Good Enough Sex" model, the point of which is to take the pressure off people to have rock-star sex. Even the rock stars aren't having that!

Oh, and to bust another myth: people are neither rock stars nor duds at sex. Sex isn't a skill that people are innately good or bad at. It's something you can practice to get more comfortable with and improve. I hope this book was a great start to your lifelong learning.

Speaking of lifelong, your enjoyment of sex doesn't need to end at a certain age; sex is something you can enjoy until a ripe, old age. In fact, research shows that women's frequency of orgasm and sexual satisfaction increases with age. This is because as women age, they generally get more comfortable with themselves and more able to say what they need sexually. You don't need to get any older to make this true of yourself. You have all the information and skills you need to do so today. You've taken your first step in learning about sexual pleasure. You've *become cliterate*!

10.

SPREAD THE WORD

Margaret Mead found that in the human female the
potentiality for orgasm is a cultural factor. If a society
considers orgasmic release of the female important, then the
essential love-making techniques which ensure the woman's
orgasm will be learned and practiced. If the female orgasm
is considered unimportant, the members of the culture will
not practice the techniques essential to orgasmic release
in the woman . . . and women are likely to be anorgasmic.

—Lonnie Barbach, *For Yourself*

As I sat down to write this chapter, I felt similar to when I dropped my
daughters off at kindergarten for their first days. As I said good-bye at the
classroom door, I felt desperate to impart a few final words of wisdom to
make sure their day went well. At the same time, I hoped that I'd already
given them the skills they needed to navigate their new world success-
fully. But here's the difference between my daughters' first days of school
and my last words written for you: I wanted my daughters to manage well
in the new world they were entering, but I want you to help me boldly
create a new world for you and for future generations of women.

This new world would be one of *orgasm equality*. It's one where we
would place the same value on women's and men's ways of achieving
sexual pleasure—and our language would reflect this. "Clitoris" would be
heard as often and with as much understanding as "penis." "Sex" would

be synonymous with consensual shared pleasure and orgasm, rather than considered an alternative word for one sexual act (i.e., intercourse) guaranteed to lead to orgasm for just one group of people (i.e., heterosexual men).

Related to these cultural changes, we wouldn't talk about girls or women "losing their virginity" anymore. Instead, we'd use the more sex-positive phrase that some are now using to denote a person's first experience with sexual intercourse: "making a sexual debut."

We wouldn't stop there. Allow me to reveal another exciting, radical idea—*drumroll please*. We'd define "sexual debut" as having one's first orgasm with another person! In other words, we'd have the fanfare currently associated with first-time heterosexual intercourse instead be about when a person has their first orgasm during partnered sex. We'd also help people prepare for this sexual coming-of-age by encouraging self-pleasure. Coming-of-age would really be cuming-of-age!

This pleasure-equality focus would permeate our culture. Instead of asking a friend "Did you have *sex*?" we'd ask "Did he (or she) give you pleasure?" and "Did you have an orgasm?" Sex education—from parents and schools—would still address intercourse, including how to prevent pregnancy, but it would also include abundant amounts of information about both male and female pleasure and orgasms. Information about the anatomy of the vulva and the clitoris would be as readily available as

Definition Difficulties

You may feel my coming-of-age definition contradicts my advice to avoid overfocusing on achieving orgasm. I considered instead defining a woman's coming-of-age as the first time a partner touches her clitoris or the first time she feels pleasure at this occurrence, but in the end, I stuck to my first-orgasm-with-another-person definition. It may not be perfect, but it applies equally well to men and women, as well as to individuals whose first sexual encounter is with someone of their own versus the other sex. It's an equal opportunity sexual debut definition!

The Sad State of Sex Education in the United States

Currently only twenty-three states in the United States mandate sex education and only thirteen require medical accuracy for the programs. Most sex education in this country is about the risks of sex (e.g., unwanted pregnancy, sexually transmitted infections) and fails to mention sexual pleasure. Even the most progressive sex education classes cover only women's internal anatomy. As stated by Peggy Orenstein (author of *Girls and Sex*) when describing U.S. sex education, it's ". . . as if the vulva and the labia, let alone the clitoris, don't exist."

information about the anatomy of the penis. And, of course, training in sexual communication would be included.

If this sounds like a completely unrealistic dream, think again. In the Netherlands, sex education in schools contains all of these elements. Strikingly, one objective of a widely used sex education program there is for students to learn that "pleasurable sex is much more than just sexual intercourse." Another program tells students, "Before you have sex with someone else it is important that you first discover your own body. That way you know what you like." And in one of Denmark's newest sex education programs, teachers show pornography to their students and then discuss how porn sex and real sex differ; in other words, they help students differentiate between fantasy and reality. Wow! It's not just Dutch and Danish school programs that are teaching such radical concepts (radical insofar as Americans are concerned). Dutch mothers talk to their daughters about pleasure, openly asking if they've had orgasms after their daughters' reveal they've had sexual encounters. Dutch fathers tell their sons it's very important that women enjoy sex as much as they do.

While a move to the Netherlands is one solution, I'd like to propose another: let's stay put and work together—young and old, men and women, lesbian and straight—to do things differently. Do you recall me saying in an earlier chapter that it's time to stop being so well adjusted to orgasm injustice? Well, borrowing from a common Independence Day quote:

> The best way to get rid of injustice is to stop it yourself. Change begins with one person.

Many writers and theorists—including Laurel Thatcher Ulrich, famous for the quote "Well-behaved women rarely make history"—state that cultural change begins with private experience. Thus, an essential (and, not to mention, fun) thing you can do to contribute to the orgasm revolution is to simply keep orgasming! Still, the more of us who start talking openly, loudly, and clearly about the clitoris and female pleasure, the more everyone will benefit.

I'm not the first person to try to raise clitoral awareness. I follow in the footsteps of brilliant women mentioned throughout this book (e.g., Shere Hite, Betty Dodson) who've been writing about the clitoris for decades. But clitoral awareness has never fully permeated our culture, nor has it resulted in long-lasting, widespread orgasm equality. Yet I feel genuinely optimistic that we are—right now—on the brink of true and lasting change. And *you* can help make that happen!

Perhaps some of you will even become inspired—as some of my students do—to become sex educators and teach about orgasm equality and female pleasure. Maybe some of you will get involved with policy work, convincing our religious institutions and schools to change their

Radical?! Really?

I've had several people refer to the concepts in this book as "radical," yet here's my hope: if enough of us get out there and spread the truth about women's pleasure, someday people will instead be saying, "*That* was considered radical back then? How weird!"

sex education policies. But there are simpler things you can do to educate everyone you know that quality sex starts with equality and to help them achieve such equality! Here's a list to get you started:

- When you see *accurate* articles about the clitoris and female pleasure, use social media to share them broadly.

- Explicitly point out media scenes that perpetuate sexual myths. For example, the next time you're watching a show with friends and there's a scene in which a woman has a screaming orgasm from intercourse alone, tell everyone that this is fake and educate them about the truth.

- Tell your friends what you've learned from this book—tell them that only about 5 percent of women reliably orgasm from thrusting alone and 95 percent need clitoral stimulation.

- Tell your friends about our new "plays" for sexual encounters.

- Start joking about men's fingers and tongues, not their penis size.

- Buy your best friend a vibrator.

- Leave this book out where people can see it and ask you about it.

- Pass this book along to a female friend, or buy her a copy of her own.

- Have a man (or men) in your life read the "Cliteracy—For Him" chapter (which you'll find in the next sextion).

- Make a copy of "The Twelve Commandments for Orgasm Equality and Quality Sex" (which you'll find on the following page) and display them somewhere people will see them and ask about them.

- Follow these commandments in your own life (and, as applicable, teach them diligently to your children, now or in the future).

Indeed, if you follow these commandments—and encourage other women and men to do the same—we'll soon become a cliterate society. We'll change history!

The Twelve Commandments for Orgasm Equality and Quality Sex

1. Whenever I see lies about female sexuality being perpetuated, I will do my best to correct them and educate those around me.

2. I will educate others about female anatomy and pleasure.

3. I will cease to use non-equality-based sexual language. I will not use the words "sex" and "intercourse" synonymously, and I will not refer to clitoral stimulation as "foreplay." I will not use the word "vagina" to represent all of a woman's genitals. I will also do my best to correct others' language.

4. I will use the word "clitoris" and all its variations openly and proudly in conversations.

5. I will use the term "making a sexual debut" and define this as a person's first orgasm with a sexual partner.

6. I will not slut shame other women, and I will do my best to confront others who do.

7. I will not tell jokes about penis size, and I will do my best to confront others who do.

8. I will do my very best to love my body and appreciate its amazing abilities, including its capacity for sexual pleasure.

9. I will continue to pleasure myself, and I will educate other women on the benefits of self-love.

10. I will take a pleasure-oriented, rather than a goal-oriented, view of sex.

11. I will choose the type of sex I want to engage in, and whatever that is, I will use both my knowledge of myself and my communication skills to make it as satisfying as it can be, with the focus on an *equitable* giving and receiving of pleasure.

12. Throughout my life, I will continue my erotic education, including seeking solutions to sexual problems as they arise.

YOU DON'T HAVE TO HAVE A CLITORIS TO BE CLITERATE

f you want to educate the men in your life, you can use the following chapter to do so. Giving it to your lover will help your own sex life. And to spread the orgasm revolution more broadly, give it to your male friends and relatives. If you want to read it before passing it along, though, know that it will be like reading a shortened version of this book. That's because it contains the same messages and information you read but in a condensed form and written for a male audience. Still, I honestly think you'll relish reading it, because it'll underscore just how much you've learned. Reading it might also further cement the knowledge and principles for becoming cliterate for you. As a bonus, you'll find some totally new information, such as advice for when men lose their erections during sex, as well as for men who think they orgasm too quickly. Whether you read it or not, I hope you'll share it with the people in your life who don't have clitorises—they can become cliterate too!

11.

CLITERACY—FOR HIM

Our society teaches us that sexual pleasure between
a man and a woman depends on the man's ability to
get and stay hard. What a demented view of sex. This
puts a lot of pressure on guys to be consummate
cocksmen. It makes us more dick-centered than
necessary, at the expense of everyone.

—Paul Joannides, *The Guide to Getting It On*

The idea that genital penetration might be seriously
overhyped is a bitter pill to swallow, especially for those
men of the world who base much of their sexual self-
esteem on the value of their penis in stimulating female
pleasure. . . . The pill doesn't have to be bitter, and once
swallowed, it can be incredibly liberating. . . . Sex is no
longer penis-dependent, and we can let go of the usual
anxieties about size, stamina, and performance.

—Ian Kerner, *She Comes First: The Thinking
Man's Guide to Pleasuring a Woman*

You're reading this chapter because you're interested in sex. I guess that
means

- you're male, and

- you're breathing.

While it's no secret that most men are pretty interested in sex, most haven't gotten sound advice that will actually make them great lovers. Congratulations. You're about to.

Let me briefly introduce myself. I'm a psychologist in private practice helping clients of all ages and walks of life enhance their lives, including their sex lives. I'm also a professor who teaches human sexuality to hundreds of college students each year. During this class, I lecture on the orgasm gap—the fact that men are having *way more* orgasms than women are. While this occurs in all kinds of sexual contexts (e.g., relationships, friends with benefits), the orgasm gap is especially wide in hookup sex. A lot of popular media explains this by male bashing, claiming that millennial-aged men care about only their own pleasure, especially during casual sex. I simply don't buy this explanation. The men I talk to genuinely want to bring women pleasure. In fact, guys who are hooking up tell me that they're constantly worried about performance. And in one research study, about two hundred men in long-term relationships said that the number one thing they wanted out of sex was to pleasure their partner. Yet most guys lack both knowledge of women's bodies and sexual communication skills. Similarly, women lack knowledge of their own bodies and communication skills to tell men what they need to orgasm. The truth is neither men nor women are to blame. This is a cultural problem—but it's fixable.

I created this book to address this societal problem and to give women the knowledge and skills needed to orgasm. But women can't do this alone. Men need to be onboard and in the bed to reap the benefits! Thus, I wrote this chapter to share with you. Think of this as the CliffsNotes version of an entire book about female orgasms, written just for you. Here's what you'll find:

1. First, I will blow (no pun intended) the number one lie you've likely learned about the importance of your penis for female pleasure.

2. You'll then learn about the true key to female orgasms, with a crash course on just where her sensitive parts are.

3. After that, you'll read about the surefire ways to put this information to use so any woman you're with experiences pleasure and orgasms.

4. Further cementing your ability to pleasure a woman, you'll get a second crash course, this one on sexual communication.

Not only will the information you learn teach you how to pleasure a woman but it's guaranteed to increase your own sexual satisfaction as well. Let's get going!

FEMALE PLEASURE: THE FICTION

If you're like most people in our culture, you've learned that intercourse is the ultimate sexual act and a man's penis is the most important tool needed for a woman's pleasure. You've probably also received the message that the bigger the better, and the longer you last (and perhaps the harder you thrust), the more pleasure a woman will have. Well, I'm here to tell you that this is **the number one lie about getting laid**!

Here's the truth: In one survey, an expert on male sexuality asked hundreds of women an open-ended question about what's most important to them during intercourse, and not one mentioned penis size. Instead, they talked about men who care about their pleasure. And in a recent online survey of over three thousand women, conducted by a group of sex educators, the overwhelming majority of women said that sexual communication skills were much more important than penis size. And in another survey, performed across multiple years of college classes and conducted by a human sexuality professor, the overwhelming majority of female students said that penis size makes *no* difference to their pleasure. While a woman can love the feelings (both emotional and physical) she gets from intercourse, it isn't usually going to result in an orgasm for her.

Penis Size: Anxiety, Actual Size, and Asinine Humor

Only about half of all men are satisfied with the size of their penises. And among the dissatisfied men, all but a few think their penis is too small and they want it to be larger. Strikingly, though, almost all men who want to be bigger are actually average size to begin with. Average circumference is 4.6 inches when erect. Average length is 3.6 inches when limp and 5.2 inches when erect. Only about three of every one hundred men have penises that are 7 inches or longer when erect (i.e., about the size we see in porn). Some rare men have penises shorter than about 1.2 inches when limp. Yet even women who've been with such men generally say it doesn't matter. They say a man's personality is much more important than the size of his dick. Given this reality, I told women readers that it was time to stop making penis size jokes. They may get a laugh, but they're not based in truth and they fuel penis size anxiety. So please join me and the women readers of this book in cutting the cock jokes. Instead, if you want to make a joke that's both funny and based on truth, brag about the flexibility of your fingers and tongue (which I'll get to shortly)!

FEMALE PLEASURE: THE FACTS

If intercourse with a big thrusting penis isn't going to cause a woman to orgasm, what is? It's stimulating her clitoris, or clit. Are you wondering what this is and where it's located? If so, you aren't alone. A recent study found that 25 percent of men were unable to locate it on a diagram. That's why there's a picture in this chapter. We'll get to that in a minute, but for now, what you need to know is that the most sensitive part of the clitoris is on the *outside* of a woman's genitals, not on the inside of her vagina where you put your dick. That's why the vast majority of women don't orgasm from just intercourse alone.

Perhaps you're wondering exactly what the "vast majority" means. Most times, when magazines talk about this, they throw around the statistic that only 25 or 30 percent of women can reach orgasm during intercourse. But, as pointed out by a scholar who analyzed the studies that came up with this statistic, there's a big problem: most of these studies don't differentiate between women who can orgasm from *just* a thrusting penis and women who orgasm during intercourse by making sure their clitoris is also being stimulated (e.g., by touching it herself or by having intercourse in a position that enables her to rub it against your penis or pubic bone). Interestingly, though, when this differentiation was made in two different recent surveys, both found that only about 15 percent of women have orgasms from thrusting alone. And the numbers decrease further when I ask my female students about their *most reliable* way to orgasm. Averaging across multiple years of anonymous polls, here's what the women in my classes say their most surefire route to orgasm is:

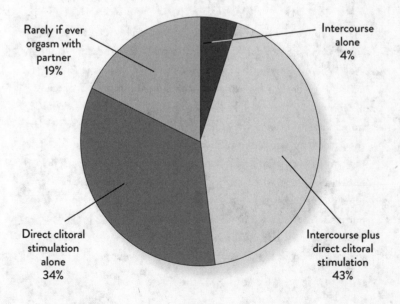

Rarely if ever orgasm with partner
19%

Intercourse alone
4%

Direct clitoral stimulation alone
34%

Intercourse plus direct clitoral stimulation
43%

Even more striking, looking only at the women who can orgasm:

> **95 percent of women need clitoral stimulation to reach orgasm!**

The clitoris is *the key* to women's orgasms. Further proof of this is the fact that only 1.5 percent of women pleasure themselves *solely* by putting something inside their vaginas. Another 12 percent sometimes or always put something inside their vaginas, yet they do this at the same time they touch their clits. And the rest—a whopping 86.5 percent—pleasure themselves by focusing exclusively on their clits. As pointed out by another professor, "one of the most striking things about female masturbation is how likely it is to produce orgasm and how little it resembles, mechanically, the stimulation received from intercourse." Thrusting gets *you* there, but not her. She needs clitoral stimulation, plain and simple.

But She Came with Me!

Maybe you're thinking that you've been sleeping with those rare women who orgasm during intercourse from your thrusting alone. Well, I hate to break it to you, but there's a good chance your partner(s) were faking. Research shows that almost 70 percent of women say they've faked orgasms during intercourse. When women are asked why they fake, they say it's because they think they *should* orgasm during intercourse and worry that if they don't, their male partner will feel bad about himself. This doesn't help either party, and when both partners take the responsibility for female orgasm off the penis, it can open up exciting avenues for mutual satisfaction. Knowing about the clitoris renders female faking unnecessary, *and* it will save you from the pressure of defining your manhood by the size and performance of your dick.

CRASH COURSE ON THE CLIT (AND OTHER PLEASURABLE PARTS)

Remember the study in which a quarter of men were unable to locate the clitoris on a diagram? Let's make sure you're not one of them. Below you'll find a simple picture of a woman's external genitals, with the clitoris and other parts labeled. Keep looking at this picture as we go through these parts, one by one. If you have a female partner (maybe the one who gave you this book), you can also ask her if you can take a look at her vulva to try to locate all the labeled parts. And while you're looking, you may as well touch and lick too—but we'll get into that in another section!

A Woman's Vulva

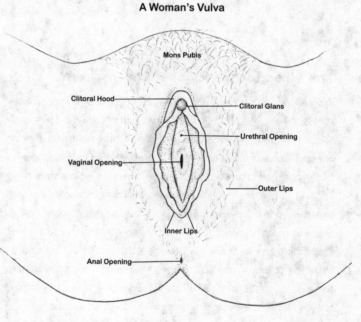

Clitoral Glans and Hood. If you've read about the clitoris before, these were the parts that were likely being referred to, since they're the only ones you can see and touch directly.

Vulva Versus Vagina: What's in a Name?

A woman's external genitals are called a vulva. Yet in our culture we call everything "down there" a vagina. By doing so, we're calling women's genitals by the place that gives men the most pleasure—and leaving women's own most erotic organ unspoken. Thus, I'd like to ask you to join me in using the terms "vulva" and "vagina" properly. Use "vulva" for her whole external genital region and "vagina" for the canal in which you stick your dick. Even more important, please start saying "clitoris" and "clit" loudly and proudly. I promise the women around you will appreciate it!

The Need for Directions "Down There"

Women vary in terms of just how their nerve endings are situated across their vulvas. Some have nerve endings spread out evenly across their clits and inner lips, and others have an especially high concentration of nerve endings in one place (e.g., to the right or to the left of their clitoral hood). These differences explain something important: the fact that *how every woman likes to be touched is unique to her*! Making things even more complicated, what any one woman needs to reach orgasm can change from one encounter to another (depending on where she is in her menstrual cycle, for example). I share this to emphasize that to bring a woman to orgasm, you have to be willing to ask for directions and feedback. The key to a female orgasm lies in the two c's: the clitoris and communication. You're getting a crash course on the clit now, and later you'll get one on communication. So by the time you're done reading, you'll have the tools you need for a woman to orgasm!

The clitoral glans (also called the tip) is a small, smooth, round bump that is jam-packed with nerves. To truly grasp the sensitivity of this organ, let me quote a Go Ask Alice! column:

> Imagine all of the nerve endings in the penis poured into an area as small as a pea.

In fact, many scientists claim that there are more touch-sensitive nerve endings on the clitoral glans than anywhere else in the human body. That's why the vast majority of women find touching the glans itself to be too intense (it can actually be painful) and they instead like to stimulate it through the hood that covers it. But some women even find that too intense for their glans to take and like more indirect touching—through their panties, for example.

The clitoral hood provides a loose covering for the clitoral glans—and it's analogous to a male foreskin (which many of you may have had removed by circumcision). In our picture of the vulva, the hood is pulled back to expose the glans. But if you were to look at real women, some would have hoods that totally cover the glans and others would have hoods that only partially cover it. When pleasuring themselves, it's common for women to lightly press their fingertip against the hood and rub small circles, round and round, thereby stimulating the glans that lies beneath the hood. Another way women stimulate their hood and glans is by touching, caressing, or even lightly tugging on their inner lips.

Inner Lips. The reason that playing with the lips stimulates the clitoris is because, as you can see by taking another look at the illustration of a woman's vulva, both the glans and hood connect to her inner lips. The inner lips are also sexually reactive in and of themselves. Like penises, inner lips are made of erectile tissue. They double or triple in size when aroused. In fact, a woman's inner lips are made of the same tissue as the head of your penis. No wonder they'll like your attention! And there's another part you might not have heard about that will appreciate some attention: her mons.

I Love Your One-of-a-Kind Lips!

Just like penises come in all shapes and sizes, so too do inner lips. Yet, akin to men's anxiety about their penises not being as large as those shown in porn, many women have angst about their lips not being as small and symmetrical as those shown in porn. And, just like real men's penises are rarely 7 inches long, real women's inner lips are rarely even and petite. In fact, it's not unusual for a woman to have one lip that's as much as twice the size of the other. So the next time you're down there, you might want to tell her that you like her one-of-a-kind lips or that you find her vulva beautiful!

Mons Pubis. This area is at the very top of a woman's vulva (above what looks like a closed slot when she's not excited). When you put your hand there, you should feel a small mound of fat, and if you press down, you'll also feel her pubic bone. A lot of women like it when you push on, pull upward, or make a circular motion on their mons. The reason this feels good is because the mons is full of nerve endings and it covers a part of the clitoris that you can't see with your naked eye. We'll talk about this internal clitoris a little later. Now let's talk about the part of her genitals that gives you (but not her) the most pleasure.

Vagina. The only part of the vagina you can see in our diagram is the opening to it. The vaginal opening also has a lot of sensitive nerve endings (although not as many as the clit), and that's why some women like to be touched there—even more than inside the vagina. Don't believe me? Next time you're using your fingers to pleasure a partner, touch around the outside of her vaginal opening instead of penetrating her. You'll probably see her squirm and moan with pleasure—even though nothing is going inside. You can also use your penis as a touching tool, since some women say they enjoy their partner teasing them with his penis at the vaginal opening before going inside.

Wait—You Missed Some Parts!

You may have noticed there are a few labeled parts in the illustration that I haven't gone over. First, the *urethral opening* is where a woman's pee comes out. Some women like to be stimulated around that opening (but some don't, so you'll have to ask with those communication skills you're going to learn). The *anal opening* is where her poop comes out—and again, some women like to be touched there. But be very careful with anal penetration. This carries the highest risk of pain and sexually transmitted infections of any sexual activity; read up on it and have a serious talk with any partner before doing it. (For information, check out *The Guide to Getting It On* by Paul Joannides [Goofy Foot Press, 2015].) Finally, the *outer lips* are simply folds of tissue that protect what's beneath them, and in our picture, they've been pulled apart so you can see the important parts we just talked about. Her outer lips are from the same tissue as your scrotum is (the sack that encases your balls)—same skin, same protective function.

The inside of the vagina is a hollow canal. When a woman isn't aroused, the walls of her vagina lie flat against each other. But when she's aroused, her vagina does two things. First, it lubricates, or gets wet. Second, it expands from about 3 to 4 inches in length to about 5 to 6 inches—long enough to accommodate your penis. These changes are really important to a woman's pleasure; if you enter her before they happen, intercourse will feel painful to her, rather than pleasurable. How do you know if she's ready? By asking—with those sexual communication skills we'll get to later. But first, more about the vagina.

There are important differences between the front and back of a woman's vagina. To understand these differences, you first have to know about its different types of nerve endings, including those that are sensitive to touch and those that are sensitive to pressure. Like the vaginal opening, the first third of the vaginal canal has a lot of touch-sensitive nerve endings. On the other hand, the inner two-thirds of the vagina has almost no touch-sensitive nerve endings and, instead, has a lot of pressure-sensitive nerve endings. In fact, there are so few touch-sensitive nerve endings in the innermost two-thirds of the vagina that one study found unaroused women couldn't even detect when they were being touched with a probe in this part of their vagina, and another source said women could have minor surgery there without anesthetic (although I wouldn't want to try this!). It's also why women can generally wear tampons without discomfort.

Lest you think the back part of the vagina is insensitive, it's not—it's just sensitive to pressure, not touch. And these pressure-sensitive nerve endings are why some women find that your penis in the back of their vagina feels really good when they're excited—and often especially while their clitoris is being stimulated at the same time.

Yep, that's right. We're back to the clitoris, because stimulating this is what will bring a woman to orgasm. To reemphasize a central point, the inside of a woman's vagina creates the ideal stimulation for your orgasm, but not for hers. Expecting her to orgasm during intercourse is like expecting yourself to orgasm while giving her oral sex—you wouldn't be able to because your most sensitive part (your penis) wouldn't be getting stimulation. In short, despite what you may think or have heard about a woman's vagina being the female equivalent of the male penis, it's not. Her clitoris—and inner lips—are!

Female Erections?!

One way the clitoris is similar to the penis is that it's made up of erectile tissue. In fact, when women are aroused, their clitorises and clitoral bulbs will get anywhere from 50 to 300 percent larger. In other words, you get an erection on the outside, and she gets one on the inside.

Now let's look at the parts of a woman's clitoris that you can't see or touch.

Internal Clitoris & Clitoral Bulbs

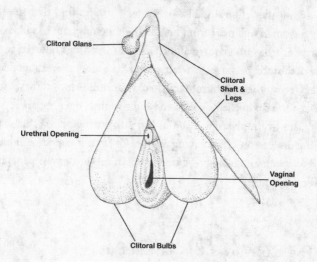

The internal clitoris is wishbone shaped—it has both legs and a shaft. The shaft sits underneath a woman's mons, further explaining why women like to be touched there. Playing with her mons stimulates her internal clit. In fact, stimulating the mons can give the internal clit its own version of an erection. Speaking of erections, notice the big teardrop-shaped organ in the diagram: the clitoral bulbs. They sit nestled under a woman's lips and are chock-full of erectile tissue. This helps explain why many women like to be rubbed under their lips (sometimes even pressing firmly); doing so may stimulate these bulbs below.

Notice also that the clitoral bulbs straddle the vagina. Some say those rare women who orgasm from penetration alone do so because a thrusting penis potentially stimulates these engorged bulbs. Still, this illustration also clearly shows why the vast majority of women *don't* orgasm from a thrusting penis alone—and it has to do with the distance between the vagina and the clitoral glans. That is, **they're too far apart**.

Look closely at the picture, and notice the distance between the vaginal opening and the glans of the clitoris. This gives you a clear visual of why penetration is not necessary for a female to orgasm. Penetration is happening too far away from where a woman's most sexually responsive organ—her clitoral glans—is. In fact, studies find that the farther away a woman's glans is from her vaginal opening, the less likely she is to orgasm from intercourse alone. This is sometimes referred to as the "rule of thumb," because the women who have more than about 2.5 centimeters (about the length from the tip of your thumb to your first knuckle) between the tip of their clitoris and their vaginal opening are less likely to orgasm from the stimulation of just a thrusting penis. This scientific finding underscores that having an orgasm from intercourse alone is related to a woman's biology—it's not something she or your penis has the power to change.

The Ear Moves the Cheek But . . .

For some women, under some circumstances, a thrusting penis pulls the inner lips, clitoral hood, and clitoral glans in just the right way for an orgasm to occur. But, using a great metaphor provided by another author, pulling her ear slightly back and forth can also pull the skin on her cheek, but if you really want her cheek to move, it's best to move it directly.

MORE FACTS (VERSUS FICTION) ON FEMALE BIOLOGY

Although not illustrated in the pictures, here's the truth about the G-spot and female ejaculation. For those of you who haven't heard of it, the G-spot is supposedly an area on the inside of a woman's vagina that (if found) will result in sheet-gripping and sheet-wetting (i.e., squirting liquid) orgasms. Well, here's the scientific truth: it's not even clear that all women have such a spot. And among those who do, only a small percentage say that stimulating it results in an orgasm. The others say it does nothing for them. Likewise, when they orgasm, some women do "ejaculate," or squirt liquid from their urethral opening (see the illustration "A Woman's Vulva," page 205, to find this body part). Yet most don't. So when squirting is filmed in porn, an actress's *vagina* is often filled up with water until she can't hold it anymore and then the camera rolls. In other words, it's not real and doesn't even come from the right hole!

REAL SEX: LET'S PLAY THIS DIFFERENTLY

Now that you know more about fake porn images, let's talk about what real sex looks like. Let's start with how it now generally plays out and then talk about ways to make it play out better—so you and your partner *both* come for real.

As you likely know from experience (and psychological research confirms this), most heterosexual sexual encounters follow what academics call the "traditional sexual script." In this script, first there is foreplay (i.e., the stuff you do to get her ready for intercourse, including touching her clit or giving her oral sex) followed by sex (i.e., intercourse, during which you have an orgasm), after which sex ends. In this script, you're responsible for your partner's orgasm and you try to "give" her one by lasting long and thrusting hard. Her role (which she may have been playing so well that you didn't know it was an act) is to protect your ego by pretending she's orgasming during intercourse, instead of having an orgasm for real. Since you now know that women don't typically orgasm from thrusting alone, it's time to rework this entire script.

Continuing the "script" metaphor, we're going to go over four modern plays. And these plays are named for when your orgasm occurs in relation to her orgasm:

- *You Come Second*

- *You Come First*

- *You Come Together*

- *Only One of You Comes*

Before reading about the four plays in more detail, let's start with Act I, which will be the same for all the plays that follow.

ACT I: "FOOLING AROUND FOR TWENTY MINUTES"

All these modern-age plays center on what you and your partner do between your legs, but most women require about twenty minutes of fooling around (making out, caressing, etc.) before you should even reach between her legs. It takes most women that long to get aroused and thus for their genitals to be lubricated enough to be comfortably touched. Yet, strikingly, in one survey about heterosexual sex, men and women said the average amount of time spent on such warming up was only five minutes. So you've seriously got to increase the time you spend on Act I!

New Plays Require New Language

We need to stop using the word "sex" to mean intercourse, because doing so gives the false impression that intercourse is the main event for *both* men and women and you now know that it's not. From now on let's use the word "sex" to denote the whole sexual encounter, not just the intercourse. And when you want to refer to "intercourse," use that word or another that means the same thing (e.g., fucking, screwing, playing hide the salami). Also, since sex will no longer mean just intercourse, we can do away with the word "foreplay," since foreplay means all that comes before intercourse. This is super important because the activities we've previously relegated to "just foreplay" (e.g., clitoral caressing, oral sex) are generally the main play for her, the ones during which she's most likely to orgasm.

Here's a sampling of things you can do to get warmed up in the first act of all the plays:

- Kiss each other on the lips—in the limitless ways that people kiss (lightly, heavily, with tongue, without tongue).

- Kiss each other on the neck and ears and other parts of the face with clothes on.

- Stroke and caress each other's bodies through your clothes.

- Grind and roll around together with your clothes on.

- Take your own or each other's clothes off.

- Stroke, kiss, and caress your partner's breasts.

- Play with your partner's nipples, maybe rolling them gently between your fingers, sucking on them, tugging on them, or giving them a little pinch if that turns her on.

- Stroke and kiss each other's naked bodies, focusing mostly on all-over body caressing but slowly moving to Act II—the scene set between your legs. (Many women say they like it when their partner touches their genitals and then returns to another area of the body and teases back and forth for a while like this.)

Act I can also include showering and bathing together, as well as laughing and joking with each other. Yes, it's A-OK for you to be playful in these modern-age sex scripts.

I hope I've given you some good ideas to start with, but please know it's impossible to make an exhaustive list of warm-up acts. Be creative and make up your own.

PLAY 1: YOU COME SECOND

In this play, you and your partner *take turns* having orgasms and you take your turn second. This is going to work great if you're with a

Different Women (and Men) Need Different Plays

To help understand how I came up with the scripts for the four plays that follow, let me share something I've discovered from talking to women. Some say that their orgasms are enhanced when they get penetration and clitoral stimulation at the same time, while others say that the feeling of a penis in their vagina makes it harder—even impossible—to reach an orgasm from clitoral stimulation. Look back at that graph at the start of this chapter and you'll clearly see this illustrated: some women say their most reliable route to orgasm is penetration plus clitoral stimulation and some say it's clitoral stimulation alone. In the plays that follow, you'll read quotes from women talking about these different styles. You'll also read about things that will appeal to you, and others you have no interest in doing. That's because I wrote these plays to be as inclusive as possible. Just skip over the stuff that doesn't interest you, knowing that another guy may think it sounds pretty good to him!

woman who orgasms most reliably from clitoral stimulation without penetration.

After the first act of "Fooling Around for Twenty Minutes," try either of the following two versions for your second act.

Act II—Version 1. You pleasure your partner *for as long as it takes her to orgasm!* You use your tongue, hands, a vibrator, your penis, water, or a combination—*whatever and however she prefers!*

> "I like him to grip my ass hard, suck on my clitoris, and just let me move!"

> "I lie on my stomach and he's on my back, reaching up under me, and he makes me come and come, and he won't stop and he won't let me up. Wow!"

> "I lie on my back with my partner between my legs, flicking his tongue very gently, over and over. I like not doing anything else except concentrating on the sensations until I orgasm."

Act II—Version 2. Your partner stimulates herself to orgasm while you watch, hold, or touch another erotic part of her body.

> "The best thing we've found so far is for me to stimulate myself directly before fucking. This lubricates and prepares my vagina for intercourse, which I then enjoy very much. And my husband enjoys watching me do this. So it works."

"As Long as It Takes"

You may be wondering just how much time "as long as it takes" is. Generally, women take anywhere from fifteen to forty minutes to reach an orgasm. But here's a cool statistic: if you spend twenty or more minutes on clitoral stimulation, about 92 percent of your female partners will orgasm. While that might sound like a long time, here's what famous sex therapist Ian Kerner said when he compared this rate of orgasm to women's usual rate of orgasm in heterosexual sex: "That's a shift of tectonic proportions—from two out of three women *not* being able to reach climax to nine out of ten achieving satisfaction—all because of a matter of minutes. Few, if any, of the world's problems can be solved with a mere twenty minutes of attention, and yet here, in the complex sociopolitical landscape of the bedroom, we have an opportunity to create bilateral satisfaction."

Act II Continued. It's your turn! What you do will depend on what you like. You could

- have intercourse.

- have your partner give you oral sex or a hand job.

- combine these activities (e.g., get oral sex and then have intercourse).

- pleasure yourself while your partner watches and touches other parts of your body.

- use sex toys designed for your pleasure, such as a prostate massager (check out men's toys at Babeland.com).

But My Boner Is Gone

Perhaps you've been wondering what to do if you lose your erection during the twenty minutes that you're pleasuring her (or any other time). First, know that it's extremely rare for a man to go through his whole life and never lose an erection. And here's the advice sex therapists give for lost erections: stay calm and continue the sexual stimulation (e.g., have your partner touch you some more). If you do this, your erection will likely come back. Therapists call this the "wax and wane" erection. You won't see it in porn, but it's for real. Therapists also advise that if you can't get your erection back, don't let it ruin a sexual encounter; ask your partner if she'd like more clitoral stimulation or maybe just a long back rub instead. And if you constantly lose erections and want help, check out *Coping with Erectile Dysfunction* by Barry McCarthy and Michael Metz (New Harbinger Publications, 2004). You can also find trained sex therapists by visiting the website of the American Association of Sexuality Educators, Counselors, and Therapists (www.aasect.org /referral-directory).

Hey, Wait—Isn't That My Job? Nope, Not Always!

If you and your partner choose a play in which she pleasures herself in your presence, please don't buy into the idea that this is a lesser form of sex than you doing the touching. It's definitely not. And for some women, especially those with self-pleasure styles that are difficult, if not impossible, for others to replicate, it's the only way they can orgasm.

> "After years of trial and error, my lover and I finally found a foolproof way for me to orgasm. We have intercourse and then before he has an orgasm, he pulls out and uses his penis to stimulate my clitoris. I guide him with my hand. I invariably orgasm this way, and while I am in the throes of it, he enters, we fuck, and he orgasms."

I hope this gives you an idea about how sex in which you come second would go. Now let's look at our second play. It's actually pretty similar to the first, except in this one, you come first.

A Five-Star Play

A woman receiving oral sex, followed by the man receiving oral sex and/or intercourse, is a favored turn-taking model for many. There's even a great book that teaches men oral sex skills: *She Comes First: The Thinking Man's Guide to Pleasuring a Woman* by Ian Kerner (William Morrow, 2004)—the same guy who just told you to give her clitoris twenty minutes of undivided attention.

PLAY 2: YOU COME FIRST

In this play, you and your partner also *take turns* having orgasms, but you take your turn first. This works well for female partners who need full-on clitoral stimulation and who have their most intense orgasms after a lot of stimulation—including, for example, clitoral stimulation that is arousing but not orgasmic, followed by intercourse. This play will also work best for women who say they can't relax and get into their own pleasure until they know you've had your orgasm.

However—as I mentioned earlier—if a woman has intercourse before she's wet enough and before her vagina elongates, this will hurt her. So you're going to have to ask her or take enough time so you know without a doubt she's ready for you. While women don't usually orgasm from intercourse alone, most like the feeling a lot and some say they crave your penis in their vagina, after they're *really* excited. Also, it's important to know that some women get excited but just don't get wet enough on their own. If you're with such a woman, please be encouraging of her using lube.

Now on to more details of the *You Come First* play. After the first act of "Fooling Around for Twenty Minutes," try either of the following two versions for your second act.

Act II—Version 1. This version of Act II involves you pleasuring your partner until you're both ready for intercourse. This could include your hands, a vibrator, or oral sex. She could also touch herself in any way that gets her excited. Perhaps pleasuring a woman is going to be arousing enough for you to become ready for intercourse. Or perhaps you'll need your partner to do something for you (e.g., touch your penis with her hand, give you oral sex, rub your penis around her vulva and tease you until she lets you in).

You and your partner then have intercourse. After you have your intercourse-based orgasm, you pleasure your partner any way she wants. This could include touching her with your hands or a vibrator, wiping her off and giving her oral sex, or hopping into the shower or bath and using

I Don't Want Her Vibrator Replacing Me!

You've likely noticed I'm including vibrators in the plays. Sometimes men get upset at the idea of using a vibrator during a sexual encounter, with the most common concern being that the vibrator will take their place. But here's the deal: Vibrators aren't replacements for men. They can't cuddle, kiss, talk, make a woman laugh, or make her feel loved. They can only give the type of intense clitoral stimulation that many women need to orgasm. Once you understand female sexual anatomy enough to know that your penis in her vagina is not going to guarantee her orgasm, you'll also understand that a vibrator on her clitoris most likely will.

Research shows that women's sexual satisfaction is highly related to their partner's knowing about and liking their vibrator use. You want her to be satisfied—after all, that's the reason you're reading this chapter! So if you have a long-term partner, talk to her about the idea of incorporating a vibrator into sex.

What about vibrators and hookup sex? One man who learned about the importance of clitoral stimulation bought a vibrator to use during hookups and says he's been "killing the game" ever since. (If you buy one, make sure to buy a sex toy cleaner and apply it after each use.)

water to help her come. (Don't worry. If she likes this, ask her to show you how.) She could also bring herself to orgasm while you watch, hold her, or touch another erotic part of her body.

> "We fool around until we're both ready. Then we put lube on his penis and all around my pussy and we screw. After he comes, he pulls out and I lie on my back and he uses my vibrator on my clit, sometimes playing with my nipples at the same time. I always come this way."

> "I have my most satisfying orgasm lying on top of my partner after he's come. He lies there exhausted and I rub my clitoris against him."

> "I need a really specific type of finger motion to orgasm and I've never been able to teach a partner to do this for me. I have to be lying on my stomach, and I rub up and down on both sides of my clit while pushing really deep and hard and rocking my hips. So with my current partner it works really well if we fool around enough to get us both ready for intercourse. We use all kinds of positions, and sometimes I also rub my clit during intercourse or use my vibrator, but I can never come that way. So after he comes, no matter what position we're in, I roll onto my tummy and finish myself off with my fingers. He lies really close to me and caresses my back and plays with my ass."

Act II—Version 2. In this version of Act II, your partner gives you oral sex or a hand job, during which you come. Then you do the same for her or she does the same for herself. As an alternative, you could stimulate yourself to orgasm while your partner watches and touches other erotic parts of your body. Then you give her an orgasm any way she wants.

> "We fool around and then I give him a blow job while I'm using my vibrator on myself. After he comes, he takes control of the vibrator and brings me to orgasm."

I hope this gives you an idea of how taking turns where you come first would transpire. Now let's talk about another way to take turns.

PLAY 3: ONLY ONE OF YOU COMES

Our third play also includes turn taking, but only one partner reaches orgasm during this sexual encounter. Truth be told, this is what's already happening in a lot of heterosexual encounters, except it's the guy having the orgasm. The unusual part is to think of this in a reverse manner: the man stimulates the woman to orgasm and gets no stimulation in return. Still, this does happen. In fact, a reader wrote about this in the comments of my *Psychology Today* blog. He said:

> It is a *shame* that the "*Love* Button" does not get attention! It is so unique, beautiful, and feminine, yet most men are oblivious to its anatomical structure and how to stimulate it. . . . Every man should find some quiet . . . time with his lover and explore her clitoris. Have her lie back and close her eyes, slowly explore and observe. Listen to her breathing, watch her chest rise with each deep breath. Hear her moans and watch her wriggle. I try to do this with my wife every Sunday morning, and it is a loving and giving experience that pays huge dividends!!

He clarified, "It is almost always an asynchronous experience and I am totally fine with that." He also asked, "How can a man be in love with a woman, sexually intimate with her, and not explore the most sensual part of her body?"

This play is all about asynchronous turn taking, which means sometimes you use the skills and methods you just learned to focus all on her, asking nothing in return for yourself—and sometimes she does the same for you. Perhaps it's obvious—unless you or your partner are the type of lovers who like only to give, not receive, pleasure, this style will generally work best for a long-term couple between whom the turn taking evens out over time. Still, instead of being the mainstay of a couple's sexual life, this type of turn taking could be done in addition to encounters that involve mutual stimulation.

Speaking of mutual stimulation, that's the focus of our next play.

PLAY 4: YOU COME TOGETHER

This play is about you coming while engaged with your partner in the same sexual act, rather than when the focus is all on one of you.

Again, after the first act of "Fooling Around for Twenty Minutes," move on to the second act. The second act has three versions, two with and one without intercourse.

Act II—Version 1. In this version of the second act, you could

- give each other oral sex simultaneously (often called "69").

- give each other hand and/or vibrator stimulation at the same time.

- lie near each other and do your own thing.

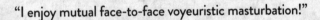

> "I enjoy mutual face-to-face voyeuristic masturbation!"

Act II—Version 2. Because of our distorted cultural perceptions of what "real sex" is (i.e., intercourse), you don't have to look very far to see countless magazine articles touting "The Best Sex Position for Her Orgasm." For example, you might have read about the "woman-on-top position" or the "coital-alignment technique" as solutions for women's "problem" of not having an orgasm during intercourse. Or maybe you've heard that it helps to put a pillow under the small of a woman's back or her rear end during missionary-style intercourse. Since this kind of advice is bountiful in the rest of the world, I'm not going to go into detail about anything like that here. Instead, I'll point out that if these tips work, they generally do so because the woman involved is getting her

Too Much Going On!

While "69" gets a fair amount of attention in the media, it doesn't work that well for many people. That's because it's hard to focus on pleasuring someone else while also being fully absorbed in your own pleasure. In the words of one woman, "It's just too much going on at once!"

clitoris stimulated by rubbing or grinding it against a part of the man's body, typically his penis or pubic bone. While this does indeed work for some women, for others it provides insufficient stimulation. So, if your partner needs more intense or direct clitoral stimulation, you'll be better off using the next version instead.

> "I have an orgasm when I assume the dominant position and rub my clitoris against his belly and pubic area."
>
> "I lie on the bottom with my legs around him, then grind my pelvis and pubic area against him."

Act II—Version 3. In this version of pairing clitoral stimulation with intercourse, you or your partner can use a hand or a vibrator. Many (but not all) women who use this method say they prefer to "do it themselves," since they best know what they need at any given moment.

> "He lies on his side close to me and facing me, and I lie on my back with one leg over his legs, angled so we can have intercourse, during which either he or I touch my clit."
>
> "I like to lie on my belly, over a pillow, and he enters me from behind. He reaches underneath me and stimulates my clitoris with his hand at the same time that he penetrates me."

There are also little-known but super-fun wearable vibrators that provide clitoral stimulation during intercourse. With one type, you wear a cock ring that has a vibrating clitoral extension attached. You place the ring (which will also enhance your erection and make you last longer) at the base of your penis with the clitoral vibrator facing in the direction where it will stimulate your partner's clitoris during intercourse. You can find these types of toys by looking in the couples toy sections at Babeland (Babeland.com) or in the wearable vibrators section at Good Vibrations (GoodVibes.com).

There is variation in these toys, both in terms of how tight or stretchy the cock ring is and the style of the clitoral vibrator attached to the cock ring, so some trial and error in purchasing may be necessary. There are also wearable vibrators that can be worn by women. If a woman you're intimate with has given you this chapter, she's read about these and I'd suggest asking her if she wants to try one out. To see some examples, check out the We-Vibe (We-Vibe-Shop.com) and the Eva (in Babeland's wearable vibrators section).

Which Intercourse Position Is Best?

You might be wondering which intercourse position is best when you're pairing clitoral stimulation with intercourse. The answer I like most comes from a woman who uses the following technique: "It can be done in almost any position with a little effort." Still, here's a handy tip for you: Ask her what she prefers. Or if you and she are comfortable with the conversation, ask her if she pleasures herself on her stomach or her back, because the closer she comes to mimicking her self-pleasure position while getting clitoral stimulation (by you or by her) during intercourse, the more likely she is to orgasm.

Simultaneous Orgasm: Not Part of the Script

It's key to not expect some magical, mythical simultaneous orgasm. If your partner orgasms during intercourse, maybe it will be before you and maybe it will be after. Either way, it's okay!

How Long Should I Last?

Now that you've given up the idea that your penis is the key to her orgasm, you can give up worries about lasting "long enough." Still, maybe you're wondering about how long men generally last during intercourse. Most men typically require 2 to 10 minutes of intercourse to reach orgasm, with a recent study finding that 5.7 minutes was the average amount of time it took hundreds of men from five different countries to orgasm—counting from the time they put their penis into a vagina until they ejaculated. Famous sex researcher Alfred Kinsey came up with a shorter time: he said the typical male lasts about 2.5 minutes. Despite these facts, likely because of unrealistic porn images, many men think they're coming too quickly. If you're one of them, you now have the remedy for that worry: simply have more realistic, as opposed to porn-based, expectations. In fact, most women say they actually *don't* want intercourse to go on and on and on (they get sore). But for a "real" problem with coming too quickly (usually defined as either less than a minute and/or feeling like you have no control over your orgasm), check out Ian Kerner's e-book (found at GoodinBed.com) called *Overcoming Premature Ejaculation* or a book by Barry McCarthy and Michael Metz (available at online booksellers) called *Coping with Premature Ejaculation* (New Harbinger Publications, 2004). You can also find sex therapists at the website of the American Association of Sexuality Educators, Counselors, and Therapists (www.aasect.org/referral-directory).

PUTTING IT ALL TOGETHER: SEX IN A CLITERATE WORLD

I hope you now have some new, fun ideas to try. There's one more thing to know: you can combine these four plays in limitless ways. Get creative! But remember, in all of these plays her orgasm is as important as yours. I know you already thought that, but now you know how to do it!

> "We go in the missionary position. He fucks me for a while, then sort of leans sideways, so I can play with my clitoris while he's still inside. When I get to a certain point, he starts fucking me again. We take turns till somebody gets tired or can't take it anymore. Sometimes I come first, and if so, I'm super sensitive inside and can feel waves of his orgasm. Sometimes he comes first and then he stays in me till the last sensations have subsided, then lies beside me, lending encouragement while I bring myself off."

Knowing how to pleasure a woman often feels easier than actually *talking* to a woman about what she likes—and this is especially true with new partners. But soon this will feel comfortable too. That's because you're about to get a crash course on simple and effective ways to find out what any partner likes.

A CRASH COURSE IN SEXUAL COMMUNICATION

Sexual communication is a subset of good general communication. You can't be a poor communicator in other aspects of your life and then expect to be great at it in bed! So before I give specific sexual communication advice, what follows are my top three general communication tips. I promise learning these will help you in all your relationships, sexual and otherwise.

First, **start sentences with "I" rather than with "you."** Starting a sentence with "you" is almost guaranteed to come across as an accusation and put the other person on the defensive. Contrast how you would react if your partner said "You never go down on me!" with her saying "I'd love you to go down on me more often." Also, putting an "I" at the start of a "you" statement doesn't count. To illustrate, "I think you're acting like an asshole" is still a "you" statement. An "I" statement would be "I feel really pissed when you [insert whatever behavior prompted the 'asshole' sentiment]."

Speaking of dealing with someone who has pissed you off, my second tip is **fight to resolve conflict**. Oftentimes, we're taught to fight to win, as well as to prove a point. This is rarely constructive and can harm relationships. People who care about each other are much better off taking the attitude that the purpose of disagreeing is to get closer rather than to win. Something that really helps is to *find the grain of truth* in what the other person is saying. In other words, when you're in conflict with someone (especially someone you care about), keep in mind that there's likely some truth in what this person is saying. If you can find it and acknowledge it, the disagreement will de-escalate. For example, say "I think you're right about . . ." or "I see your point." Likewise, *reflect what you hear*. Reflection is using your own words to repeat what someone said and, if possible, to also acknowledge their emotions. Reflection is extremely useful when talking to someone, especially a woman, about something she's upset about. You've probably heard women complain that men give them advice when they just want to be comforted. Well, reflection is the solution! Instead of saying "I think you should . . ." say "Wow. That sounds really distressing."

Third, to avoid upsetting others, **don't ask questions that aren't actually questions**. The receiver is likely to hear these as criticism. As an example, asking "Why'd you do that?" is almost surely going to result in the other person feeling defensive. Saying "I'm feeling upset that you did . . ." is a lot more likely to lead to a productive conversation. Also, think about the question "Do you want to have sex?" It's not really a question at all; instead, it's usually a statement about your desire for sex. It often means you want to have sex and hope that she does too, but it can sometimes mean you aren't in the mood and hope she isn't either.

Now let's talk about good sexual communication. Sexual communication includes talking before, during, and after sex, as well as at nonsexual times and places. Let's go over all four.

Talking Before Sex. The notion of talking before sex goes against another false idea you might have and that is that sex is supposed to be spontaneous. Well, sorry to blow another unrealistic belief, but sex is rarely unplanned. To illustrate, think about going out for the night, maybe with a long-term girlfriend or to meet up with someone you just met on Tinder. You start the evening off knowing you want to have sex—it doesn't just happen without forethought. And once you realize this and let go of the unrealistic notion that sex *should* be spontaneous, it opens the door to helpful talks that occur *before* a sexual encounter. These talks are useful because in real life, unlike in the movies, one partner may want to have sex and the other may want to study, work, watch TV, or just go to sleep. Also, learning to talk before sex can help you get (and give) consent. Sex educators are increasingly teaching people to explicitly—verbally—ask for consent before a sexual encounter, as well as emphasizing that individuals have the right to revoke consent at any point in an encounter. (To learn more about consent skills, check out a series of four really cool videos by Planned Parenthood called Consent 101, which you can find on YouTube.) Now that I've hopefully convinced you about the importance of talking before sex, let's discuss the reverse.

Talking After Sex. Many couples benefit from talking immediately after sex (or soon after waking up from their post-sex nap!). While this may be easier to do in longer-term relationships, it can be very helpful after any encounter. A female client of mine recently told me that after a first-time hookup, her male partner said, "I got the feeling you weren't comfortable." She replied honestly, telling him that she didn't feel at ease, and that she requires a slower start-up than they had. They had a really nice talk about this. They then hung out together the rest of the weekend, including having another sexual encounter. After that encounter, they agreed that the sex had been much better! Clearly, processing a sexual encounter after it occurs can be great even in the context of a hookup or a new relationship. It's also helpful in longer-term relationships. It can lead you and your partner to make improvements the next time or allow you to feel more confident in continuing to do what you're doing. Of course, if you run into a more serious problem during sex with a partner, it's best to talk it through outside the bedroom. That's our next topic.

Kitchen-Table Sex Talks. These talks don't have to take place at the kitchen table; they can occur in any nonsexual location. They can be general, positive discussions of things you want to try to make good sex even better. Or they can be used to solve problems. In fact, it's best not to bring up sexual dissatisfaction or any other difficult topic in bed, because it may create a negative association with a place you want to be fun, exciting, and positive. No matter where you have such "kitchen-table sex talks" (e.g., on a walk, in the car, at the actual kitchen table), when trying to problem-solve, the key is to use the general communication skills discussed earlier. Say, for example, "I think it would help me get turned on if you . . ." rather than "You don't know how to turn me on." One really fun topic for kitchen-table talks is sexual fantasies. When partners share sexual fantasies, it can open the door to trying fun new things together. Of course, sharing a fantasy doesn't mean you'll actually engage in it. It needs to be okay for either you or your partner to give a nonjudgmental "No" to trying out the other person's fantasy. If you want to talk about sexual fantasies, say something like "Do you have any fantasies you want to try out?" or "I have a fun idea. Let's share our secret sexual fantasies with each other."

But, here's one almost universal female fantasy that goes hand in hand with the plays we just went over: make sure she knows that her orgasm is important to you and that you're willing to do what she needs to get her there. To this end, communicate with your partner, outside of bed, about the stimulation she needs to orgasm. Have a kitchen-table sex talk focused on this. For example, you could open the conversation by saying something like "I'd like you to orgasm and I want to talk about what you need." Alternatively, if you want your partner to teach you *exactly* how she stimulates her clitoris, something that works wonders is to tell her that you'd love to watch her pleasure herself while you observe. If she's willing (and don't push if she isn't), I promise it will be both educational and arousing.

Another equally instructive and exciting option is for you and your partner to watch a realistic video of women masturbating and to talk about it. I'd specifically suggest you pay the fee to watch any (or all!) of the over fifty videos of women touching their clits at OMGYes.com. If you aren't involved in a relationship, the videos at OMGYes will still be extremely helpful for you to watch alone. They'll show you twelve common ways women touch their clits while masturbating. There's even touchscreen technology to help you practice techniques on a virtual vulva and to get feedback as you do. Practicing on a virtual clit will no doubt make you more skilled when you touch a real one. On that topic, here's the moment perhaps you've been waiting for. . . . *Here it comes, here it comes, here it comes*. . . . Let's talk about communicating *during* sex!

In-the-Midst Sex Talks. The tips in this section are useful for both communicating your desires and learning about hers while having sex. But since our focus is on bringing her to orgasm (which, if you're like most men, you find much more elusive than having your own orgasm), the advice I've included will help you encourage a woman to tell you how she likes to be touched. It won't be hard (there I go with the puns again) for you to extrapolate these ideas to telling her what you want too.

First, you can:

Let her fingers do the talking.

In other words, put your hand on top of your partner's as a signal that you want her to show you how she likes to be touched. When she does, follow her lead in terms of location, pressure, and motion. You can then find out if you've got it right by actually asking!

Indeed, another way to communicate sexually is:

Use your words.

Except for really explicit dirty talk, talking during sex is rarely portrayed in either porn or mainstream films. Yet it can be one of the most effective ways to discover what a woman needs to orgasm. Most of these communications will be brief, but they can make a big difference. For example, you can say something like "Tell me what you like" or "I want you to tell me if you like this" or "I want to pleasure you. Show me how you like it." Such talk is necessary because, again, every woman likes something different. Remember, because each woman's nerves are positioned differently, they will each like to be touched in different ways (with panties on, with panties off) and with different pressures (hard, soft) and rhythms (fast, slow). Most women also need something different as they get closer to orgasm than they do at the start of getting aroused. But, here's a word of advice: Start out gently on her clit and let her tell you when to touch harder. Clits are delicate organs, and so:

It's better for her to say "More" than "Ouch."

In sum, it's truly impossible to know what a woman wants unless you have her show or tell you; this is especially true for new partners. Once you know her way, you may talk less, but since what a woman needs changes from one encounter to another, it's always good to be willing to ask if how you're touching her feels good. It's also helpful to ask what intercourse positions she likes (especially if she'll want to reach her clit during intercourse). Try a simple "Let's do it how you want." Plus, know that you can also briefly talk during sex to check something out and make sex better, such as saying "I feel like this isn't working for you. Tell me what to do different." If this sounds unromantic, think about how much more romantic it is than a woman faking an orgasm with you!

But no more worries about that. You now have enough knowledge about women's bodies and sexual communication to help a female partner orgasm for real. Woo-hoo! Good for you!

But I Want More!

This chapter summarized the main points of a whole book. So, if you're intrigued and want more information, I'd recommend reading select chapters of *Becoming Cliterate*. Specifically, for more information on female anatomy, read chapter 4. You can also read more about the ways women masturbate at the start of chapter 6. For more information on communication, read chapter 8. And to learn a really simple, effective way to focus on your sensations during sex (rather than worrying about if you're doing it right), check out the section on mindfulness in chapter 5. And, what about if you want more information on sexuality in general and male sexuality in particular? I recommend the many relevant chapters in Paul Joannides's *The Guide to Getting It On*. Also, though it was originally published decades ago, *The New Male Sexuality* by Bernie Zilbergeld (Bantam, 1999) remains full of relevant and useful information for men today.

COOL TIDBITS FOR YOUR LADY BITS

Vulvas and vaginas do some awesome stuff, and there are cool things you can do to keep them as healthy as possible. In fact, there are so many that I can't include them all, but in this appendix you'll find an assortment of useful information, including details about grooming, smells, farts (yes, vaginas fart!), lubricants, and exercises.

BARE OR HAIR DOWN THERE?

The topic of genital hair removal can be sensitive and touchy (and I don't just mean the "Ouch!" of waxing). Often women either don't talk about what they do with their hair down there or get into a heated (like the hot wax) discussion about why they do this (For themselves? For a partner?). Sometimes this heated discussion includes a focus on how this genital fashion trend started and is perpetuated (e.g., the hairless, prepubescent look that dominates porn and the big business that hair removal now is). I'm not going to get more into this topic, except to encourage you to read a little about this on your own (just do a web search for "genital hair removal and feminism").

To lighten up the topic of genital hair a bit, did you know that when you get to be my age, you'll no longer need to worry about what do with all the hair down there? It will start to fall out on its own. My mother says that when it does, it hits the floor and bounces back up, attaching itself to your chin. Now, there's something to look forward to!

Since loss of genital hair is in the far future for most of you, let's talk about two more currently relevant topics, including what other women do and advice from health experts on what they recommend you do. First, despite media images leading us to believe that almost every gal is bare down there, there's actually a lot of variety in what women do. One study found that among twenty-five- to twenty-nine-year-old women, about 12 percent go bare most of the time and 16 percent don't remove any hair at all. The rest remove some hair sometimes. To remove hair, women use a variety of methods—most commonly shaving or waxing. Gynecological experts, however, warn of the dangers of shaving and waxing, such as razor burns, painful ingrown hairs, micro-tears, and, most important, an increased risk of both minor and serious infections (including a couple of sexually transmitted ones). Some women's health experts advocate a total ban on hair removal, while others say there might be benefits of having less—but not totally missing—pubic hair. Here's something most experts seem to agree on: the safest route is carefully trimming your hair with scissors or a bikini trimmer, rather than completely removing it.

SELF-CLEANING AND NOT SMELLY

Your vagina is like a self-cleaning oven. The bacteria inside the vagina naturally destroy potentially harmful bacteria from outside the vagina. This is why douching is *not* a good idea (unless your doctor recommends it). Douching washes away that good bacteria inside the vagina. Also, there's evidence that douching can wash harmful bacteria up into the uterus and fallopian tubes, resulting in a higher rate of STIs and infections. So please don't believe that crap about your vagina being dirty and smelly.

Vaginas naturally have a marvelous, musky odor. Studies show that this odor is a sexual stimulant for men. However, in order to sell products (douches, deodorant sprays, scented pads), advertisers tell you that this odor has to be masked. Just like douching, feminine deodorant sprays and scented pads are bad for your vaginal health. They can increase infections and mask the smell of an actual infection.

Please get acquainted with your own unique vaginal scent, so when it changes and actually smells funky, you'll know to see a doctor about a possible infection. Similarly, your vagina secretes stuff all month long, so get familiar with your typical discharges too, and if they change, see a doctor.

WHO FARTED IN THE TENT?

Recall that when a woman is sexually aroused, her vagina turns into a tent—the front narrows and the back lengthens and expands. Well, your vagina also makes farting noises. But farts that come out of your vagina differ from the ones that come out of your ass: they don't smell. Vaginal farts are actually called "queefs," although some nickname them "varts." You're especially likely to vart after intercourse and vaginal tenting. That's because the thrusting penis pulls air into your vagina, and the air gets trapped in the tented back part. When your vagina shrinks back to its original size (i.e., the walls collapse against each other like a fire hose), air is released. Still, anything that pulls air up into your vagina (e.g., certain yoga positions) can result in vaginal farts. One of my daughter's friends discovered this when she was a preteen and liked to entertain friends by queefing on purpose. However, many women don't know how common queefing is and so they're embarrassed, but it is perfectly normal and nothing to be ashamed of!

MY TENT NEEDS TO BE MORE WET

Do you also remember that the tent gets wet (i.e., lubricates), and that some women need or like to add additional lubricant? There are oil-based, water-based, and silicone lubes, plus hybrid lubes that mix a water base with some silicone. It's good to know a little about all the types.

Oil-Based Lubes. Lubes with an oil base cause problems for many women, including irritations and infections. They're not safe for use with latex condoms; they'll break the material down.

No Cooking Oils on Your Coochie

Except for pure coconut oil, it isn't healthy to use cooking oils, such as olive, vegetable, or almond. The same goes for products from your medicine cabinet, such as shea butter or petroleum jelly. Pure vitamin E oil is safe but sticky and hard to wash off, so it's not recommended, although lubes containing vitamin E are fine.

Water-Based Lubes. Made of water and other ingredients (more on that shortly), these lubes wipe off more easily than other types, but many women don't find them slippery or long lasting enough for penetrative sex. They're compatible with all sex toys and almost all condoms, but check the bottle, because some haven't been tested and a few shouldn't be used with polyisoprene condoms.

Silicone Lubes. These are slippery and long lasting, so they're good for penetrative sex. Because of this, however, they won't wash off with water alone (i.e., you'll need to use soap and water to wipe them off). They can be used with latex and polyisoprene condoms. An important caution is that silicone lubricants can damage silicone sex toys. You can cover your toys with a condom to avoid damage, or you can do a spot test. Specifically, put a drop of the silicone lubricant on a part of the toy that won't touch your body. Then wait at least five minutes and wipe the lubricant off the toy. If you see a discoloration or a raised or sticky area (or any other reaction), do not use the lube and toy together. Instead, use a water-based or compatible hybrid lubricant, or cover the toy with a condom before using it with that particular silicone lubricant.

Hybrid Lubes. Designed to combine the best aspects of water-based and silicone lubes (i.e., easy to wipe off and slippery/long-lasting, respectively), these lubes are good for penetrative sex. They can be used with almost all condoms and most silicone sex toys, but make sure to check the bottle or online store selling the lube to be sure.

What Are the "Other Ingredients"? Some water-based lubricants contain the ingredient glycerin, which makes the lube feel more slippery.

While many women have no problem with glycerin, for some it increases their proneness to infections, especially yeast infections. That's why you'll often see lubricants advertised as "glycerin-free."

Also, some water-based and hybrid lubes have other ingredients that aren't good for vaginal or vulva health, can cause pain or irritation, and can increase the risk of sexually transmitted infections. Both Babeland and Good Vibrations list the ingredients of their lubes, and here are ingredients to avoid:

- capsaicin
- chlorhexidine gluconate
- lidocaine
- menthol
- nonoxynol-9
- polyquaternium-7, -10, or -15

Some lubes also contain preservatives that people with skin sensitivities or allergies react to. If you have sensitivities, test some of the lube under your arm first to make sure you don't have a reaction.

Want even more safety information on lubes? Check out the "Sex Info" sections at Babeland (www.Babeland.com) and Good Vibrations (www .GoodVibes.com). Also, both online shops are great places to buy lube because they include information not only on ingredients, but on compatibility with sex toys and condoms.

PELVIC FLOOR PILATES

As you know, orgasm involves the pleasurable feeling of your muscles contracting in your genitals. Specifically, three layers consisting of fourteen muscles surround your urethra, anus, and vaginal opening. These muscles are collectively called pelvic floor muscles. Strengthening them (through Kegel exercises) can make your orgasms feel bigger and stronger. What follows is the best advice for learning to do Kegels

Don't Stop the Pee

You may have read elsewhere that you should find your pelvic floor muscles by stopping your urine midstream. Pelvic floor physical therapists don't recommend this, because you won't actually identify all the muscles that way. And doing this consistently can actually cause you to hold urine back without realizing it, which can result in urinary tract infections (UTIs).

that I've ever seen, adopted from a brochure available at A Woman's Touch (SexualityResources.com).

Identify your muscles:

- The best way to find these muscles is to insert one or two lubricated fingers into your vagina and try to squeeze your pelvic muscles around your fingers. When you feel a tightening and lifting around your fingers, you've found the right muscles.

Do your first Kegel:

- Lie down on your back. This takes the weight off your muscles.

- Contract and hold the pelvic muscles you just located for five seconds. It should feel like you're pulling the muscles up and in toward your belly button. Focus on tightening only the pelvic floor muscles, and don't flex the muscles in your abdomen, thighs, or buttocks.

  - As you practice, it will help to put your hand on these areas to make sure you aren't flexing these muscles.

- Release the muscles by just letting go. Don't bear down or push out.

- After you've relaxed the muscles, take a five-second deep belly breath to make sure you're truly relaxing all your muscles. (You've

When *Not* to Exercise

These exercises strengthen pelvic floor muscles, but some women have muscles that are too tight and some have muscles that spasm. This can result in an inability to have penetrative sex or pain with arousal, penetration, and/or orgasm. Other health issues can also cause these same symptoms, so your first step is to see a physician and verify that your pelvic floor muscles are the cause of your genital pain and/or discomfort. If they are, check out the books in the "Additional Resources" appendix (page 243) and find a qualified pelvic floor physical therapist.

now completed your first Kegel exercise, which includes a muscle contraction, a muscle release, and a deep belly breath.)

Start exercising and build your strength:

- Do two sets of five repetitions of the five-second hold-and-release Kegel that you just learned. Do this twice a day.

- Gradually increase the contractions until you can hold them for ten seconds. When you do this, also increase your deep belly-breath release to ten seconds.

- Build up to doing two sets of ten repetitions of a ten-second hold-and-release Kegel, and do this twice a day.

Add a new exercise:

- Once you're comfortable with these exercises, add Kegel "flicks" to your routine. While still lying down, tighten your pelvic floor muscles quickly and then just relax—all while breathing normally. This should take about three seconds. Do twenty of these, and when you finish, take one deep belly breath. Do this twice a day.

Change positions and places:

- Once you're comfortable with all these exercises, try them in a seated position.

- Once you're used to that, do the Kegels at any place and any time. No one can tell you're doing them, making them especially fun to do if you're bored in class or at a meeting.

Use Kegels with a partner:

- Once you know how to use your pelvic floor muscles, you and a male partner might enjoy it if you squeeze and release them during intercourse. While intercourse is not the source of most female orgasms, it's still quite a fun activity and this muscle action could make it more fun! Of course, the squeezing motion isn't limited to penises; you can do this around the finger of any gender partner.

Want more tips to help you care for your lady bits? Check out *Read My Lips: A Complete Guide to the Vagina and Vulva* by Debby Herbenick and Vanessa Schick, and "Vulva Care: Keeping Your Kitty Happy" in the eighth edition of *The Guide to Getting It On*. And for more resources for keeping your kitty purring, read on.

ADDITIONAL RESOURCES

I hope you've found the information in this book useful and you're now feeling sexually empowered, confident, and satisfied. I'm also hoping this book has spurred your interest in learning more about sexuality and other topics related to your overall well-being (e.g., communication, mindfulness). Maybe you'll become a self-help or sex nerd like me. If so, you'll find plenty of resources in this appendix to get you started on this fun-filled journey.

ALL THINGS SEXUAL

Books and Websites

- *The Guide to Getting It On* by Paul Joannides (Waldport, OR: Goofy Foot Press, 2017)

- Website with blogs and downloadable e-books on a variety of topics:

  - Good in Bed: Your Guide to a Better Sex Life, www.goodinbed.com

- Online sex stores with information on a variety of topics:

  - A Woman's Touch Sexuality Resource Center, www.SexualityResources.com

- Babeland, www.Babeland.com

- Good Vibrations, www.GoodVibes.com

FEMALE SEXUAL CONCERNS

Genital Pain, Vaginismus, and Pelvis Floor Muscle Treatment

The following website has a section of self-help books. As a starting place, I'd suggest *Heal Pelvic Pain* by Amy Stein, DPT (New York: McGraw-Hill, 2009), although there are many other excellent books in their online bookstore:

- National Vulvodynia Association, https://www.nva.org

To find a physical therapist experienced in treating pelvic floor muscles, try these organizations:

- American Physical Therapy Association, https://www.apta.org

- Interstitial Cystitis Association, http://www.ichelp.org

Low Sexual Desire

- *A Tired Woman's Guide to Passionate Sex: Reclaim Your Desire and Reignite Your Relationship* by Laurie B. Mintz (Avon, MA: Adams Media, 2009)

- *Reclaiming Your Sexual Self: How You Can Bring Desire Back into Your Life* by Kathryn Hall (Hoboken, NJ: Wiley, 2004)

OVERALL WOMEN'S HEALTH

- *Our Bodies, Ourselves: A New Edition for a New Era,* 4th edition, by The Boston Women's Health Book Collective and Judy Norsigian (New York: Touchstone, 2005)

BODY IMAGE

- *Body Image Workbook: An Eight-Step Program for Learning to Like Your Looks* by Thomas Cash (Oakland, CA: New Harbinger, 2008)

COMMUNICATION AND INTIMACY SKILLS

- *The Dance of Connection: How to Talk to Someone When You're Mad, Hurt, Scared, Frustrated, Insulted, Betrayed, or Desperate* by Harriet Lerner (New York: William Morrow, 2002)

- *The Dance of Intimacy: A Woman's Guide to Courageous Acts of Change in Key Relationships* by Harriet Lerner (New York: Harper Perennial, 1990)

MINDFULNESS AND MEDITATION

Books and Audibles

- *8 Keys to Practicing Mindfulness: Practical Strategies for Emotional Health and Well-Being* by Manuela Mischke-Reeds (New York: W. W. Norton and Dreamscape Media, 2015)

- *Wherever You Go, There You Are: Mindfulness Meditation in Everyday Life* by Jon Kabat-Zinn (New York: Hyperion, 2005; Macmillan Audio, 2000)

- *Guided Mindfulness Meditation: A Complete Guided Mindfulness Meditation Program* by Jon Kabat-Zinn (Louisville, CO: Sounds True, 2005)

Apps

- Headspace, https://www.headspace.com

- Insight Timer, https://insighttimer.com

Book and Companion Online Course

- *10% Happier: How I Tamed the Voice in My Head, Reduced Stress Without Losing My Edge, and Found Self-Help That Actually Works—A True Story* by Dan Harris (New York: Dey Street, 2014)

- 10% Happier: Meditation for Fidgety Skeptics, https://www.10percenthappier.com

STRESS MANAGEMENT

- *The Relaxation and Stress Reduction Workbook* by Martha Davis, Elizabeth Robbins Eshelman, and Matthew McKay (Oakland, CA: New Harbinger, 2008)

SEXUALITY AND DISABILITY ISSUES

- Dr. Mitchell Tepper: Regain That Feeling, http://www.drmitchelltepper.com

PLEASURING MEN

- *Passionista: The Empowered Woman's Guide to Pleasuring a Man* by Ian Kerner (HarperCollins, 2008)

SEXUAL ABUSE RECOVERY

If you turned to this appendix to find resources for recovering from sexual abuse, the following three self-help books are excellent. Additionally, for this concern, therapy is strongly recommended. Please also see the next section on finding a qualified therapist.

- *The Courage to Heal: A Guide for Women Survivors of Child Sexual Abuse*, 20th anniversary edition, by Ellen Bass and Laura Davis (New York: William Morrow, 2008)

- *The Courage to Heal Workbook: A Guide for Women and Men Survivors of Child Sexual Abuse* by Laura Davis (New York: Harper Perennial, 1990)

- *The Sexual Healing Journey: A Guide for Survivors of Sexual Abuse*, 3rd edition, by Wendy Maltz (New York: William Morrow, 2012)

FINDING A QUALIFIED THERAPIST

It's possible that reading this book has made you aware that you need to seek counseling for more serious problems in your life, including, but not limited to, healing from sexual trauma or relationship issues. Although having such a realization is difficult, it's a brave and positive step. The next step is to find a good therapist. I have outlined how to do so in the following steps, which apply equally well to finding an individual or a couples counselor.

Get a Few Names

To find a good therapist, word-of-mouth is the best way. If you have a friend who's in therapy and feels positively about it, ask them for their therapist's name and number. If you don't know anyone who's in therapy but you know and trust someone working in the service sector—anyone from your hairdresser to your doctor—ask if they have other clients who have spoken positively about being in therapy. If so, see if they can get the name and phone number of this recommended therapist for you. You can also check *Psychology Today*'s online referral service, which sorts therapists by zip code and provides descriptions of their training and specialties (https://therapists.psychologytoday.com/rms). If you're seeking help for a sexual problem, search the online directory of the American Association of Sexuality Educators, Counselors, and Therapists for professionals certified in sex therapy (https://www.aasect.org/referral -directory). No matter what your source, your goal is to get at least one— ideally two or three—names of recommended therapists.

College and University Counseling Centers

If you're a student at a college or university, they'll likely have a counseling center that is free or has a minimal charge for students. Such centers generally have well-trained therapists. So a terrific option is to simply make an appointment, and skip to the following section about what therapy feels like and your role in it.

Call the Therapist and Listen to Your Reaction

Your next step is to call the therapist or therapists. A good therapist should be willing to chat with you for a few minutes to answer your questions and help you determine if he or she is qualified to help you. Here is a list of potential questions to ask:

- Have you ever worked with someone with _____?
  (Fill in the issue here, such as body-image issues or childhood sexual abuse.)

- What is your approach to this type of problem?

- What is your general therapy style?

- Are you and your services covered by my insurance company? If not, can you recommend any therapists who are?

Look for a therapist who is licensed to practice and has training and experience with your concern. I also recommend looking for someone who conveys that they'll take an active approach in therapy. While it's critical to feel connected and understood, having a therapist who does nothing but empathize with your concerns isn't likely to help you change.

Also, both while on the phone and during your first sessions, pay attention to your internal reactions. Though it's important to find a well-trained therapist, the "click" or chemistry that you feel with the therapist is equally essential.

WHAT THERAPY FEELS LIKE AND YOUR ROLE IN IT

It's vital that you be open and honest with your therapist. While developing trust takes time, your therapist can only help you if you truthfully reveal your feelings, thoughts, and behaviors. You should be able to speak the previously unspeakable when you're with your therapist, and you should feel both understood and challenged to make changes in your life. Therapy doesn't always feel comfortable, however. A good therapist will sometimes challenge you and confront you. Even so, you should always feel that your therapist has your best interests at heart. If you aren't making progress in therapy, talk to your therapist about this. A good therapist will want to hear your perceptions of how things are going and work with you to make appropriate changes to the process of therapy if needed. If you're open to the process of therapy and you find a good therapist, therapy can be truly life altering.

ACKNOWLEDGMENTS

A few pages cannot reflect the enormity of my gratitude to those who assisted and supported me. First are two people without whom this book would not have become a reality: my determined and skilled agent, Deborah Ritchken, and my talented and visionary editor, Hilary Lawson. Deborah provided discerning feedback on my original proposal and tirelessly championed it. My editor at HarperOne, Hilary Lawson, was much more than an editor throughout the writing process—she was a kindred spirit ("a sister from another mister") in terms of working styles, vision for this book, and beliefs about our current cultural milieu and female pleasure. She was *always* there with sage advice when I needed something—be it reassurance or concrete suggestions. Her keen insight, sheer brilliance, and ability to simultaneously see the big picture and the small details shaped and improved this book beyond measure. Indeed, I consider *Becoming Cliterate* to not be my book, but *our* book.

Another person who deserves ownership of this book is Juliana Guitelman, my extraordinarily talented student and research assistant. Juliana read, edited, and talked ideas through for countless hours—providing honest and insightful feedback, not only about content but about how to "say it to millennials." Juliana is a true champion of female pleasure, and her passion and insights substantially enhanced this book. Juliana also recruited two others who were instrumental to this book: Kelsi Quicksall, who prepared the beautiful illustrations (patiently reworking them as I continually changed my mind about what I wanted), and Kelsey Wonderlin, who also read every word (sometimes multiple times) and provided a second, astute millennial opinion and voice.

Thanks to several colleagues including Steve Weinberg for his early and ongoing support and guidance, and David Knox and Joan Price for championing this idea in its early stages. Thanks to Eve Adams for her perspective on lesbian sexuality. Gratitude to Logan Neser and Jennifer Vencill for their invaluable assistance in addressing issues pertaining to this book and gender-diverse individuals. Thanks to Leland Price for providing a panel from her empowering site, Gynodiversity, and to Beverly Whipple, Ellen Barnard, and Kathleen Green for answering questions and reading portions for accuracy. Thanks to Paul Joannides for this same editing and answering, and also for being my go-to expert for all things sexual, as well as for normalizing my struggles along the way. A special thanks to Ian Kerner—*who coined the words "cliterate" and "cliteracy"*—and who so generously allows others, including myself, to use them. Much gratitude also goes to those pioneers I've never met but whose work paved the way, including but not limited to Shere Hite, Betty Dodson, Lonnie Barbach, Rebecca Chalker, and the women of the Federation of Feminist Women's Health Centers. I stand on your shoulders, as I try to advance the efforts that you began.

I am very thankful to my department chairperson, Lise Abrams, who tangibly supported this project by generously rearranging my duties so I'd have the time to write. And, speaking of tangible support, thanks to the team at HarperOne, who worked behind the scenes on copyediting, design, and the like.

Gratitude also goes to my talented graduate students—Meena, Tessa, Kati, Rachel, Jackeline, Sarah, Hanna, and Hannah—some of whom talked through ideas with me, some of whom read different sections, and all of whom were patient and understanding when I was less available than usual.

Similar gratitude goes to many cherished friends. Some read and edited parts of this book, some talked through ideas, and all cheerleaded and encouraged me, supported me, understood my temporary absences from their lives, and provided me with a haven of love and laughter when I surfaced for air: Cyd, Berta, Gerry, Karen, Mary Anne, Mike, Nancy, Ryan, Shelly, Tamara, and Tina. My sister, Sari, goes in this same category—she is both a lifelong friend and a cherished family member.

Special gratitude to my mother and father. Thank you for raising me to believe I could achieve my dreams, as well as to believe that sex is something that should be enjoyable and be openly discussed. Thank you for teaching me the value of improving the lives of others. Certainly, you never imagined I'd do this by raising clitoral awareness, yet you've encouraged and been proud of my work.

Abundant love and gratitude goes to my husband and daughters. Thank you, Glenn, for being my best friend and soul mate, and for supporting me and this book through every up and down, every step along the way. Thank you, Jennifer and Allison, for your ideas, suggestions, love, and support. Thank you for encouraging me to pursue my dreams, and most of all, for the daily ways that you enrich my life by virtue of your presence in it; it's an absolute joy to be your mother.

Finally, thanks to those who need to remain nameless—the women and men who permitted me to use their experiences in this book, including the many students in my human sexuality courses who consented to using their anonymous responses in my writing.

BIBLIOGRAPHY

Chapter 1: The Pleasure Gap

Armstrong, Elizabeth A., Paula England, and Alison C. K. Fogarty. "Accounting for Women's Orgasm and Sexual Enjoyment in College Hookups and Relationships." *American Sociological Review* 77, no. 3 (2012): 435–62.

Backstrom, Laura, Elizabeth A. Armstrong, and Jennifer Puentes. "Women's Negotiation of Cunnilingus in College Hookups and Relationships." *Journal of Sex Research* 49, no. 1 (2012): 1–12.

Breslaw, Anna, Marina Khidekel, and Michelle Ruiz. "Cosmo Survey: Straight Single Women Have the Fewest Orgasms." *Cosmopolitan* online, March 16, 2015. http://www.cosmopolitan.com/sex-love/news/a37812/cosmo-orgasm-survey/.

Cooper, Erin B., Allan Fenigstein, and Robert L. Fauber. "The Faking Orgasm Scale for Women: Psychometric Properties." *Archives of Sexual Behavior* 43, no. 3 (2014): 423–35.

England, Paula, and Jonathan Bearak. "The Sexual Double Standard and Gender Differences in Attitudes Toward Casual Sex Among U.S. University Students." *Demographic Research* 30, no. 46 (2014): 1327–38.

Fugl-Meyer, Kerstin S., Katarina Oberg, Per Olov Lundberg, Bo Lewin, and Axel Fugl-Meyer. "On Orgasm, Sexual Techniques, and Erotic Perceptions in 18- to 74-Year-Old Swedish Women." *Journal of Sexual Medicine* 3, no. 1 (2006): 56–68.

Garcia, Justin R., Elisabeth A. Lloyd, Kim Wallen, and Helen E. Fisher. "Variation in Orgasm Occurrence by Sexual Orientation in a Sample of U.S. Singles." *Journal of Sexual Medicine* 11, no. 11 (2014): 2645–52.

Ingham, Roger. "'We Didn't Cover That at School': Education *Against* Pleasure or Education *for* Pleasure?" *Sex Education* 5, no. 4 (2005): 375–88.

Live Science Staff. "Orgasm and Desire Top List of Women's Sex Concerns." Live Science, July 27, 2010. http://www.livescience.com/6764-orgasm-desire-top-list-women-sex-concerns.html.

Migdol, Erin. "This Is What Hollywood Keeps Getting Wrong About the Female Orgasm." Women. *Huffington Post*, February 3, 2015. http://www.huffingtonpost.com/2015/02/03/this-is-what-hollywood-ke_n_6603582.html.

Morgan, Teesha. "The Most Common Questions a Sex Therapist Hears." Chatelaine, July 5, 2011. http://www.chatelaine.com/health/sex-and-relationships/the-most-common-questions-a-sex-therapist-hears/.

O'Connor, Maureen. "The Case for Teaching Girls to Masturbate in Sex Ed." The Cut. *New York Magazine* online, March 31, 2016. http://nymag.com/thecut/2016/03/why-not-teach-girls-to-masturbate-in-sex-ed.html.

Reece, Michael, Debby Herbenick, J. Dennis Fortenberry, Brian Dodge, Stephanie A. Sanders, and Vanessa Schick. "National Survey of Sexual Health and Behavior (NSSHB)." Center for Sexual Health Promotion, Indiana University. Accessed May 8, 2016. http://www.nationalsexstudy.indiana.edu/.

Silverberg, Cory. "New Sex Survey Offers Snapshot of 21st Century American Sex." Dating and Relationships. About.com. Accessed May 8, 2016. http://sexuality .about.com/od/sexualscience/a/Sex-Suveys-Offer-Snapshot-Of-American -Sex.htm.

Sullivan, Clayton. *Rescuing Sex from the Christians*. New York: Continuum International Publishing Group, 2006.

Teen Futures Media Network. "Body Image Lesson: Images of Women in the Media." College of Education, University of Washington. Accessed June 26, 2016. http://depts.washington.edu/sexmedia/educators/bodyimage/lesson -objectification.php.

Tiggemann, Marika, and Elyse Williams. "The Role of Self-Objectification in Disordered Eating, Depressed Mood, and Sexual Functioning Among Women: A Comprehensive Test of Objectification Theory." *Psychology of Women Quarterly* 36, no. 1 (2012): 66–75.

Zietsch, Brendan P., Geoffrey F. Miller, J. Michael Bailey, and Nicholas G. Martin. "Female Orgasm Rates Are Largely Independent of Other Traits: Implications for 'Female Orgasmic Disorder' and Evolutionary Theories of Orgasm." *Journal of Sexual Medicine* 8, no. 8 (2011): 2305–16.

Chapter 2: Dirty Talk

Brown, Lisa. "Lisa Brown: Silenced for Saying (Shock!) 'Vagina.'" CNN website, June 21, 2012. http://www.cnn.com/2012/06/21/opinion/brown-kicked-out -for-saying-vagina/.

Christina, Greta. "Are We Having Sex Now or What?" *Greta Christina* (blog). Accessed January 5, 2016. http://www.gretachristina.com/arewe.html.

Kobola, Frank. "10 Vagina Things Guys Don't Care About." *Cosmopolitan* online, July 30, 2015. http://www.cosmopolitan.com/sex-love/news/a44100/vagina -things-guys-dont-care-about/.

Kort, Joe. "The BRO Phenom, and the Demise of Sexual Labeling: An App That Connects Straight Men for Sex Is Challenging Simple Definitions." The Blog. *Huffington Post,* January 26, 2016. http://www.huffingtonpost.com/joe-kort-phd /the-bro-phenom-and-the-de_b_9072324.html.

Lerner, Harriet. "Raising Vulva Consciousness: Go For It!" *Psychology Today* online, January 15, 2014. https://www.psychologytoday.com/blog/the-dance -connection/201401/raising-vulva-consciousness-go-it.

Michelson, Noah. "There's Something Lily-Rose Depp Wants You to Know About Her Sexuality." Queer Voices. *Huffington Post,* February 6, 2016. http://www.huffingtonpost.com/entry/lily-rose-depp-clarifies-comments -sexuality_us_56b5fa2fe4b04f9b57d9cb71.

"Orgasm Myths and Facts Quiz: Test Your Smarts About Sexual Climax." WebMD. Accessed December 10, 2015. http://www.webmd.com/sex-relationships/rm -quiz-orgasms.

Rosenbloom, Stephanie. "What Did You Call It?" Fashion and Style. *New York Times* online, October 28, 2007. http://www.nytimes.com/2007/10/28/fashion/28 vajayjay.html?pagewanted=all.

Salvin, Peter. "Toward a More Just Society and Health Care System: The Role of Academic Medical Centers." AAMC Chair's Address. November 8, 2015. https://www.aamc.org/download/448304/data/11082015.pdf.

Sanders, Stephanie A., Brandon J. Hill, William L. Yarber, Cynthia A. Graham, Richard A. Crosby, and Robin R. Milhausen. "Misclassification Bias: Diversity in Conceptualisations About Having 'Had Sex.'" *Sexual Health* 7, no.1 (2010): 31–34.

tigtog. "FAQ: What is Male Privilege?" *Finally, a Feminism 101 Blog.* March 11, 2017. Accessed December 4, 2017. https://finallyfeminism101.wordpress.com/2007/03/11 /faq-what-is-male-privilege/.

"V Is for Vulva." V Is for Vulva. Accessed January 7, 2016. http://visforvulva.tumblr .com/ [site discontinued].

Waskul, Dennis D., Phillip Vannini, and Desiree Wiesen. "Women and Their Clitoris: Personal Discovery, Signification, and Use." *Symbolic Interaction* 30, no. 2 (2007): 151–74.

Chapter 3: It's Been Going On Too Long!

Angel, Katherine. "The History of 'Female Sexual Dysfunction' as a Mental Disorder in the 20th Century." *Current Opinion in Psychiatry* 23, no. 6 (2010): 536–41.

Castleman, Michael. "'Hysteria' and the Strange History of Vibrators." *All About Sex* (blog). *Psychology Today* online, March 1, 2013. https://www .psychologytoday.com/blog/all-about-sex/201303/hysteria-and-the-strange -history-vibrators.

Clitoraid website. Accessed January 5, 2016. http://www.clitoraid.org/.

GatorWell Health Promotion Services—Health Data. "Sexual Health Student Survey 2009." University of Florida. Accessed January 6, 2016. http://gatorwell.ufsa.ufl .edu/health_data#sexual_health_student_survey.

Hitschmann, Eduard, and Edmund Bergler. *Frigidity in Women: Its Characteristics and Treatment.* Washington, D.C., and New York: Nervous and Mental Disease Publishing, 1936.

Huhner, Max. *The Diagnosis and Treatment of Sexual Disorders in the Male and Female Including Sterility and Impotence.* Philadelphia: F. A. Davis, 1937.

Masters, William H., and Virginia E. Johnson. *Human Sexual Response.* Boston: Little, Brown, 1966.

Siragusa, Marco. "Study Challenges Popular Perception of New 'Hookup Culture' on College Campuses." Press release for the American Sociological Association. August 13, 2013.

Vatsyayana, Mallanaga. *Kamasutra.* Edited and translated by Wendy Doniger and Sudhir Kakar. Oxford: Oxford University Press, 2003.

"Welcome to G-Spot Amplification." TheG-Shot.com. Accessed May 8, 2016. http://thegshot.com/.

Wolf, Naomi. *Promiscuities: The Secret Struggle for Womanhood*. New York: Random House, 1997.

Wolf, Naomi. *Vagina: A New Biography*, revised and updated edition. New York: Ecco, 2013.

Chapter 4: Let's Look Under the Hood

"All About the Vulva and the Vagina." Mini-Guides. Good in Bed. Accessed July 1, 2016. http://www.goodinbed.com/miniguides/2010/01/all-about-the-vulva-and -the-vagina.php#genitalchange.

Barnard, Ellen. E-mail message to the author. July 6, 2016.

Breslaw, Anna. "Sex Talk Realness: Is Squirting Fake?" *Cosmopolitan* online, November 21, 2013. http://www.cosmopolitan.com/sex-love/advice/a5085 /squirting-sex-realness/.

Castleman, Michael. "How the Menstrual Cycle Affects Women's Libido." *All About Sex* (blog). *Psychology Today* online, March 15, 2015. https://www .psychologytoday.com/blog/all-about-sex/201503/how-the-menstrual -cycle-affects-womens-libido.

Castleman, Michael. "So *That's* How It Feels . . ." *All About Sex* (blog). *Psychology Today* online, July 1, 2012. https://www.psychologytoday.com/blog/all -about-sex/201207/so-thats-how-it-feels.

Chandra, Anjani, William D. Mosher, and Casey Copen. *Sexual Behavior, Sexual Attraction, and Sexual Identity in the United States: Data from the 2006–2008 National Survey of Family Growth*. National Health Statistics Reports, no. 36. Hyattsville, MD: National Center for Health Statistics, 2011. http://www.cdc .gov/nchs/data/nhsr/nhsr036.pdf.

Colson, M. H. "Female Orgasm: Myths, Facts, and Controversies." *Sexologies* 19, no. 1 (2010): 8–14.

Crouch, N. S., R. Deans, L. Michala, L. M. Liao, and S. M. Creighton. "Clinical Characteristics of Well Women Seeking Labial Reduction Surgery: A Prospective Study." *BJOG: An International Journal of Obstetrics and Gynaecology* 118, no. 12 (2011): 1507–10.

"Emma." Large Labia Project. Accessed January 28, 2016. http://largelabiaproject.org/.

"Female Genital Anatomy." Boston University School of Medicine: Sexual Medicine. November 26, 2002. http://www.bumc.bu.edu/sexualmedicine /physicianinformation/female-genital-anatomy/.

"Female Orgasms: Myths and Facts." Society of Obstetricians and Gynaecologists of Canada. Accessed April 13, 2016. http://sogc.org/publications/female -orgasms-myths-and-facts/.

Gerson, Merissa Nathan. "How Orgasm Could Dull Pain." *The Atlantic* online, May 12, 2014. http://www.theatlantic.com/health/archive/2014/05/how-orgasm -could-dull-pain/361470/.

Goddard, Amy Jo, and Kurt Brungardt. *Lesbian Sex Secrets for Men, Revised and Expanded*. New York: Plume, 2015.

Gravina, Giovanni Luca, Fulvia Brandetti, Paolo Martini, Eleonora Carosa, Savino M. Di Stasi, Susanna Morano, Andrea Lenzi, and Emmanuele A. Jannini.

"Measurement of the Thickness of the Urethrovaginal Space in Women with or without Vaginal Orgasm." *Journal of Sexual Medicine* 5, no. 3 (2008): 610–18.

Gynodiversity website. Accessed January 28, 2016. http://gynodiversity.tumblr.com/.

Herbenick, Debby. "The Magic of Tenting." My Sex Professor, November 5, 2007. http://mysexprofessor.com/how-to-have-sex/the-magic-of-tenting/.

Hillin, Taryn. "Is Female Ejaculation Real? Here's What We Know." Fusion, February 3, 2015. http://fusion.net/story/37002/female-ejaculation-squirting -study/.

Jannini, Emmanuele A., Odile Buisson, and Alberto Rubio-Casillas. "Beyond the G-Spot: Clitourethrovaginal Complex Anatomy in Female Orgasm." *Nature Reviews Urology* 11, no. 9 (2014): 531–38.

Joannides, Paul. E-mail message to the author. May 10, 2016.

Moran, Clair, and Christina Lee. "What's Normal? Influencing Women's Perceptions of Normal Genitalia: An Experiment Involving Exposure to Modified and Nonmodified Images." *BJOG: An International Journal of Obstetrics and Gynaecology* 121, no. 6 (2014): 761–66.

O'Connell, Helen E., Kalavampara V. Sanjeevan, and John. M. Hutson. "Anatomy of the Clitoris." *Journal of Urology* 174, no. 4, pt. 1 (2005): 1189–95.

Pappas, Stephanie. "Does the Vaginal Orgasm Exist? Experts Debate." Live Science, April 9, 2012. http://www.livescience.com/19579-vaginal-orgasm-debate.html.

Puppo, Vincenzo, and Giulia Puppo. "Anatomy of Sex: Revision of the New Anatomical Terms Used for the Clitoris and the Female Orgasm by Sexologists." *Clinical Anatomy* 28, no. 3 (2015): 293–304.

Puts, David A., Khytam Dawood, and Lisa L. M. Welling. "Why Women Have Orgasms: An Evolutionary Analysis." *Archives of Sexual Behavior* 41, no. 5 (2012): 1127–43.

Schick, Vanessa R., Brandi N. Rima, and Sarah K. Calabrese. "E Vulva Lution: The Portrayal of Women's External Genitalia and Physique Across Time and the Current Barbie Doll Ideals." *Journal of Sex Research* 48, no. 1 (2011): 74–81.

Schick, Vanessa R., Sarah K. Calabrese, Brandi N. Rima, and Alyssa N. Zucker. "Genital Appearance Dissatisfaction: Implications For Women's Genital Image Self-Consciousness, Sexual Esteem, Sexual Satisfaction, and Sexual Risk." *Psychology of Women Quarterly* 34, no. 3 (2010): 394–404.

The Sex Counselor. "How Do I Know If I've Had an Orgasm?" A Woman's Touch Sexuality Resource Center. Accessed April 13, 2016. https://sexualityresources .com/ask-sex-counselor/orgasms/how-do-i-know-if-ive-had-orgasm.

The Sex Counselor. "The Myth of the Magic Button: The G, A, and U 'Spots' Explained." A Woman's Touch Sexuality Resource Center. Accessed June 28, 2016. https://sexualityresources.com/ask-sex-counselor/sex-tips-tricks-techniques /myth-magic-button-g-u-spots-explained.

Shih, Cheryl, Christopher J. Cold, and Claire C. Yang. "Cutaneous Corpuscular Receptors of the Human Glans Clitoris: Descriptive Characteristics and Comparison with the Glans Penis." *Journal of Sexual Medicine* 10, no. 7 (2013): 1783–89.

Zimmer, Carl. "Scientists Ponder an Evolutionary Mystery: The Female Orgasm." *New York Times,* August 1, 2015. http://www.nytimes.com/2016/08/02/science

/scientists-puzzle-over-a-biological-mystery-the-female-orgasm.html?smid
=nytcore-ipad-share&smprod=nytcore-ipad&_r=0.

The-Clitoris.com website. Accessed January 28, 2016. http://www.the-clitoris.com/
[site discontinued].

Chapter 5: Training the Sex Organ Between Your Ears

Brotto, Lori A., Rosemary Basson, and Mijal Luria. "A Mindfulness-Based Group
Psychoeducational Intervention Targeting Sexual Arousal Disorder in Women."
Journal of Sexual Medicine 5, no. 7 (2008): 1646–59.

Dayton, Tian. "Exercise: The Best Antidepressant Ever?" The Blog. *Huffington Post,*
June 20, 2008. http://www.huffingtonpost.com/dr-tian-dayton/exercise-the-best
-antidep_b_106683.html.

"Entitled." Urban Dictionary. Accessed March 2, 2016. http://www.urbandictionary
.com/define.php?term=entitled.

Fredrickson, Barbara L., and Tomi-Ann Roberts. "Objectification Theory." *Psychology
of Women Quarterly* 21, no. 2 (1997): 173–206.

Harvard Medical School. "Exercise and Depression." Excerpt from Special Health
Report *Understanding Depression.* Boston: Harvard Health Publications, 2009.
http://www.health.harvard.edu/mind-and-mood/exercise-and-depression
-report-excerpt.

Khazan, Olga. "For Depression, Prescribing Exercise Before Medication." *The
Atlantic* online, March 24, 2014. http://www.theatlantic.com/health/archive
/2014/03/for-depression-prescribing-exercise-before-medication/284587/.

Laan, Ellen, and Alessandra H. Rellini. "Can We Treat Anorgasmia in Women? The
Challenge to Experiencing Pleasure." *Sexual and Relationship Therapy* 26, no. 4
(2011): 329–41.

Mintz, Laurie B. *A Tired Woman's Guide to Passionate Sex.* Avon, MA: Adams Media,
2009. Substantial portions of the mindfulness concepts in this chapter were
adapted from this book.

Mintz, Laurie B., and Nancy E. Betz. "Sex Differences in the Nature, Realism, and
Correlates of Body Image." *Sex Roles* 15, no. 3 (1986): 185–95.

Peplau, Letitia Anne. "Human Sexuality: How Do Men and Women Differ?" *Current
Directions in Psychological Science* 12, no. 2 (2003): 37–40.

Pujols, Yasisca, Cindy M. Meston, and Brooke N. Seal. "The Association Between
Sexual Satisfaction and Body Image in Women." *Journal of Sexual Medicine* 7,
no. 2, pt. 2 (2010): 905–16.

Smith, Jeremy Adam. "Mindful Sex?" My Empowered World. 2013. http://my
empoweredworld.com/relationships/mindful-sex/.

Vagianos, Alanna. "Amy Schumer to Women Everywhere: 'You're Entitled to
Orgasm.'" Women. *Huffington Post,* July 07, 2015. http://www.huffingtonpost
.com/2015/07/07/amy-schumer-entitled-to-orgasm_n_7743282.html.

"Walk of No Shame with Amber Rose." Digg video, 1:52. Accessed June 18, 2016.
http://digg.com/video/amber-rose-walk-of-no-shame.

Weiss, Suzannah. "3 Ways to Be Sexually Empowered Without Being Sexually
Entitled." Everyday Feminism, January 11, 2016. http://everydayfeminism
.com/2016/01/sexual-empowerment-entitlement/.

Wilson, Jeff. "Mindful Sex." *OUPblog*. Oxford University Press, July 22, 2014.
http://blog.oup.com/2014/07/mindful-sex/.

Chapter 6: Taking Matters into Your Own Hands

A Woman's Touch Sexuality Resource Center. *Tips for First-Time Vibrator Users*.
Online pamphlet. Accessed July 2, 2016. https://sexualityresources.com/sites
/default/files/documents/TipsFirsttimeVibes13.pdf.

A Woman's Touch Sexuality Resource Center. *Vibrators*. Online pamphlet. Accessed
July 2, 2016. https://sexualityresources.com/sites/default/files/documents
/Vibrators13.pdf.

Babeland website. Accessed March 2, 2016. http://www.babeland.com/.

Cass, Vivienne. *The Elusive Orgasm*. Cambridge, MA: Da Capo Press, 2007.

"Female Orgasm." Good in Bed. Accessed June 13, 2016. http://www.goodinbed.com
/miniguides/2010/01/female-orgasm.php.

"50 Great Names for Female Masturbation." Ed Uncovered. Accessed July 22, 2016.
http://eduncovered.com/50-great-names-for-female-masturbation-2015-03-31.

Herbenick, Debra, Michael Reece, Stephanie Sanders, Brian Dodge, Annahita
Ghassemi, and J. Dennis Fortenberry. "Prevalence and Characteristics of Vibrator
Use by Women in the United States: Results from a Nationally Representative
Study." *Journal of Sexual Medicine* 6, no. 7 (2009): 1857–66.

Katehakis, Alexandra, and Tom Bliss. *Mirror of Intimacy: Daily Reflections on
Emotional and Erotic Intelligence*. Los Angeles: Center for Healthy Sex, 2014.

Palaniappan, Meenakshi, Laurie Mintz, and Rachel Heatherly. "Bibliotherapy
Interventions for Female Low Sexual Desire: Erotic Fiction Versus Self-Help."
Sexual and Relationship Therapy 31, no. 3 (2016): 344–58.

Ross, Carlin. "Betty's Rock 'n Roll Orgasm Technique." *Betty Dodson with Carlin Ross*.
Better Orgasms. Better World. Accessed December 6, 2017. http://www.dodson
andross.com/blogs/carlin-ross/2013/02/bettys-rock-n-roll-orgasm-technique.

"Shop, Adult Toys, Vibrators." A Woman's Touch Sexuality Resource Center website.
Accessed March 2, 2016. https://sexualityresources.com/shop/category/adult-toys
/category/vibrators-0.

Silverberg, Cory. "Why Can't I Have an Orgasm?" About Dating and Relationships.
About.com, December 5, 2015. http://sexuality.about.com/od/orgasms/a/i_cant
_orgasm.htm?utm_content=20160302.

Squires, Bethy. "Why Girls Hump Pillows and Stuffed Animals." Broadly. Vice.com,
March 22, 2016. https://broadly.vice.com/en_us/article/why-girls-hump
-pillows-and-stuffed-animals?utm_source=broadlynlus.

Chapter 7: Equal Opportunity Orgasms

Cox, Tracey. "I'll Have What She's Having! Research Says Female Same Sex Couples
Are More Satisfied Between the Sheets than Straight Women." *Daily Mail* online,
September 11, 2014. http://www.dailymail.co.uk/femail/article-2750931/I-ll-s
-having-Research-says-female-sex-couples-satisfied-sheets-straight-women.html.

Editors. "45 Best Sex Positions Every Couple Should Try." *Men's Health,* December 29,
2014. http://www.menshealth.com/sex-women/45-sex-positions-guys-should
-know/cat.

Fahs, Breanne, and Eric Swank. "Adventures with the 'Plastic Man': Sex Toys,
Compulsory Heterosexuality, and the Politics of Women's Sexual Pleasure."
Sexuality and Culture 17, no. 4 (2013): 666–85.

Joannides, Paul. E-mail message to the author. February 16, 2016.

"Masturbation—3 Ways to Make It Feel More Like a Vagina." Ask Dan and Jennifer.
Accessed June 19, 2016. https://askdanandjennifer.com/sex-intimacy
/masturbation-how-to-masturbate/masturbation-3-ways-to-make-it-feel-more
-like-a-vagina-video/.

Schnarch, David. "Sexual Relationships Always Consist of 'Leftovers.'" *Psychology
Today* online, June 1, 2011. https://www.psychologytoday.com/blog/intimacy
-and-desire/201106/sexual-relationships-always-consist-leftovers.

Vingiano, Ali. "This Hands-Free Vibrator Could Close the Pleasure Gap in the
Bedroom." BuzzFeed, October 25, 2014. http://www.buzzfeed.com/alisonvingiano
/dame-products-eva-sex-toy#.riGYo6Avv.

Chapter 8: The Other C

Levin, Roy J. "Vocalised Sounds and Human Sex." *Sexual and Relationship Therapy*
21, no. 1 (2006): 99–107.

Maurer, Harry. *Sex: An Oral History.* New York: Viking, 1994.

Mintz, Laurie B. *A Tired Woman's Guide to Passionate Sex.* Avon, MA: Adams Media,
2009. Substantial portions of this chapter were adapted from this book.

Passie, Torsten, Uwe Hartmann, Udo Schneider, and Hinderk M. Emrich. "On
the Function of Groaning and Hyperventilation During Sexual Intercourse:
Intensification of Sexual Experience by Altering Brain Metabolism Through
Hypocapnia." *Medical Hypotheses* 60, no. 5 (2003): 660–63.

Chapter 9: Your Endless Erotic Education

Castleman, Michael. "Vibrators: Myths vs. Truth." *All About Sex* (blog). *Psychology
Today* online, February 15, 2011. https://www.psychologytoday.com/blog/all
-about-sex/201102/vibrators-myths-vs-truth.

Corrina, Heather. "Do Vibrators Cause a Loss of Sensitivity?" Scarleteen.
February 23, 2014. http://www.scarleteen.com/article/advice/do_vibrators
_cause_a_loss_of_sensitivity.

Katehakis, Alexandra, and Tom Bliss. *Mirror of Intimacy: Daily Reflections on
Emotional and Erotic Intelligence.* Los Angeles: Center for Healthy Sex, 2014.

McCarthy, Barry, and Maria Thestrup. "Integrating Sex Therapy Interventions
with Couple Therapy." *Journal of Contemporary Psychotherapy* 38, no. 3 (2008):
139–49.

OBOS Sexuality and Relationships Contributors. "All About Orgasms: Why We
Have Them, Why We Don't, and How to Increase Pleasure." Our Bodies

Ourselves. October 15, 2011. http://www.ourbodiesourselves.org/health-info /all-about-orgasms/.

Silverberg, Cory. "Can I Become Addicted to My Vibrator?" About Dating and Relationships. About.com. Accessed April 13, 2016. http://sexuality.about.com /od/sexualhealthqanda/f/vibrator_addict.htm.

Trompeter, Susan E., Ricki Bettencourt, and Elizabeth Barrett-Connor. "Sexual Activity and Satisfaction in Healthy Community-Dwelling Older Women." *American Journal of Medicine* 125, no. 1 (2012): 37–43.

Wismeijer, Andreas A. J., and Marcel A. L. M. van Assen. "Psychological Characteristics of BDSM Practitioners." *Journal of Sexual Medicine* 10, no. 8 (2013): 1943–52.

Chapter 10: Spread the Word

Ferguson, Rebecca M., Ine Vanwesenbeeck, and Trudie Knijn. "A Matter of Facts . . . and More: An Exploratory Analysis of the Content of Sexuality Education in the Netherlands." *Sex Education* 8, no. 1 (2008): 93–106.

"Laurel Thatcher Ulrich." *Wikipedia.* Accessed April 13, 2016. https://en.wikipedia .org/wiki/Laurel_Thatcher_Ulrich.

Chapter 11: Cliteracy—For Him

Alice. "Vagina More Pleasurable Than Clitoris?" New Q&As. Go Ask Alice! Accessed May 8, 2016. http://goaskalice.columbia.edu/answered-questions /vagina-more-pleasurable-clitoris.

Notopoulos, Katie. "14 Women Tell What It's Like Having Sex with a Micropenis." BuzzFeed. October 15, 2014. http://www.buzzfeed.com/katienotopoulos/14 -women-tell-what-its-like-having-sex-with-a-micropenis#.rgJlzBOx4.

Smith, Robyn. "Going Out with a Bang: It's Been a Pleasure." *Independent Florida Alligator.* December 3, 2015. http://www.alligator.org/opinion/columns/article _a8077900-9a41-11e5-aca9-47d44c7e0f6d.htm.

Sources Used in Multiple Chapters of *Becoming Cliterate*

Books

Barbach, Lonnie Garfield. *For Yourself: The Fulfillment of Female Sexuality.* Garden City, NY: Doubleday, 1975.

Block, Jenny. *O Wow: Discovering Your Ultimate Orgasm.* Berkeley, CA: Cleis Press, 2015.

Chalker, Rebecca. *The Clitoral Truth: The Secret World at Your Fingertips.* New York: Seven Stories Press, 2000.

The Federation of Feminist Women's Health Centers. *A New View of a Woman's Body: A Fully Illustrated Guide.* New York: Simon and Schuster, 1981.

Herbenick, Debby, and Vanessa Schick. *Read My Lips: A Complete Guide to the Vagina and Vulva.* Lanham, MD: Rowman and Littlefield, 2011.

Hite, Shere. *The Hite Report: A Nationwide Study of Female Sexuality.* New York: Seven Stories Press, 2004.

Joannides, Paul. *The Guide to Getting It On.* Waldport, OR: Goofy Foot Press, 2015.

Kerner, Ian. *She Comes First: The Thinking Man's Guide to Pleasuring a Woman.* New York: William Morrow, 2004.

King, Bruce M., and Pamela C. Regan. *Human Sexuality Today.* Upper Saddle River, NJ: Pearson, 2014.

Kinsey, Alfred C. *Sexual Behavior in the Human Female.* Bloomington: Indiana University Press, 1953.

Komisaruk, Barry R., Beverly Whipple, Sara Nasserzadeh, and Carlos Beyer-Flores. *The Orgasm Answer Guide.* Baltimore: Johns Hopkins University Press, 2010.

Ladas, Alice Kahn, Beverly Whipple, and John D. Perry. *The G-Spot: And Other Recent Discoveries About Human Sexuality.* New York: Henry Holt, 2005.

Lehmiller, Justin J. *The Psychology of Human Sexuality.* Hoboken, NJ: Wiley-Blackwell, 2013.

Lloyd, Elisabeth A. *The Case of the Female Orgasm: Bias in the Science of Evolution.* Cambridge, MA: Harvard University Press, 2005.

Solot, Dorian, and Marshall Miller. *I Love Female Orgasm: An Extraordinary Orgasm Guide.* Cambridge, MA: Da Capo Press, 2007.

Winston, Sheri. *Women's Anatomy of Arousal: Secret Maps to Buried Pleasure.* Kingston, NY: Mango Garden Press, 2010.

Magazine and Scholarly Articles

Covert, Jerilyn. "Inside the Orgasm Lab." *Men's Health.* Accessed December 7, 2017. https://www.menshealth.com/sex-women/inside-the-orgasm-lab.

Garcia, Justin R., Chris Reiber, Sean G. Massey, and Ann M. Merriwether. "Sexual Hookup Culture: A Review." *Review of General Psychology* 16, no. 2 (2012): 161–76.

Herbenick, Debra L. "The Development and Validation of a Scale to Measure Attitudes Toward Women's Genitals." *International Journal of Sexual Health* 21, no. 3 (2009): 153–66.

Herbenick, Debra L., Michael Reece, Stephanie A. Sanders, Brian Dodge, Annahita Ghassemi, and J. Dennis Fortenberry. "Women's Vibrator Use in Sexual Partnerships: Results from a Nationally Representative Survey in the United States." *Journal of Sex and Marital Therapy* 36, no. 1 (2010): 49–65.

Hite, Shere. "Female Orgasm Today: The Hite Report's Research Then and Now." *On the Issues Magazine,* Summer 2008. http://www.ontheissuesmagazine.com/july08/july2008_6.php.

Mark, Kristen. "Good in Bed Survey on Penis Perceptions." Good in Bed. Accessed May 8, 2016. http://www.goodinbed.com/good-in-bed-survey-on-penis-perceptions/index.php.

Muehlenhard, Charlene L., and Sheena K. Shippee. "Men's and Women's Reports of Pretending Orgasm." *Journal of Sex Research* 47, no. 6 (2010): 552–67.

Nuzzo, Regina. "Female Orgasms and a 'Rule of Thumb.'" *Los Angeles Times* online, February 11, 2008. http://www.latimes.com/health/la-hew-ordistance11feb11-story.html.

Orenstein, Peggy. "When Did Porn Become Sex Ed?" Sunday Review. *New York Times* online, March 19, 2016. Accessed April 13, 2016. http://mobile.nytimes .com/2016/03/20/opinion/sunday/when-did-porn-become-sex-ed.html?smid =tw-share.

Salisbury, Claire M. A., and William A. Fisher. "'Did You Come?' A Qualitative Exploration of Gender Differences in Beliefs, Experiences, and Concerns Regarding Female Orgasm Occurrence During Heterosexual Sexual Interactions." *Journal of Sex Research* 51, no. 6 (2013): 616–31.

Veale, David, Sarah Miles, Gordon Muir, and John Holdsoll. "Am I Normal? A Systematic Review and Construction of Nomograms for Flaccid and Erect Penis Length and Circumference in Up to 15,521 Men." *BJU International* 115, no. 6 (2015): 978–86.

Wade, Lisa. "The Orgasm Gap: The Real Reason Women Get Off Less Often than Men and How to Fix It." Sex and Relationships. AlterNet. April 3, 2013. http://www.alternet.org/sex-amp-relationships/orgasm-gap-real-reason-women -get-less-often-men-and-how-fix-it.

Wade, Lisa D., Emily C. Kremer, and Jessica Brown. "The Incidental Orgasm: The Presence of Clitoral Knowledge and the Absence of Orgasm for Women." *Women and Health* 42, no. 1 (2005): 117–38.

Waldinger, Marcel D., Joe McIntosh, and Dave H. Schweitzer. "A Five-Nation Survey to Assess the Distribution of the Intravaginal Ejaculatory Latency Time Among the General Male Population." *Journal of Sexual Medicine* 6, no. 10 (2009): 2888–95.

Wallen, Kim, and Elisabeth A. Lloyd. "Female Sexual Arousal: Genital Anatomy and Orgasm in Intercourse." *Hormones and Behavior* 59, no. 5 (2011): 780–92.

Videos

"Celebrating Orgasm: Carol." Betty Dodson with Carlin Ross video, 14:46. Accessed January 5, 2016. http://dodsonandross.com/boutique/videos/celebrating-orgasm -carol.

OMGYes website. Accessed March 2, 2016. https://www.omgyes.com.

Websites

Betty Dodson with Carlin Ross website. http://dodsonandross.com/.

Appendix A: Cool Tidbits for Your Lady Bits

De Costa, April. "5 Unintended Consequences of America's War on Pubic Hair." Sex and Relationships. AlterNet. May 22, 2013. http://www.alternet.org/sex -amp-relationships/5-unintended-consequences-americas-war-pubic-hair.

Gibson, Emily. "The War on Pubic Hair Must End." KevinMD.com. April 29, 2011. http://www.kevinmd.com/blog/2011/04/war-pubic-hair.html.

Kelly, Denise. "Reasons for Pubic Hair." Livestrong.com. July 06, 2015. http://www
.livestrong.com/article/207980-reasons-for-pubic-hair/.

Sanghani, Radhika. "Pubic Hair: 8 Things You Need to Know Before You Shave."
Women's Health. *The Telegraph* online, September 10, 2014. http://www.telegraph
.co.uk/women/womens-health/11087771/Pubic-hair-8-things-you-need-to-know
-before-you-shave.html.

The Sex Counselor. "Pelvic Floor Health for Women." Accessed March 21, 2016.
https://sexualityresources.com/content/pelvic-floor-health-women.

Appendix B: Additional Resources

Mintz, Laurie B. *A Tired Woman's Guide to Passionate Sex*. Avon, MA: Adams Media,
2009. Substantial portions were adapted from this book.

INDEX

self-induced, 108
sexologists on, 41–42, 48–49
sex-positive thinking and, 94
sexual trauma and, 13
simultaneous with partner, 149, 184, 227
time required for, 26, 108, 134, 217
types of, *14*, 79–82, *203*
vaginal, *14*, 16, 45–46, 72, 109, 137, 201, *203*
variability in, 64, 135, 137, 206, 216
orgasm, language of, 79–80
orgasm, male
experience of, 7–13, 47, 86, 130, 139–40, 185
in intercourse, 7–10, 22, 139–40
pleasure gap and, 7–13, 130
pornographic portrayal of, 227
premature ejaculation and, 227
privileged over female orgasm, 22, 33–34, 48–49, 90–91
time required for, 185, 227
orgasm equality
"as long as it takes" approach, 134, 138, 141, 216, 217
defined, 48, 189–90
entitlement to pleasure, 90–94, 129, 172
in hookup sex, 47–48
in language of sex, 23–24, 34–35, 189–90
in male and female orgasm experience, 86
vs. orgasm injustice, 49
through cliteracy, 8, 13–17, 189–94, 200
through new sexual scripts (*See* sexual scripts, new)
through sexual communication (*See* communication, sexual)
twelve commandments for, 194
varying levels of enjoyment within, 188
orgasm gap. *See* pleasure gap
orgasmic meditation (OM), 147
orgasm injustice, 49
orgasm problems. *See also* pleasure gap
during hookup sex, 9
medications and, 119

prevalence of, 19
relationship issues and, 10
sexual trauma and, 13, 111
tips for, 118–23
orgasms, coming together, 148–52, 224–27
orgasms, simultaneous, 149, 184, 227
orgasms, single-partner only, 146–47, 223–24
orgasms, taking turns
from female perspective, 138–46
from male perspective, 215–22
Our Bodies, Ourselves (Boston Women's Health Book Collective), 244
Overcoming Premature Ejaculation (Kerner), 227
O Wow (Block), 107

pain
G-spot and, 75
during intercourse, 60, 142, 143, 241
resources for, 244
panties, crotchless vibrating, 151
paraurethral gland, 75–76, 77
Passion: Erotic Romance for Women (Bussel), 119
Passionista (Kerner), 246
pelvic floor muscles
contracting and relaxing, 121, 242
contraction during orgasm, 82–83
resources about, 244
strengthening, 239–42
penetration. *See also* intercourse
anal, 59, 141, 209
in blended orgasm (*See* blended orgasm)
indirect clitoral stimulation with, 42, 72–74, 81, 149, 211–12, 224–25
as insufficient for female orgasm, 8, 13, 15, 72–73, 210, 212
in lesbian sex, 15–16, 141
in masturbation, 16, 109, 115, 123, 135
orgasm from, *14*, 16, 72, 109, 137, *203*
in orgasm hierarchy, 135
pain with, 60, 142, 143, 241
sex toys for, 15–16, 60, 141

penis
  analogous to inner lips, 65
  avoiding jokes about, 186, 194, 202
  clitoral stimulation with, 140, 219, 225
  engorgement of, 185, 218, 227
  language for, 27, 32
  pornographic images of, 185, 227
  sensitivity of, 62
  size of, 46, 185–86, 201–2
pillows, masturbating with, 109, 110, 123
pleasure, sexual
  absent in sex education, 191
  age and, 188
  as better focus than orgasm, 91, 201
  body love and, 99, 194
  entitlement to, 90–94, 129, 172
  inequity in (*See* pleasure gap)
  making noise and, 172
  mindfulness and, 101
  new sexual scripts for (*See* sexual
    scripts, new)
  overcoming double standards, 93–97
  resources for, 243–44, 246
  sex-positive thinking and, 90–93
  shame and guilt about, 100
  varying levels of, 188
pleasure gap (orgasm gap)
  cultural reasons for, 7–13, 47, 48–49
  defined, 7, 200
  in hookup sex, 7, 9, 12, 47, 200
  solutions to (*See* orgasm equality;
    sexual scripts, new)
  statistics, 8–9, 19
  stories about, 18–19
pornography
  female ejaculation in, 78, 213
  female genitals misrepresented in, 57,
    64–65, 78, 213
  female orgasm misrepresented in,
    45–46, 78, 213
  feminist, 119
  hair removal and, 235
  less suitable for masturbation, 116
  male genitals misrepresented in, 185,
    227
  male timing misrepresented in, 227
  pleasure gap perpetuated by, 9–10, 11

prevalence of, 45
  in sex education, 191
  sexual communication absent in, 233
  vibrators used in, 40
positions for masturbation, 109, 121–22,
    123
positions for sex
  clitoral stimulation and, 149, 151, 226
  media focus on, 148–49, 224
  "69," 148, 224
  talking about, 173–74
privilege, male sexual, 33–34, 48–49,
    90–91
Promiscuities (Wolf), 49
prostate stimulation, 76
Psychology Today, 28, 146, 223, 247
pudendum, 38

"queefs," 237
questions, statements disguised as,
    161–62, 229–30

Read My Lips (Herenick, Schick), 242
Reclaiming Your Sexual Self (Hall), 244
reconditioning pleasure styles, 135
reflection, *vs.* advice, 166, 229
Regain that Feeling (Tepper), 246
relationships
  vs. hookup sex, 46–47, 94–95
  orgasm problems and, 10
  sexual quality in, 95
  sexual routines in, 152, 183
Relaxation and Stress Reduction
    Workbook, The (Davis, et. al), 246
relaxation techniques, 120–21, 122–23
religion, shame and, 100, 106–7
resources, 243–49
Rose, Amber, 96–97
"rule of thumb," 73, 212

same-sex sex. *See* lesbian sex
Schick, Vanessa, 242
Schumer, Amy, 90
science. *See* sexology

scrotum, 58, 209
self-examination, *68,* 68–71, *70, 71,* 118
self-love. *See* masturbation
self-talk
    body image and, 99
    sex-positive, 92–94, 99, 100–101, 172
    sexual abuse and, 111
sex, anal. *See* intercourse, anal
sex, double standards about, 11, 47, 92
sex, hookup. *See* hookup sex
sex, kinky, 187
sex, language of
    awareness of, 26
    cultural problems reflected by, 33–35
    equality in, 23–27, 34–35, 189–90
    foreplay, 22–23
    inclusivity in, 24–25
    vs. intercourse, 21–27, 35, 214
    orgasm, 79–80
sex, lesbian, 15–16, 25, 115, 141, 147, 177
sex, myths about. *See* myths, sex-related
sex, oral. *See* oral sex
sex, partnered. *See also* intercourse
    allowing time for, 26, 134, 214, 217
    communication and (*See*
      communication)
    duration of, 185, 201
    "good enough" model for, 188
    inclusivity of, 25, 132, 133
    vs. intercourse, 21–27, 35, 214
    as learned skill, 188
    making noise during, 172
    mindfulness during, 101–4, 174
    new sexual scripts for (*See* sexual
      scripts, new)
    orgasm equality in (*See* orgasm
      equality)
    planning, 169–70
    positions for, 149, 151, 173–74, 224, 226
    routines in, 152, 183
    self-stimulation during, 129–30, 139,
      143, 144, 145, 224, 225
    spontaneity myth, 169, 174, 230
    traditional sexual script for, 22–23,
      130, 213
    twelve commandments for quality,
      194

variation in quality and enjoyment of,
    152, 175, 183, 188
sex, solo. *See* masturbation
"sex" (term), 21–22, 34
sex education, 12, 190–91, 243–44
Sex for One (Dodson), 43
sexiness, media images of, 11
sexology
    Hite, 42, 73–74, 109
    intercourse bias in, 41
    Kinsey, 41, 185, 227
    Masters and Johnson, 41–42, 48–49
sex-positive language, 190
sex-positive thinking
    benefits of, 101
    body positivity through, 97–100
    entitlement to pleasure in, 90–93
    overcoming double standards with,
      93–97
sex sounds, 172
sex therapy, 10, 246, 247–49
sex toys, 115, 140, 150, 151, 218. *See also*
    dildos; vibrators
sexual abuse, 13, 111, 246–47
sexual activities, *vs.* sexual orientation,
    25
sexual communication. *See*
    communication, sexual
sexual consent, 170, 187, 230
"sexual debut," 190
sexual desire, low, 119, 244
sexual fantasy, 79, 118–19, 169, 231
Sexual Healing Journey (Maltz), 13, 247
sexual orientation, *vs.* sexual activities, 25
sexual pleasure. *See* pleasure, sexual
sexual problems. *See also* orgasm
    problems; pleasure gap
    erectile dysfunction, 218
    vs. normal or kinky sex, 187
    resources for, 244, 246–48
sexual response cycle, 83
sexual script, traditional, 22–23, 130, 213
sexual scripts, new
    coming together, 148–52, 224–27
    single-partner orgasms, 146–47,
      223–24
    taking turns, 138–46, 215–22

University of Florida/Bernard Brzezinski

LAURIE MINTZ, Ph.D., is a college professor at the University of Florida who teaches the psychology of human sexuality to hundreds of students a year and has over twenty years of experience working with private clients on general and sexual issues. Dr. Mintz has received numerous professional and teaching awards, and is a Fellow of the American Psychological Association. She has published more than fifty research studies, seven book chapters, and writes a popular *Psychology Today* blog. She has been quoted extensively in the media, including in outlets such as *Parenting, Cosmopolitan, Prevention, Women's Day, Women's Health, Men's Health*, CNN.com, Oprah.com, and *The Huffington Post.*